Learning Unix for Mac OS X Tiger

Other Macintosh resources from O'Reilly

Related titles

AppleScript: The Missing Manual

AppleScript: The Definitive Guide

iBook Fan Book

iPod Fan Book

Mac OS X Tiger Pocket Guide

Mac OS X Tiger for Unix Geeks

Mac OS X: The Missing Manual, Tiger Edition

Mac OS X Power Hound

Mac OS X Hacks

PowerBook Fan Book

Macintosh Books Resource Center

mac.oreilly.com is a complete catalog of O'Reilly's books on the Apple Macintosh and related technologies, including sample chapters and code examples.

A popular watering hole for Macintosh developers and power users, the Mac DevCenter focuses on pure Mac OS X and its related technologies including Cocoa, Java, AppleScript, and Apache, just to name a few. Its also keenly interested in all the spokes of the digital hub, with special attention paid to digital photography, digital video, MP3 music, and QuickTime.

Conferences

O'Reilly brings diverse innovators together to nurture the ideas that spark revolutionary industries. We specialize in documenting the latest tools and systems, translating the innovator's knowledge into useful skills for those in the trenches. Visit *conferences.oreilly.com* for our upcoming events.

Safari Bookshelf (*safari.oreilly.com*) is the premier online reference library for programmers and IT professionals. Conduct searches across more than 1,000 books. Subscribers can zero in on answers to time-critical questions in a matter of seconds. Read the books on your Bookshelf from cover to cover or simply flip to the page you need. Try it today with a free trial.

Learning Unix for Mac OS X Tiger

Dave Taylor

O'REILLY®

Beijing · Cambridge · Farnham · Köln · Paris · Sebastopol · Taipei · Tokyo

Learning Unix for Mac OS X Tiger
by Dave Taylor

Published by O'Reilly Media, Inc., 1005 Gravenstein Highway North, Sebastopol, CA 95472.

O'Reilly Media, Inc. books may be purchased for educational, business, or sales promotional use. Online editions are also available for most titles (*safari.oreilly.com*). For more information, contact our corporate/institutional sales department: (800) 998-9938 or *corporate@oreilly.com*.

Editor:	Chuck Toporek
Production Editor:	Philip Dangler
Cover Designer:	Emma Colby
Interior Designer:	David Futato

Printing History:

May 2002:	First Edition. Originally published under the title *Learning Unix for Mac OS X*.
January 2003:	Second Edition. Originally published under the title *Learning Unix for Mac OS X*.
December 2003:	Third Edition. Originally published under the title *Learning Unix for Mac OS X Panther*.
June 2005:	Fourth Edition.

RepKover™

This book uses RepKover™, a durable and flexible lay-flat binding.

ISBN-10: 0-596-00915-1
ISBN-13: 978-0-596-00915-1
[M]   [5/07]

Table of Contents

Preface

Odds are good that you're already running Mac OS X (that's "oh-ess ten," not "oh-ess ex," by the way) and have been for a while. In fact, if you've purchased new Apple hardware in the last few years, you haven't had a choice but to jump into this new world of operating systems. If you're like most people, there was a bit of psychic jarring when you left the familiar Mac OS 9 behind; Mac OS X is a remarkable achievement—fast, stable, and very powerful—so the transition has been most worthwhile.

On a daily basis, the major change in Mac OS X is the graphical interface, known as Aqua, which has new buttons, a new appearance, and even an entirely different multiuser architecture that was never before a core part of the Mac OS. What you might not have realized, however, is that it was the underpinnings of the operating system that changed the most in the update to Mac OS X, and that you now have a tremendously powerful OS that can run thousands of open source applications downloaded free from the Net and a command-line interface that makes even the most complex task a breeze. Tasks that Windows users wouldn't even dream of attempting and that old Mac users would be allocating hours or even days to accomplish.

If you want to learn the key phrases, beneath Mac OS X lies an operating system called Unix (pronounced "you-nicks"); specifically UC Berkeley's BSD Unix and the Mach kernel, a multiuser, multitasking operating system. Being *multiuser* means Mac OS X allows multiple users to share the same system, each with their own settings, preferences, and separate filesystems, secured from another user's prying eyes. Being *multitasking* means Mac OS X can easily run many different applications at the same time, and if one of those applications crashes or hangs, the entire system doesn't need to be rebooted like it did in the past. Instead, you just force quit the application that's causing the "Spinning Beach Ball of Death" (you know, when the mouse pointer turns into a wildly spinning color wheel that just won't stop rotating) and move along like nothing ever happened.

The fact that Mac OS X has Unix under the hood doesn't matter to users who simply want to use its slick graphical interface to run their applications or manage their files. But it opens up a world of possibilities for users who want to dig a little deeper. The Unix command-line interface, which is accessible through the Terminal application (*/Applications/Utilities*), provides an enormous amount of power for intermediate and advanced users. What's more, once you've learned to use Unix in Mac OS X, you'll also be able to use the command line in other versions of Unix, such as FreeBSD (which is where Mac OS X derives its Unix core) or even Linux.

This book is designed to teach Macintosh users the basics of Unix. You'll learn how to use the command line (which Unix users refer to as the *shell*) and the filesystem, as well as some of Unix's most useful commands. I'll also give you a tour of some great applications you can download off the Internet and run within X11, the Unix graphical interface that's included with your Mac OS X system (a free, but optional install with Mac OS X, discussed in detail in Chapter 9). Unix is a complex and powerful system, so I can only scratch only the surface, but I'll also tell you how to deepen your Unix knowledge once you're ready for more.

Who This Book Is For

This book is for savvy Mac users who are comfortable enough in their own skin (the Finder and other GUI applications), but also want to learn more about the "Power of Unix" that Apple keeps talking about. Here, you'll learn all the basic commands you need to get started with Unix. Instead of burying you with lots of details, I want you to be comfortable in the Unix environment as soon as possible. So I cover each command's most useful features instead of describing all its options in detail. And let me tell you, Unix has thousands of commands with millions of options. It's very powerful! But, fortunately, it's just as powerful and helpful even if you just focus on a core subset and gradually learn more as you need additional power and capabilities.

Who This Book Isn't For

If you're seeking a book that talks about how to build Mac software applications, this isn't your book (although it's quite helpful for developers to have a firm grasp of Unix essentials, because you never know when you're going to need them). If you're a complete beginner and are occasionally stymied by where the second mouse button went, this might be a better book to put on the shelf until you're more comfortable with your Macintosh.

Finally, if you live and breathe Unix every day, this book is probably too basic for you. I also don't cover either Unix system administration or Mac system administration from the command line. For example, if you already know what a PID is and how to *kill* a program, this book is probably beneath your skill level. But if you don't know what that means, or if you're somewhere in between, you've found the right book!

A Brief History of Unix

The Macintosh started out with a single-tasking operating system that allowed simple switching between applications through an application called the Finder. More recent versions of Mac OS have supported multiple applications running simultaneously, but it wasn't until the landmark release of Mac OS X that true multitasking arrived in the Macintosh world. With Mac OS X, Macintosh applications run in separate memory areas; the Mac is a true multiuser system that also finally includes proper file-level security.

To accomplish these improvements, Mac OS X made the jump from a proprietary underlying operating environment to Unix. Mac OS X is built on top of Darwin, a version of Unix based on BSD 4.4 Lite, FreeBSD, NetBSD, and the Mach microkernel.

Unix itself was invented more than 35 years ago for scientific and professional users who wanted a very powerful and flexible OS. It has evolved since then through a remarkably circuitous path, with stops at Bell Telephone Labs, UC Berkeley, research centers in Australia and Europe, and also received some funding from the U.S. Department of Defense Advanced Research Projects Agency (DARPA). Because Unix was designed by experts for experts (or "geeks," if you prefer), it can be a bit overwhelming at first. But after you get the basics (from this book!), you'll start to appreciate some of the reasons to use Unix:

- It comes with a huge number of powerful programs. You can get many others for free on the Internet. (The Fink project, available from Source-Forge—*http://fink.sourceforge.net*—brings many open source packages to Mac OS X.) You can thus do much more at a much lower cost. Another place to explore is the cool DarwinPorts project, where a dedicated team of software developers are creating Darwin versions of many popular Unix apps (*www.opendarwin.org/projects/darwinports*).

- Unix is pretty much the same, regardless of whether you're using it on Mac OS X, FreeBSD, or Linux, or even in tiny embedded systems or a giant supercomputer. After you read this book, you'll not only learn how to harness the "Power of Unix," but you'll also be ready to use many other kinds of Unix-based computers without learning new commands for each one.

Versions of Unix

There are several versions of Unix. Some past and present commercial versions include Solaris, AIX, and HP/UX. Freely available versions include Linux, NetBSD, OpenBSD, and FreeBSD. Darwin, the free Unix version underneath Mac OS X, was built by grafting an advanced version called Mach onto BSD, with a light sprinkling of Apple magic for the Aqua interface.

Although GUIs and advanced features differ among Unix systems, you should be able to use much of what you learn from this introductory handbook on any system. Don't worry too much about what's from what version of Unix. Just as English borrows words from French, German, Japanese, Italian, and even Hebrew, Mac OS X's Unix borrows commands from many different versions of Unix—and you can use them all without paying attention to their origins.

From time to time, I explain features of Unix on other systems. Knowing the differences can help you if you ever want to use another type of Unix system. When I write "Unix" in this book, I mean "Unix and its versions," unless I specifically mention a particular version.

Interfaces to Unix

Unix can be used as it was originally designed: on typewriter-like terminals, from a prompt on a command line. Most versions of Unix also work with window systems (or GUIs). These allow each user to have a single screen with multiple windows—including "terminal" windows that act like the original Unix interface.

Mac OS X includes a simple terminal application for accessing the command-line level of the system. That application is called the Terminal and is closely examined in Chapter 2.

And while you can use your Mac quite efficiently without issuing commands in the Terminal, that's where we'll spend all of our time in this book. Why?

- Every modern Macintosh has a command-line interface. If you know how to use the command line, you'll always be able to use the system.

- If you become a more advanced Unix user, you'll find that the command line is actually much more flexible than the graphical Mac interface. Unix programs are designed to be used together from the command line—as "building blocks"—in an almost infinite number of combinations, to do an infinite number of tasks. No windowing system I've seen has this tremendous power.

- You can launch and close any Mac program from the command line.

- Once you learn to use the command line, you can use those same techniques to write *scripts*. These little (or big!) programs automate jobs you'd have to do manually and repetitively with a window system (unless you understand how to program a window system, which is usually a much harder job). See Chapter 11 for a brief introduction to scripting.

- In general, text-based interfaces are much easier than graphical computing environments for visually impaired users.

We aren't saying that the command-line interface is right for every situation. For instance, using the Web—with its graphics and links—is usually easier with a GUI web browser within Mac OS X. But the command line is the fundamental way to use Unix. Understanding it will let you work on any Unix system, with or without windows. A great resource for general Mac OS X information (the GUI you're probably used to) can be found in *Mac OS X: The Missing Manual* by David Pogue (Pogue Press/O'Reilly).

How This Book Is Organized

This book will help you learn Unix on your Mac fast. As a result, the chapters are organized in a form that gets you started quickly and then expands your Unix horizons, chapter by chapter, until you're comfortable with the command line and with X11-based open source applications and able to push further into the world of Unix. Specific commands are previewed in earlier chapters, for example, and then explained in detail in later chapters (with cross references so you don't get lost). Here's how it's all laid out:

Chapter 1, *Why Use Unix?*
> Graphical interfaces are useful, but when it's time to become a power user, really forcing your Mac to do exactly what you want, when you want it, nothing beats the power and capability of the Unix command line. You'll see exactly why that's the case in this first chapter.

Chapter 2, *Using the Terminal*
> It's not the sexiest application included with Mac OS X, but the Terminal, found in the */Applications/Utilities* folder, opens up the world of Unix on your Mac. This chapter explains how to best use it and customize it for your own requirements.

Chapter 3, *Exploring the Filesystem*
> Once you start using Unix, you'll be amazed at how many more files and directories are on your Mac, information that's hidden from the graphical interface user. This chapter takes you on a journey through your Mac's filesystem, showing you how to list files, change directories, and explore the hidden nooks and crannies of Tiger.

Chapter 4, *File Management*

Now that you can move around in your filesystem, it's time to learn how to look into individual files; copy or move files around; and even create, delete, and rename directories. This is your first introduction to some of the most powerful Unix commands, too, including the text-based *vi* editor.

Chapter 5, *Finding Files and Information*

If you've ever looked for a file with the Finder or Spotlight, you know that some types of searches are almost impossible. Looking for a file that you created exactly 30 days ago? Searching for that file with the Finder will prove to be an exercise in futility. But that's exactly the kind of search you can do with Unix's *find*, *locate*, and *grep* commands, as well as Spotlight's command-line utilities.

Chapter 6, *Redirecting I/O*

One of the most powerful elements of the Unix command line is that you can easily combine multiple commands to create new and unique "super-commands" that perform exactly the task you seek. You'll learn exactly how you can save a command's output to a file, use the content of files as the input to Unix commands, and even hook multiple commands together so that the output of one is the input of the next. You'll see that Unix is phenomenally powerful, and easy, too!

Chapter 7, *Multitasking*

As mentioned earlier, Unix is a *multitasking* operating system that allows you to have lots of applications running at the same time. In this chapter, you'll see how you can manage these multiple tasks, stop programs, restart them, and modify how they work, all from the Unix command line.

Chapter 8, *Taking Unix Online*

Much of the foundation of the Internet was created on Unix systems, and it's no surprise that you can access remote servers, surf the Web, and interact with remote filesystems all directly from the command line. If you've always wanted more power when interacting with remote sites, this chapter dramatically expands your horizons.

Chapter 9, *Of Windows and X11*

The graphical interface in Mac OS X is the best in the industry. Elegant and intuitive, it's a pleasure to use. But it turns out that there's another, Unix-based graphical interface lurking in your Mac system, called the X Window System, or X11 for short. This chapter shows you how to install X11 from Tiger's install DVD and gives you a quick tour of some of the very best X11 applications available for free on the Internet.

Chapter 10, *Open Source Software Via Fink*

We Mac OS X users are spoiled with the Software Update utility and commercial application installers. However, the world of X11 and open source applications is more anarchic, which is why it's a blessing that a team of talented Mac programmers have created a software distribution and installation tool called Fink. Learning about Fink is a smart move for any Mac Unix user who wants to experience the full range of free software in the market.

Chapter 11, *Where to Go from Here*

With all its commands, command-line combinations, and the addition of thousands of open source utilities free for the downloading, you can spend years learning how to take best advantage of the Unix environment. In this final chapter, I offer you some directions for your further travels, including recommendations for favorite books, web sites, and similar.

Conventions Used in This Book

The following typographical conventions are used in this book:

Plain text

Indicates menu titles, menu options, menu buttons, and keyboard accelerators (such as Alt and Control).

Italic

Indicates new terms; example URLs; email addresses; filenames; file extensions; pathnames; directories; and Unix commands, utilities, and options.

`Constant width`

Indicates commands and options in code samples, variables, attributes, values, the contents of files, or the output from commands.

`Constant width bold`

Shows commands or other text that should be typed literally by the user.

`Constant width italic`

Shows text that should be replaced with user-supplied values.

Menus/navigation

Menus and their options are referred to in the text as File → Open, Edit → Copy, etc. Arrows are also used to signify a navigation path when using window options; for example, System Preferences → Screen Effects → Activation means you would launch System Preferences, click on the icon for the Screen Effects preferences panel, and select the Activation pane within that panel.

Pathnames

Pathnames are used to show the location of a file or application in the filesystem. Directories (or folders for Mac and Windows users) are separated by forward slashes. For example, if you see something like "launch the Terminal application (*/Applications/Utilities*)" in the text, that means the Terminal application can be found in the Utilities subfolder of the Applications folder.

↵

A carriage return (↵) at the end of a line of code is used to denote an unnatural line break; that is, you should not enter these as two lines of code, but as one continuous line. Multiple lines are used in these cases due to printing constraints.

Menu symbols

When looking at the menus for any application, you will see some symbols associated with keyboard shortcuts for a particular command. For example, to open a document in Microsoft Word, you could go to the File menu and select Open (File → Open), or you could issue the keyboard shortcut, ⌘-O.

Figure P-1 shows the symbols used in the various menus to denote a keyboard shortcut.

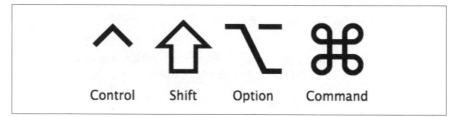

Figure P-1. Keyboard accelerators for issuing commands

Rarely will you see the Control symbol used as a menu command option; it's more often used in association with mouse clicks to emulate a right click on a two-button mouse or for working with the *bash* shell.

$, #

The dollar sign ($) is used in some examples to show the user prompt for the *bash* shell; the hash mark (#) is the prompt for the *root* user.

  This icon signifies a tip, suggestion, or general note.

This icon indicates a warning or caution.

Using Code Examples

This book is here to help you get your job done. In general, you may use the code in this book in your programs and documentation. You do not need to contact us for permission unless you're reproducing a significant portion of the code. For example, writing a program that uses several chunks of code from this book does not require permission. Selling or distributing a CD-ROM of examples from O'Reilly books does require permission. Answering a question by citing this book and quoting example code does not require permission. Incorporating a significant amount of example code from this book into your product's documentation does require permission.

We appreciate, but do not require, attribution. An attribution usually includes the title, author, publisher, and ISBN. For example: *"Learning Unix for Mac OS X Tiger*, Fourth Edition, by Dave Taylor. Copyright 2005 O'Reilly Media, Inc., 0-596-00915-1."

If you feel your use of code examples falls outside fair use or the permission given above, feel free to contact us at *permissions@oreilly.com*.

Safari® Enabled

 When you see a Safari® Enabled icon on the cover of your favorite technology book, that means the book is available online through the O'Reilly Network Safari Bookshelf.

Safari offers a solution that's better than e-Books: it's a virtual library that lets you easily search thousands of top tech books, cut and paste code samples, download chapters, and find quick answers when you need the most accurate, current information. Try it for free at *http://safari.oreilly.com*.

Comments and Questions

Please address comments and questions concerning this book to the publisher:

> O'Reilly Media, Inc.
> 1005 Gravenstein Highway North
> Sebastopol, CA 95472
> (800) 998-9938 (in the United States or Canada)
> (707) 829-0515 (international or local)
> (707) 829-0104 (fax)

We have a web page for this book, where we list errata, examples, and any additional information. You can access this page at:

> *http://www.oreilly.com/catalog/ltigerunix*

To comment or ask technical questions about this book, send email to:

> *bookquestions@oreilly.com*

For more information about our books, conferences, Resource Centers, and the O'Reilly Network, see our web site at:

> *http://www.oreilly.com/*

You can also contact the author on his own web site:

> *http://www.AskDaveTaylor.com/*

The Evolution of This Book

This book is loosely based on the popular O'Reilly title *Learning the Unix Operating System*, by Jerry Peek, Grace Todino, and John Strang (currently in its fifth edition). There are lots of differences in this book to meet the needs of Mac OS X users, but the fundamental layout and explanations are the same. The Tiger edition is the fourth Mac OS X custom edition of this title. As Mac OS X keeps getting better, so does this little book.

Acknowledgments

I'd like to acknowledge the work of Chuck Toporek, my editor at O'Reilly. I would also like to express my gratitude to Brian Jepson, my co-author on the previous editions of this book. Brian, I'm sorry your cat's no longer featured in the GIMP section! Thanks also to Christian Crumlish for his backroom assistance, and to Tim O'Reilly for the opportunity to help revise the popular *Learning the Unix Operating System* book for the exciting Mac OS X world. Oh, and a big thumbs up to Linda, Ashley, Gareth, and Kiana for letting me type, type, and type some more, ultimately getting this book out the door in a remarkably speedy manner.

## CHAPTER 1

Why Use Unix?

Why would any sane person want to type in a bunch of funny looking Unix commands when you can just use the mouse? After all, Mac OS X has one—if not *the*—best looking user interface out there, so what would compel you, a Mac user through and through, to use the Unix command line? That's a tough sell, but you can boil it down to just one word: Power.

Lying underneath Mac OS X Tiger's purring Aqua interface is a powerful Unix system, ready to leap into action at a moment's notice. All you have to do is *command* Unix to take action. One of the greatest pleasures of using Unix within Mac OS X is that you get the benefit of a truly wonderful graphical environment and the underlying power of the Unix command line. There's no denying it's a match made in heaven. Even Apple promotes Mac OS X with the tagline:

"The simplicity and elegance of the Mac, and the Power of Unix."

This chapter sets the stage for the rest of the book, answering the question: "Why use Unix when you have a perfectly good Mac graphical interface?" It's an important question, and I think that within just a few minutes, you'll agree that joining the Unix world is really like learning you have a completely separate, and even more powerful, operating system lurking in your machine.

The Power of Unix

Why you should have to remember commands and type them in is an obvious thing to question. If you're a long-time Macintosh person who is familiar and happy with the capabilities and logic of the Aqua interface, you might need some convincing that *Unix is your friend*. Here's why: dipping into the primarily text-based Unix tools on your Mac OS X system gives you more power and control over both your computer and your computing environment. There are other reasons, including:

- There are thousands of open source and otherwise freely downloadable Unix-based applications. Can't afford Adobe Photoshop but still want a powerful graphics editor? The GNU Image Manipulation Program (GIMP) offers a viable solution (see Chapter 10).
- Want to search for files by when or who created them? Difficult in the Finder or Spotlight, but it's a breeze with Unix (see Chapter 5).
- And how about managing your files and file archives in an automated fashion? Tricky to set up with the GUI tools, but in Unix, you can set up a cron job to handle this at night while you sleep (see Chapter 5 as well).

Fundamentally, Unix is all about power and control. As an example, consider the difference between using Force Quit from the Apple menu and the Unix programs *ps* and *kill*. While Force Quit is more attractive, as shown in Figure 1-1, notice that it lists only graphical applications.

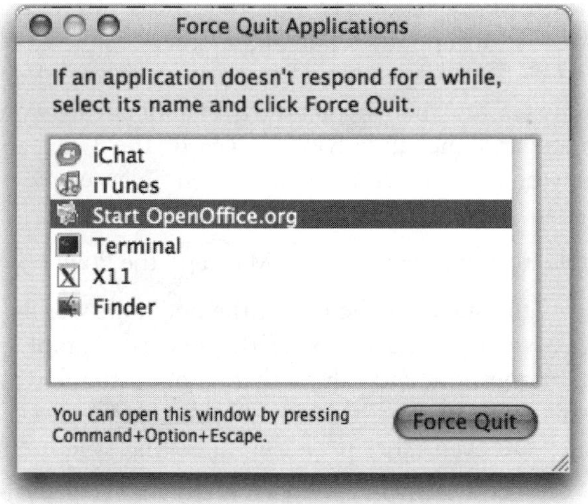

Figure 1-1. Force Quit doesn't show all running applications

By contrast, the *ps* (*processor status*) command used from within the Terminal application (*/Applications/Utilities/Terminal*) shows a complete and full list of every application, utility, and system process running on your Mac, as shown here:

```
$ ps -ax
  PID  TT  STAT     TIME COMMAND
    1  ??  S<s   0:00.31 /sbin/launchd
```

```
  31 ??  Ss      0:00.56 /usr/sbin/syslogd -m 0 -c 5
  37 ??  Ss      0:02.30 kextd
  41 ??  Ss      0:03.48 /usr/sbin/configd
  42 ??  Ss      0:00.47 /usr/sbin/coreaudiod
  43 ??  Ss      0:00.76 /usr/sbin/diskarbitrationd
...
 375 p2  Ss      0:00.03 login -p -f taylor
 376 p2  S+      0:00.04 -bash
 437 p3  Ss      0:00.05 -bash
 455 p3  R+      0:00.01 ps -ax
```

That's more than the few applications Force Quit shows you. Of course, the next thing that's running through your head is "Sure, but what does all that output in the Terminal mean to me, and what do I do with it?" This is the key reason to learn and work with the Unix side of Mac OS X: to really know what your Mac's doing and be able to make it match what you want and need your Mac to do.

Okay, now let's go back and look at the output from running the *ps -ax* command. First off, you'll see that we added some *options* (or *flags* or *switches*) to the *ps* command; the options are the *-ax* bit. The *-ax* option tells *ps* to display all of the programs and processes being run by all of the users (including you and the system, itself) on the system. When the Terminal displays the results of the *ps -ax* command, you'll see that it adds a "header" to the output:

```
$ ps -ax
 PID TT  STAT     TIME COMMAND
   1 ??  S<s   0:00.31 /sbin/launchd
```

Think of the headers the same way you would when looking at an Excel spreadsheet with a bunch of columns. Each column in that spreadsheet should have a column head to help define what you see underneath. The same applies here. In the very first line of the information returned, you'll see PID, TT, STAT, TIME, and COMMAND. These relate to:

PID

    The command's process identification number (or PID for short).

TT

    The terminal type the process is running in; if you see two question marks (??), that means the process is running outside of a Terminal window or display.

STAT

    Tells you the status of the command.

TIME

Tells you the amount of time it took to run that particular process, or how long that process has been running in minutes and seconds. For example, the 0:00.31 you see in the output means that it took, roughly, a third of a second for the *launchd* process to start and run.

COMMAND

Gives you the entire pathname to the process that's running; for example, */sbin/launchd* tells you that the process that's running is *launchd* (a *daemon*, or system service, as noted by the *d* at the end of its name), which is located in the */sbin* directory.

Great! So now you know what all that means, but you still don't know how this relates to Force Quit, right? Well, be patient, we're getting there.

Once you know a process's PID number, you can then issue the Unix *kill* command to, well, kill that process. For example, let's say that Microsoft Word decided to lock up on you and you're stuck with the Spinning Beach Ball of Death (SBBoD) syndrome. After you finish screaming, you need to *kill* Microsoft Word, but in order to do so, you first need its process number. For this, we'll add the *grep* command, which is basically a Unix search tool that you use to search for words or numbers in files, or in this case, the output of a command:

```
$ ps -ax | grep Word
2847 ??  S    134:05.69 /Applications/Microsoft Office X/Microsoft Word
/Application
3665 std  R+     0:00.00 grep Word
```

This tells us that Microsoft Word's PID is 2847, as noted by the first set of numbers in the command's output. Now all you need to do to *kill* Word is issue the following command:

```
$ kill 2847
```

After typing that and hitting the Return key (an activity known as "entering a command"), Microsoft Word promptly quits, closing all its windows without first saving any of your previous work. But since Word was locked in a deep freeze, you wouldn't have been able to save your changes anyway, right? And if you had used the Force Quit window, you wouldn't be able to save changes there, either.

Batch Renames and Extracting File Lists

Here's another example. Suppose you just received a CD-ROM from a client with hundreds of files all in the main folder. Now let's say you only need those files that have *-nt-* or *-dt-* as part of their filenames, and that you want to copy them from the CD to your Home directory. Within the Finder, you'd be doomed to going through the list manually, a tedious and error-prone process. But on the Unix command line, this becomes a breeze:

```
$ cd /Volumes/MyCDROM
$ cp *-dt-* *-nt-* ~
```

The first command, *cd /Volumes/MyCDROM*, takes you to the Volumes directory, which is where the CD (named *MyCDROM*) is actually mounted on your Mac's filesystem. The second command, *cp *-dt-* *-nt-* ~*, breaks down as follows:

cp
> This is Unix's copy command.

-dt- *-nt-*
> This tells the *cp* command to look for any items on the CD that have either *-dt-* or *-nt-* in their filenames. Unix recognizes the asterisks (*) as wildcards as part of the search string. By placing an asterisk before and after each item (**-dt-** and **-nt-**), you're telling Unix to find any file that has either *-dt-* or *-nt-* anywhere in its filename.

~
> The tilde character (or squiggle, in Unix-speak) simply refers to a user's Home folder (or directory).

> By placing the tilde (~) at the end of the command line, you're telling *cp* to locate any file that has *-dt-* or *-nt-* in its filename, and copy those files to your Home directory.

Fast, easy, and doable by any and all Mac OS X users.

There are a million reasons why it's helpful to know Unix as a Mac OS X power user, and you'll see them demonstrated time and again throughout this book.

Finding Hidden Files

You might not realize it if you only work in the Finder, but your system has thousands of additional files and directories that you can find much more easily on the command line. These hidden files are known in the Unix world as *dot files*, because the file or directory has a period (.) as the first letter of its name. For example, in your Home directory you have a file called *.bash_profile* that contains specific instructions on how you want your Terminal session set up. But when you view your Home folder in the Finder, this file is hidden, as shown in Figure 1-2. Instead, all you see are the default set of folders (Desktop, Documents, Library, Movies, Music, Pictures, Public, and Sites) and a file called *myopen*.

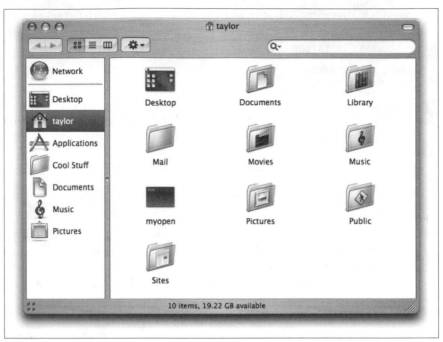

Figure 1-2. The Finder doesn't show hidden files that you can see in the Terminal with standard Unix commands

To view the dot files in the Terminal, type the file listing command (*ls*), along with its *–a* option (for *list all*, which shows me the hidden dot files), and suddenly you realize that there are lots more files in that directory:

```
$ ls -a
.               .bash_history   .ssh            Mail
..              .gimp-1.2       .sversionrc     Movies
.DS_Store       .kde            .viminfo        Music
.ICEauthority   .pine-debug1    .xscrabble.save Pictures
.Trash          .pinerc         Desktop         Public
.Xauthority     .profile        Documents       Sites
.angband        .qt             Library         myopen
```

Though I don't always need the power, I like knowing that I can get to, view, and even edit every file on my computer if I need to. All I need to do is launch the Terminal application, type in a few simple commands, and I'm on my way.

Folders or Directories?

If you're new to the whole Unix thing, you're going to need to learn Unix-speak. In the graphical world, such as with Mac OS 9 or Mac OS X, you're used to working with a graphical user interface (GUI) that lets you see everything visually. When you create a new file, it gets stored in a folder of some sort, even if you save the file to your Desktop (which is, in its own right, a folder).

But in Unix-land, folders are referred to as *directories*. That's right, folders and directories are one and the same. It's an odd sort of translation, but when Unix was first developed, there was no GUI; all you had was a text-based terminal to type into, and you were darn happy to have that. Directories were set up as part of the hard drive's *filesystem*, or the structure in which directories and files are stored on the system. And the way you get to a folder (er, directory) in Unix is to enter its *file path*, using forward slashes between the directory names. For example, the file path to your Home directory (again, think folder) is actually:

    /Users/your_name

Where *your_name* would be replaced by your short username (in my case, taylor). (There is, of course, an easier way to denote your Home directory, but we'll get to that at a later time.)

At the very bottom of your Mac's hard drive, you have the root directory, otherwise denoted with a single forward slash (/). As noted in the example above, all you need to do is place the folder/directory name in between the slashes.

This takes a little getting used to, but once you get the hang of entering Unix file paths, you'll find that it's actually a faster way to get around (particularly if you can type faster than it takes you to move the mouse around in the graphical world).

Just remember: folders are directories, and when working on the Unix side of your Mac, we'll refer to folders as directories throughout the book.

Thousands of Free Applications

This should appeal to anyone who is a part of the Macintosh community: by warming up to Unix and its command line, you are joining the much-lauded open source movement, since Mac OS X is based on an open source Unix operating system, called Darwin. What's excellent is that there are thousands of different applications available for open source operating systems, including design, development, scientific, and business applications that compare quite favorably to expensive commercial alternatives. Also, don't make the mistake of assuming that all open source applications are command-line applications! Some of the very best applications, like The GIMP graphics editor (*www.gimp.org*) and the NeoOffice/J suite (*www. neooffice.org*) are designed to work within either X11 or directly in Mac OS X's Aqua GUI environment.

Commands Included with Unix

While this book covers only about 50 of the most basic Unix commands, there are over a thousand Unix commands included with Mac OS X—and you can't see some of these commands without accessing the command line. From sophisticated software development environments to web browsers, file transfer utilities to encryption and compression utilities, almost everything you can do in the Aqua interface—and more—can be done with a few carefully chosen Unix commands.

Displaying All Unix Commands

To quickly see all of the binary executables—Unix programs—on your system, open the Terminal and hit the Tab key twice. You'll be asked if you want the system to "Display all 1157 possibilities? (y or n)". If you do, hit the Y key; if not, hit N.

Before the commands are displayed in the Terminal, however, you'll first be prompted (asked) to make a choice:

```
$
Display all 1099 possibilities? (y or n)
```

If you press the **n** key on your keyboard, you'll be taken back to a command prompt and nothing else happens. However, if you press the **y** key, you'll see a double-column of the Unix commands stream past in the Terminal window. At the bottom of the screen, you'll see:

```
--More--
```

This lets you know that there's more to display. If you hit the spacebar, the next "page" of commands scrolls into view. Keep pressing the spacebar to view the entire list of commands; or, if you're getting tired of that, just hit Control-C to cancel the output and go back to the command prompt.

If you're a software developer or just curious about programming, for example, you'll want to install the optional Xcode Tools, included with Mac OS X Tiger. The Xcode Tools give you a full, professional-grade software development environment that lets you develop new applications in Objective-C, C, or C++. Pretty nice for something included free with your computer, eh?

If you're eager to install Xcode Tools right now, flip forward to "Xcode" in Chapter 4.

Downloading Unix Software from the Web

While Mac OS X is a capable Unix system from the get-go, there are many, many wonderful Unix-based applications you can download and add to your system, too, and almost all of them are free for the downloading. In addition to command-line tools and utilities, there are hundreds of graphical applications built within the X Window System, a standard Unix graphical interface that Apple includes with your Mac OS X system!

 Learn how to install X11 in "Installing X11" in Chapter 9.

Two standout applications in the X11 world are NeoOffice/J, a complete and robust replacement for the Microsoft Office Suite (that's free!), and The GIMP, an awkwardly named photo and graphics editor that compares quite favorably to Adobe Photoshop. Both are examined in Chapter 9.

Chapter 10 talks about the Fink program, a tool that makes it a breeze for you to find, download, and install these thousands of free applications from the Web, including both OpenOffice and The GIMP. Chapter 10 alone will pay for this book a hundred times over!

Power Internet Connections

If you're someone who uses the Internet daily, you already know that there are a bunch of useful Mac OS X applications available to help you be efficient. But lots of them seem to have a price tag attached, even a simple FTP program like Fetch (*www.fetchworks.com*). But why spend $25 on an application when you can use Mac OS X Tiger's built-in *ftp* command-line utility for free!

For example, if you wanted to download the cover image for this book from O'Reilly's web site, you could use the following commands (as noted in **bold** type):

```
MacDave:~ taylor$ ftp ftp.oreilly.com
Connected to tornado.east.ora.com.
220 ProFTPD 1.2.10 Server (ftp.oreilly.com) [172.31.173.9]
Name (ftp.oreilly.com:taylor): anonymous
```

```
331 Anonymous login ok, send your complete email address as your password.
Password: [Type in your email address here]
ftp> cd /pub/graphics/book-covers/low-res
ftp> get 0596009151.gif
local: 0596009151.gif remote: 0596009151.gif
229 Entering Extended Passive Mode (|||38666|)
150 Opening BINARY mode data connection for 0596009151.gif (217245 bytes)
100% |********************************|   212 KB   45.72 KB/s   00:00 ETA
226 Transfer complete.
217245 bytes received in 00:04 (44.22 KB/s)
ftp> bye
221 Goodbye.
```

That downloads the image file for the cover of this book to your Mac, which is nice, but what if you want to *look* at it? Sure, you could go to the Finder, find the file, and then double-click on the file's icon to open it in Preview, but that's a lot of work. However, with a little help from Unix, you can just type in the following command:

```
MacDave:~ taylor$ open 0596009151.gif
MacDave:~ taylor$
```

The *open* command, which is special to Mac OS X, examines the file it's supposed to open (*0596009151.gif*), detects which application should open it by default (something you can see in a file's Get Info window), and then opens the file in Preview—all in a fraction of a second! See how much time Unix just saved you (not to mention the $25!)?

From logging in to your Mac from remote locations to transferring files from your system to a server using an encrypted connection, Mac OS X's Unix command line is quite powerful. But don't take my word for it. Chapter 8 takes you on a detailed tour of command-line Internet utilities.

A Simple Guided (Unix) Tour

Enough talking about what Unix can do, it's time to flex your fingers, open up your Mac, and try a few commands so you can get a sense of how it all works!

The first step is to launch the Terminal application, through which you'll interact with the command shell, the program within which you type in your commands and the responses are shown. Terminal is tucked into the Utilities folder in your Applications folder, which you can quickly get at from the Finder with the Shift-⌘-U keyboard shortcut.

Since you'll be using the Terminal application a lot throughout this book (and hopefully in the future, as you grow more comfortable with Unix), you should drag the Terminal's icon to the Dock so it's always at the ready. Or, if the Terminal's already running, you can Control-click on its application in the Dock and select "Keep in Dock" from its contextual menu, as shown in Figure 1-3.

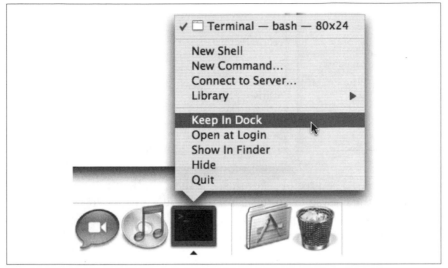

Figure 1-3. Control-click the Terminal's Dock icon, and select "Keep In Dock" from its contextual menu so it will always be there when you need it

Throughout the following example, type in the commands you see in **bold**, pressing the Return key after each one (again, this is known as "entering a command" in Unix-speak). Preceding each command, I've included some comments to let you know what you're about to do:

Without any arguments, the *cd* command moves you to your Home directory:

```
$ cd
```

The *pwd* (or *present working directory*) command shows you the path for the directory you're currently in:

```
$ pwd
/Users/taylor
```

Use the *ls* command to list the files in your Home directory; compare this listing with the picture of the Finder window shown in Figure 1-2. If you omit the *-a* option, then all the hidden dot files stay hidden in this directory:

```
$ ls
Desktop      Mail      Pictures      myopen
Documents    Movies    Public
Library      Music     Sites
```

Now let's change directories to your Library folder:

```
$ cd Library
```

Use the *ls* command again to see what's inside (there's very little here you'll need to mess with):

```
$ ls
Application Support    FontCollections    Preferences
Assistants             Fonts              Printers
Audio                  Icons              Recent Servers
Autosave Information   Indexes            Safari
Caches                 Internet Plug-Ins  Snapz Pro X
Classic                Keyboard Layouts   Sounds
ColorPickers           Keychains          Syndication
Cookies                Logs               iMovie
Documentation          Mail               iTunes
Favorites              Metadata
```

Now let's go back a directory. For this, use the .. shortcut for moving up one directory in the filesystem. In this case, since you were in your Library folder (*/Users/taylor/Library*, or just *~/Library*), the following command moves you back to your Home directory (as noted by the *pwd* command that follows):

```
$ cd ..
$ pwd
/Users/taylor
```

Finally, when it's time to quit Terminal, use the *exit* command rather than just quitting the application with ⌘-Q:

```
$ exit
```

Don't worry if you aren't sure exactly what each of those commands does: we'll explore each one in great detail as the book proceeds.

The 10 Most Common Unix Commands

If you want to just jump in and try things out, here are the 10 most common commands with a very short summary of what each does:

ls
> List files or directories.

cp original_file copied_file
> Copies the *original_file* (or files) from one location to another.

mv original_file new_file
> Move a file or files; the original is deleted once complete.

rm filename
> Remove a file, set of files or folders full of files.

Use the *rm* command with caution; there's no "Trash" where things are moved to. Once you've used *rm* to delete something, it's gone forever.

pwd

> Display your present working directory; this is where you currently are in the filesystem.

cd directory_name

> Change to the specified directory in the filesystem. Without any arguments, it's a shortcut for changing back to your Home directory.

man command_name

> Access Mac OS X's built-in documentation for the Unix commands. To read the man page for the *ls* command, for example, type in **man ls**.

more filename

> Display a long text file, one screen at a time. Pressing the spacebar gets the next page when you're ready, and pressing Q at any time quits the program and returns you to the command prompt.

grep pattern

> Search for the specified pattern across as many files as you desire. A fast way to find that email message you sent to Uncle Linder, for example.

top

> Shows you which applications and processes are running on your system, including those that the Finder's Force Quit window ordinarily hides.

There's a whole world of Unix inside your Mac OS X system, and it's time for you to jump in and learn how to be more productive, more efficient, and gain remarkable power as a Mac user. Ready? Let's go!

## CHAPTER 2

Using the Terminal

With a typical Unix system, a staff person has to set up an account for you before you can use it. With Mac OS X, however, the operating system installation process automatically creates a default user account. The account is identified by your *username*, which is usually a single word or an abbreviation. Think of this account as your office—it's your personal place in the Unix environment.

When you log into your Mac OS X system, you're automatically logged into your Unix account as well. In fact, your Desktop and other customized features of your Mac OS X environment have corresponding features in the Unix environment. Your files and programs can be accessed either through the Finder or through a variety of Unix command-line utilities that you can use in Mac OS X's Terminal application.

In this chapter, you'll not only learn about the Terminal and how to customize it for your own needs, but you'll also gain an understanding of the command-line nature of Mac OS X when accessed through the Terminal. If you're used to moving your mouse around and clicking on buttons, this might seem wonderfully—or awkwardly—retro, but like any other powerful environment, the difference between the Finder and the Terminal are part of what makes the Terminal, and Unix, so remarkably powerful.

Launching the Terminal

The way you use Unix on Mac OS X is through an application, known as the Terminal. The Terminal application is located in the Utilities folder (*/Applications/Utilities*). To launch the Terminal, open a Finder window, use the Shift-⌘-U keyboard shortcut (which takes you right to the *Utilities* folder), and then locate and double-clicking on the Terminal application, as shown in Figure 2-1. It starts up presenting you with a dull, uninspiring white window with black text that says "Welcome to Darwin!" and a shell prompt.

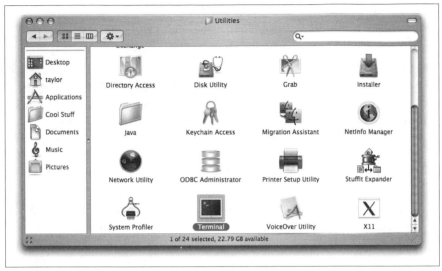

Figure 2-1. Finding Terminal in the Utilities folder

 By default, Terminal uses *bash* as its shell. If you'd like to configure it to use a different shell, you can do so by selecting Terminal → Preferences and specifying the shell to use. I talk about that in the sidebar "What is a Shell?" later in this chapter.

Most Mac OS X applications you've run to this point probably have a pretty graphical interface and allow you to move the cursor around with your mouse or trackpad. Move it over something you want and you can simply click for the action to take place. The Terminal is different, though, and your mouse gets a rest for a while as you type in the commands on your keyboard, ending each line with a Return.

Syntax of a Unix Command

Unix command lines can be simple, one-word entries such as the *date* command. They can also be more complex; you may need to type more than the command or program name.[*]

---

[*] The command can be the name of a Unix program (such as *date*), or it can be a command that's built into the shell (such as *exit*). You probably don't need to worry about this!

A Unix command can have *arguments*. An argument can be an option or a filename. The general format for a Unix command line is:

```
command option(s) filename(s)
```

There isn't a single set of rules for writing Unix commands and arguments, but these general rules work in most cases:

- Enter commands in lowercase.

- *Options* modify the way in which a command works. Options are often single letters prefixed with a dash (-, also called "hyphen" or "minus") and set off by any number of spaces or tabs. Multiple options in one command line can be set off individually (such as *-a -b*). In most cases, you can combine them after a single dash (such as *-ab*), but most commands' documentation doesn't tell you whether this will work; you'll have to try it.

  Some commands also have options made from complete words or phrases and starting with two dashes, such as *--delete* or *--confirm-delete*. When you enter a command line, you can use this option style, the single-letter options (which each start with a single dash), or both.

- The argument *filename* is the name of a file you want to use. Most Unix programs also accept multiple filenames, separated by spaces or specified with wildcards (see Chapter 8). If you don't enter a filename correctly, you may get a response such as "*filename*: no such file or directory" or "*filename*: cannot open."

  Some commands, such as *who*, have arguments that aren't filenames.

- You must type spaces between commands, options, and filenames. You'll need to "quote" filenames that contain spaces. For more information, see Chapter 4.

- Options come before filenames.

- In a few cases, an option has another argument associated with it; type this special argument just after its option. Most options don't work this way, but you should know about them. The *sort* command is an example of this feature: you can tell *sort* to write the sorted text to a filename given after its *-o* option. In the following example, *sort* reads the file *sortme* (given as an argument), and writes to the file *sorted* (given after the *-o* option):

  ```
  $ sort -o sorted -n sortme
  ```

  I also used the *-n* option in that example. But *-n* is a more standard option; it has nothing to do with the final argument *sortme* on that command line. So, I also could have written the command line this way:

  ```
  $ sort -n -o sorted sortme
  ```

Don't be too concerned about these special cases, though. If a command needs an option like this, its documentation will say so.

- Command lines can have other special characters, some of which you'll see later in this book. They can also have several separate commands. For instance, you can write two or more commands on the same command line, each separated by a semicolon (;). Commands entered this way are executed one after another by the shell.

Mac OS X has a lot of commands! Don't try to memorize all of them. In fact, you'll probably need to know just a few commands and their options. As time goes on, you'll learn these commands and the best way to use them for your job. I cover some useful commands in later chapters.

Let's look at a sample command. The *ls* program displays a list of files. You can use it with or without options and arguments. If you enter:

    $ ls

you'll see a list of filenames. But if you enter:

    $ ls -l

there will be an entire line of information for each file. The *-l* option (a dash and a lowercase letter "L") changes the normal *ls* output to a long format. You can also get information about a particular file by using its name as the second argument. For example, to find out about a file called *chap1*, enter:

    $ ls -l chap1

Many Unix commands have more than one option. For instance, *ls* has the *-a* (all) option for listing hidden files. You can use multiple options in either of these ways:

    $ ls -a -l
    $ ls -al

You must type one space between the command name and the dash that introduces the options. If you enter **ls-al**, the shell reports back with:

    ls-al: command not found

Exercise: Entering a Few Commands

The best way to get used to the Terminal is to enter some commands. To run a command, type the command and then press the Return key. Remember that almost all Unix commands are typed in lowercase. Try issuing the commands shown in Table 2-1 to see what results you see in the Terminal.

Table 2-1. Sample Unix commands to test out

Task	Command
Get today's date.	*date*
List logged-in users.	*who*
Obtain more information about users.	*who -u, finger,* or *w*
Find out who is at your terminal.	*who am i*
Enter two commands in the same line.	*who am i;date*
Mistype a command.	*woh*

In this session, you've tried several simple commands and seen the results on the screen.

Types of Commands

When you use a program, you'll want to know how to control it. How can you tell it what job you want done? Do you give instructions before the program starts, or after it's started? There are several general ways to give commands on a Mac OS X system. It's good to be aware of them.

Graphical programs

Some programs work only within the graphical window environment (on Mac OS X, this is called Aqua). On Mac OS X, you can run these programs using the *open* command. For instance, when you type *open -a Chess* at a command prompt, the Chess application (*/Applications*) launches. It opens one or more windows on your screen. The program has its own way to receive your commands—through menus and buttons on its windows, for instance. Although you can't interact with these programs using traditional Unix utilities, Mac OS X includes the *osascript* utility, which lets you run AppleScript commands from the Unix shell.

Noninteractive Unix programs

You can enter many Unix commands at a shell prompt. These programs work in a window system (from a Terminal window) or from any terminal. You control those programs from the Unix command line—that is, by typing options and arguments from a shell prompt before you start the program. After you start the program, wait for it to finish; you generally don't interact with it.

Interactive Unix programs

Some Unix programs that work in the Terminal window have commands of their own. (If you'd like some examples, see Chapters 3 and 4.) These programs may accept options and arguments on their command lines. But, once you start a program, it prints its own prompt and/or menus, and it understands its own commands. It also takes instructions from your keyboard that weren't given on its command line.

For instance, if you enter **ftp** at a shell prompt (refer back to the example in Chapter 1), you'll see a new prompt from the *ftp* program. At this prompt, you'll enter certain FTP commands for transferring files to and from remote systems. When you enter the special command **quit** to quit the *ftp* program (or you can use **bye**), *ftp* stops prompting you for more input. Once you quit FTP, you're returned to the standard Unix shell prompt, where you can enter other Unix commands.

Changing the Terminal's Preferences

To change the Terminal's preferences, go to Terminal → Window Settings; this opens the Terminal Inspector window, as shown in Figure 2-2.

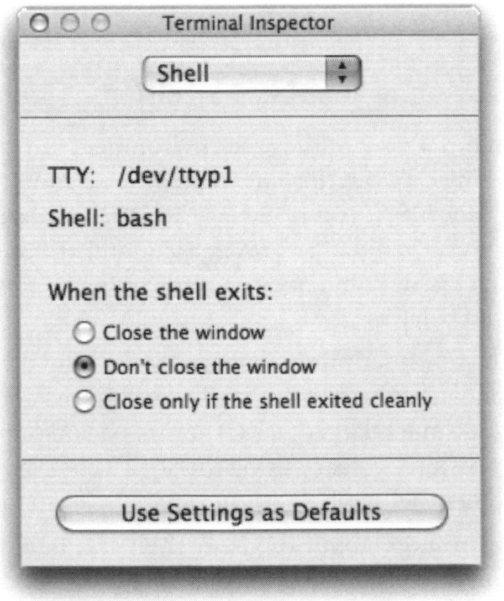

Figure 2-2. The Terminal Inspector window lets you configure the settings for your Terminal windows

At the top of the window, there's a pop-up list that lets you select which options to configure: Shell, Processes, Emulation, Buffer, Display, Color, Window, and Keyboard. The names suggest what each does, but let's have a closer look anyway, particularly since some of these settings definitely *should* be changed (in my view).

Any changes you make within the Terminal Inspector will affect only the current Terminal window. To make these settings apply to all Terminal windows in the future, click "Use Settings as Defaults."

Shell

When you first open the Terminal Inspector, the Shell settings are displayed, as shown in Figure 2-2. This panel specifies which virtual Terminal device (or *tty*, pronounced "tee-tee-why") and shell are associated with the current Terminal window. In addition, it allows you to choose one of the following options for when the shell exits:

- Close the window.
- Don't close the window.
- Close the window only if the shell exited cleanly (that is, returned a *zero status code*, which means that all the applications gracefully shut down).

What Is a Shell?

A *shell*, at least in the Unix world, is the environment in which you work on the Unix side of things. To put this into context, when you're using the Aqua user interface for Mac OS X, you're using Mac OS X's native "environment." With Unix, however, everything is text-based, and the shell offers you an interface in which to issue commands, and to configure how your shell environment works and behaves.

Shells also offer their own scripting language, which allows you to write miniprograms for mundane things, such as displaying a message to tell you to clean the cat box, or much larger tasks, such as backing up your computer. With shell scripts, you're basically using the shell's environment to run Unix commands—or other shell scripts—to automate tasks and processes.

If you want to learn more about the *bash* shell and how to program shell scripts with it, look to *Learning the bash Shell*, by Cameron Newham and Bill Rosenblatt (O'Reilly, 2005). Don't let the age of this book fool you; it's packed with lots of useful information that still applies to using *bash* under Mac OS X. And if you want to see what you can do with shell scripts, I'd recommend picking up a copy of *Wicked Cool Shell Scripts* (No Starch Press, 2004), authored by yours truly.

If you like to study what you've done and want to be forced to close the Terminal windows yourself, the "Don't close the window" option is for you. Otherwise, either of the other two will work fine.

 Personally, I like to use "Close the window" so I don't have to worry about whether something went wrong and I just didn't notice.

If you want to change the login shell for future Terminal windows, open up the Terminal → Preferences dialog box, as shown in Figure 2-3.

```
○○○                    Terminal Preferences

  When creating a new Terminal window:
    ⦿ Execute the default login shell using /usr/bin/login
    ○ Execute this command (specify complete path):
    ┌──────────────────────────────────────────┐
    │ /bin/bash                                  │
    └──────────────────────────────────────────┘
    Declare terminal type ($TERM) as:  [ xterm-color        ▲▼]

    ☐ Open a saved .term file when Terminal starts:
    ┌────────────────────────────────────┐  ┌─────────┐
    │                                      │  │ Select... │
    └────────────────────────────────────┘  └─────────┘
```

Figure 2-3. Terminal Preferences

The choice of shells in Mac OS X Tiger are: */bin/bash*, */bin/csh*, */bin/ksh*, */bin/tcsh*, */bin/zsh*, and */bin/sh*. Unix fans will no doubt find a shell to their liking, but if you're just learning, stick with *bash* (*/bin/bash*) and you'll be able to follow every example in this book without a hiccup.

Processes

The Processes window (shown in Figure 2-4) lists all the Unix programs, or *processes*, running under in the Terminal window, and lets you specify what to do when you close a window.

The Processes window is split into two sections:

Currently Running Processes
> This area lists any Unix processes currently running on your Mac. Without any other Unix programs running, you should at least see the *login* and *bash* processes listed in this display.

Figure 2-4. Processes

Prompt before closing window

> This section offers three options that let you choose whether or not the Terminal prompts you before closing its windows. If there's something still running in the window, a dialog box pops up asking if you're sure you want to quit. This feature is very helpful if you are prone to accidentally clicking the wrong window element or pushing the wrong key sequence.

> Set "Prompt before closing window" to "Always" if you'd like Terminal to always ask before closing the window, or set it to "Never" to prevent it from ever asking. You can also use the "If there are processes other than" setting (the default) to ignore the programs shown in the list (you can also add or remove items from this list).

Emulation

These preferences, shown in Figure 2-5, don't need to be altered by most users.

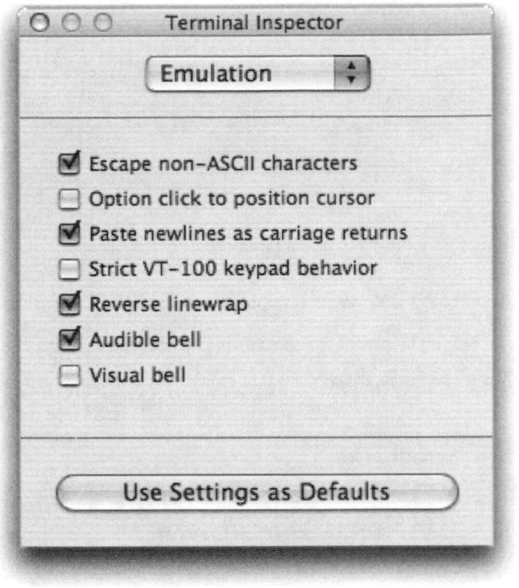

Figure 2-5. Emulation

Some PowerBook G4s have a long delay before emitting audio. If you have one of these and you feel it's a problem, deselect "Audible bell" to neatly sidestep the issue. This also has a nice side effect of preventing people around you from knowing when you've made a mistake.

It's best to leave "Paste newlines as carriage returns" checked, so you can ignore the difference in end-of-line sequences in Mac files versus Unix files, and to avoid selecting "Strict VT-100 keypad behavior" because it can get in the way of some of the newer Mac OS X Unix utilities. Whether you enable "Option click to position cursor" depends on whether you're a Unix purist (for whom the "good old keyboard" works just fine), or whether you're trying to simplify things. Beware that if you do enable Option-click positioning, it won't work in all cases—only when you're in a full-screen application such as Emacs or *vi*.

Buffer

The scrollback buffer allows you to scroll back and review earlier commands and command output. The settings in this area probably don't need changing, as shown in Figure 2-6.

The default value of 10,000 lines should be more than enough for most people. If your Mac doesn't have a lot of memory, though, you can put in a smaller number or completely disable the scrollback buffer, rather than specify a size.

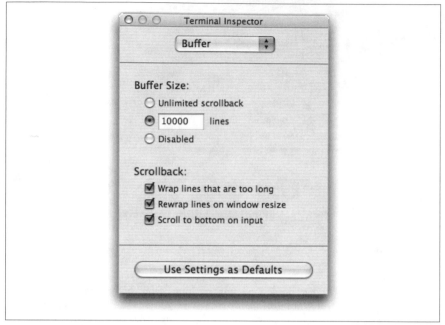

Figure 2-6. Buffer settings

You can also choose whether the Terminal should wrap long lines (not all Unix programs will wrap long lines: the extra text instead disappears off the edge of the window if this option isn't set), or whether you should automatically jump to the bottom of the scroll buffer upon input (if you've scrolled back to examine something that transpired earlier in your session). These options are set by default, and you should probably leave them that way.

The buffer itself is a storage space where the Terminal program can keep track of lines of text displayed that are no longer visible due to newer text being shown. It's what becomes visible as you use the scrollbar in the Terminal.

Display

One area that you'll probably fine-tune more than others is Display, as shown in Figure 2-7. Here, you can specify a different (or larger) font, define the shape of your cursor within the Terminal window, and control character set encoding. I always choose "Blink" to make my Terminal cursor easy to find. (It's worth noting that the arrow cursor that you're used to with the graphical interface is not the same cursor. Terminal, being a text-based environment, has a text-based cursor, too, a big gray block by default.)

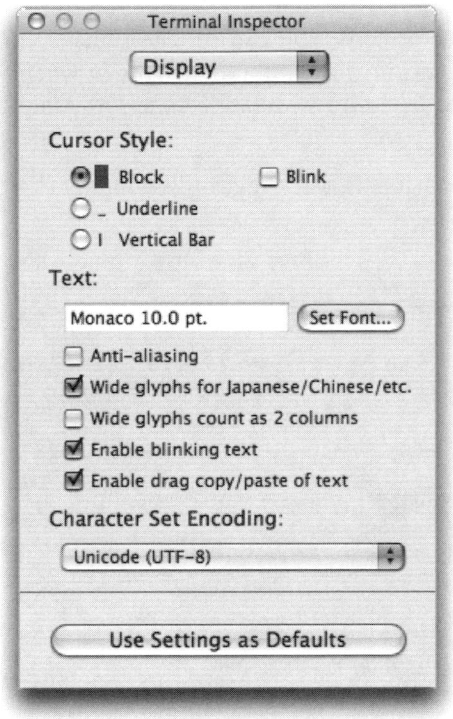

Figure 2-7. Display settings

While you can choose any font available on your system, you'll find that your display ends up quite wonky and unreadable if you don't stick with monospace or fixed-width typefaces. Monaco is a good choice, and is the default typeface for the Terminal application. Others you can choose include Courier or Courier New, after selecting the "Set font" button.

Finally, you can specify a nonstandard string encoding if you're working with an unusual language or font. The default Unicode (UTF-8) encoding works in most situations, so unless you know what you're doing or have specific needs, the default should work just fine.

Color

The Color settings, shown in Figure 2-8, let you change the colors for:

- The cursor
- Normal text

- Bold text
- Any text you select in the Terminal window
- The Terminal window's background

In addition to these options, you can set the transparency of the Terminal window, which comes in handy for those times when you want to issue some commands you see on a web site (such as Mac OS X Hints, *www. macosxhints.com*).

The default color scheme is black text on a white background, as shown in Figure 2-8.

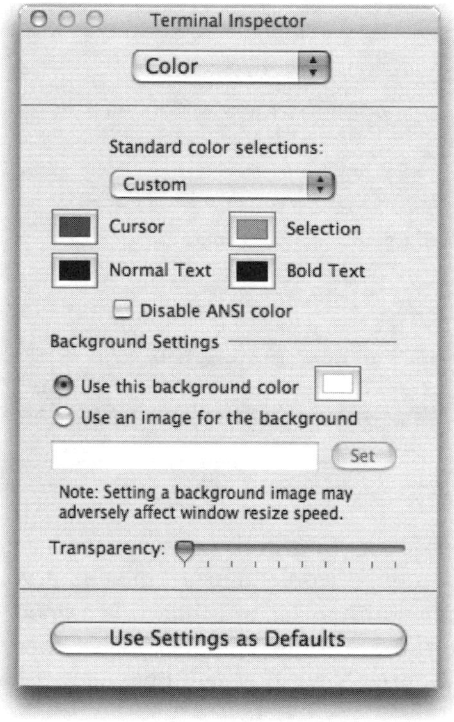

Figure 2-8. Color settings

The default color settings display black text on a white background, but you might find that light text on a dark background is easier to read for extended periods. One suggested setting is to have the background very dark blue, the cursor yellow, normal text light yellow, bold text light green, and the selection dark green.

End-of-Line Sequences Explained

Almost every time you look at a text file on your screen, it'll be laid out exactly as intended, with each line ending and the text continuing on the beginning of the following line. To accomplish this, the computer actually saves an invisible *end-of-line* character, which is then used later to ascertain where each of the file's lines of text ends.

The problem is that Unix and Macs use different characters for this task. Not such good planning, but there's quite a lot of history behind this problem. On the Mac side, all you have to know is if you see ^M in your file and the computer seems to have forgotten where all the lines end, you have an end-of-line mismatch. Nothing too dreadful, and you can easily fix it by using the following command:

```
tr '\015' '\012' < inputfile > inputfile.new
```

It's worth experimenting with the different predefined color settings. I particularly like green on black and white on blue, but your tastes will undoubtedly vary!

Window

If you have a large display or are running at a higher resolution than 800 × 600, you'll find it quite helpful to enlarge the Terminal window to offer a bigger space within which to work. The default is 80 characters wide by 24 lines tall, as shown in Figure 2-9.

The title of each Terminal window can be fine-tuned as well. You might find the device name (what you'd get if you typed **tty** at the shell prompt), the window dimensions, and the Command key option (this shows you which command sequence lets you jump directly to that Terminal window from any other Terminal window you might be using) all particularly helpful.

If you want to change the Terminal window title at any point, you can use the Set Title option either by choosing it from the File menu or by typing Shift-⌘-T.

Keyboard

The final Terminal Inspector pane is the Keyboard pane (see Figure 2-10), which offers control over which key performs which function within the Unix environment. However, switching something without knowing how it's used can be quite problematic, so I recommend that you don't change any of these settings unless you know exactly what you're doing.

Figure 2-9. Window preferences

Features of the Terminal

There are quite a few nifty Terminal features worth mentioning before I move further into the world of Unix.

Secure Keyboard Entry

While the vast majority of Mac OS X users ignore this feature, the Terminal has a very nice security feature called Secure Keyboard Entry (enable it with File → Secure Keyboard Entry). When enabled, Secure Keyboard Entry ensures that keyboard "sniffers" (or other applications that monitor your keystrokes) cannot see what you type within the Terminal. This means that the Mac OS X utility that calculates whether your computer is in use or ready to sleep won't know you're working, for example, but that could be a small price to pay for the added security of circumventing possible spyware on your system.

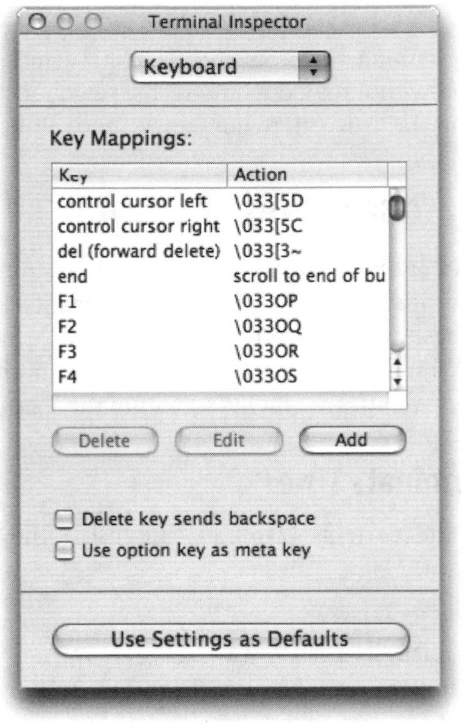

Figure 2-10. Keyboard preferences

In addition to using the Secure Keyboard Entry option from the File menu, some other features you'll find quite useful include:

File → New Command

If you need to run a Unix command but don't want to launch a new Terminal window or have its output in the current window (manpages are an excellent example), you'll appreciate knowing about the New Command option from the File menu. Choose that, enter the command you'd like to run, and its output will be displayed in a new window that you can then easily close without affecting anything else.

Edit → Paste Escaped Text

One of the common challenges of working with Unix within the Mac OS X environment is that the Finder has no problems with spaces embedded in filenames, but Unix can be rather testy about even a single space. When you're copying and pasting filenames, however, you don't have to worry about remembering to escape each and every space: just use Paste Escaped Text, and a filename like *taylor/Desktop/My Favorite Martian* is automatically pasted as *taylor/Desktop/My\ Favorite\ Martian*.

Edit → Keyboard Selection

If you want to just copy and paste what you've selected from a window, rather than everything visible in the Terminal window, use Paste Keyboard Selection without a Copy and it'll save you a step. The keyboard shortcut for this one is worth remembering, too: Shift-⌘-V.

Customizing Your Terminal Session

There are a number of different ways that you can customize your Terminal session beyond what's shown so far in this chapter. These are more advanced techniques, and you can safely flip past them if they seem too complex (though I'd still encourage you to read through the material, just so you can see what capabilities are included within the Terminal application).

Setting the Terminal's Title

You can change the current Terminal title using the following cryptic sequence of characters:

```
echo '^[]2;My-Window-Title^G'
```

To type the ^[characters in *bash*, use the key sequence Control-V Escape (press Control-V and release, then press the Escape key). To type ^G, use Control-V Control-G. The *vi* editor supports the same key sequence.

Such cryptic sequences of characters are called *ANSI escape sequences*. An ANSI escape sequence is a special command that manipulates some characteristic of the Terminal, such as its title. ^[is the ASCII ESC character (which begins the sequence), and ^G is the ASCII BEL character. (The BEL character is used to ring the Terminal bell, but in this context, it terminates the escape sequence.)

Using AppleScript to Manipulate the Terminal

AppleScript is a powerful programming language used to automate Mac OS X applications. The Mac OS X Terminal is one such application. You can run AppleScript commands at the shell prompt using the *osascript* utility. The \ character tells the shell that you want to enter a single command on several lines (when you use this, the shell will prompt you with a ? character):

```
osascript -e \
'tell app "Terminal" to set option of first window to value'
```

For example, to minimize your current Terminal window:

```
$ osascript -e \
> 'tell app "Terminal" to set miniaturized of first window to true'
$
```

For a complete list of properties you can manipulate with AppleScript, open the Script Editor (*/Applications/AppleScript*) and select File → Open Dictionary. Open the Terminal dictionary and examine the properties available under *window*, as shown in Figure 2-11. If a property is marked r/o, it is read-only, which means you can't modify it on the fly.

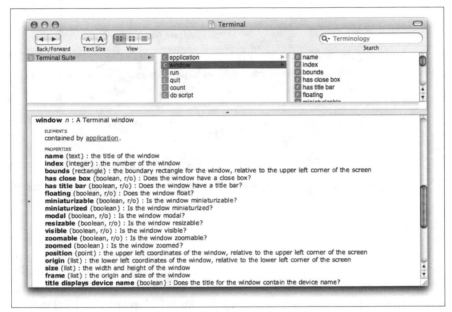

Figure 2-11. The Terminal's AppleScript dictionary

Working with .term Files

One useful feature of the Terminal is the ability for you to create a specific Terminal window, customize its appearance and behavior, and then save that configuration as a *.term* file. Later, simply double-click on the *.term* file and you'll have your Terminal window back and ready to go, exactly as you set it up previously. Even better, you can set up multiple windows and have them all saved into a single *.term* file and then collectively relaunched when you restart the Terminal program.

As an example, I have set up the main Terminal window exactly as I prefer—large, blue text on a white background—and would like to save it as a *.term* file. To accomplish this, choose File → Save As. You'll be prompted with the dialog shown in Figure 2-12.

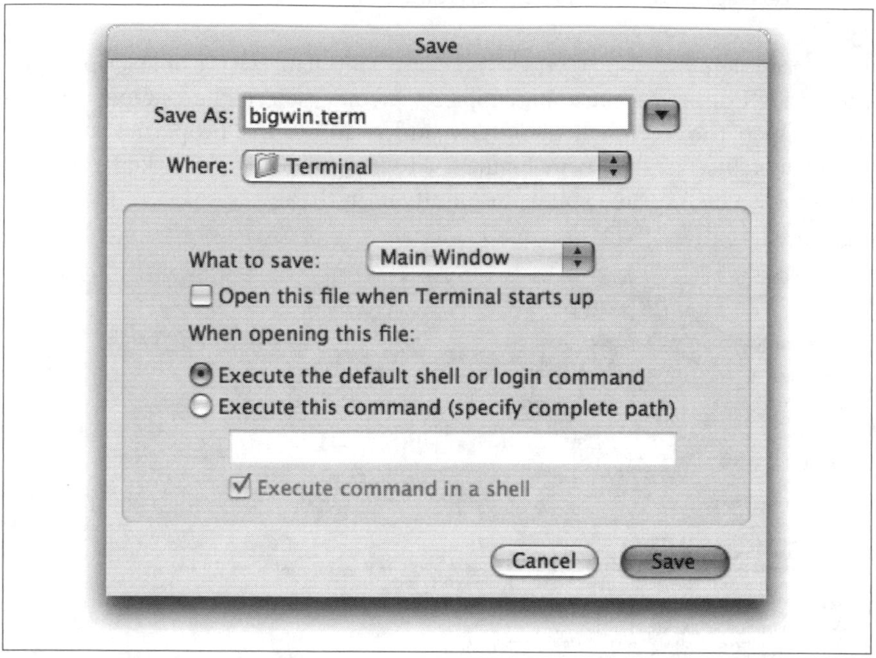

Save

Save As: bigwin.term

Where: 🖥 Terminal

What to save: Main Window

☐ Open this file when Terminal starts up

When opening this file:

⦿ Execute the default shell or login command
◯ Execute this command (specify complete path)

☑ Execute command in a shell

Cancel   Save

Figure 2-12. Saving a .term file

Perhaps the most interesting option is the checkbox "Open this file when Terminal starts up." Set things up the way you want and automatically, every time you start up Terminal, you could find a half dozen different size and different color windows on your Desktop, all ready to go. Further, notice that instead of having a shell, you could have some start up running specific commands. A popular command to use is *top* or *tail -f /var/log/ system.log*, to help keep an eye on how your system is performing. Explore the pop-up menu, too; that's where you choose a single window to save as a *.term*, or specify "All Windows" to save them all in a single *.term* file.

If you find yourself working a lot with *.term* files, you'll want to check out Terminal Pal, a helpful utility for managing your *.term* files (*www.freshlysqueezedsoftware.com/products/ freeware*).

Working with the Terminal

To get into the Unix environment, launch the Terminal application (go to Finder → Applications → Utilities → Terminal).

> If you expect to use the Terminal a lot, drag the Terminal icon from the Finder window onto the Dock or choose "Keep in Dock" by clicking on the app icon in the Dock while Terminal is running. You can then launch Terminal with a single click.

Once Terminal is running, you'll see a window like the one in Figure 2-13.

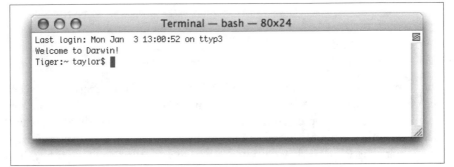

Figure 2-13. The Terminal window

You can have a number of different Terminal windows open, if that helps your workflow. Simply use ⌘-N to open each one, and ⌘-~ to cycle between them without removing your hands from the keyboard.

Once you have a window open and you're typing commands, it's helpful to know that regular Mac OS X copy and paste commands work, so it's simple to send an email message to a colleague showing your latest Unix interaction, or to paste some text from a web page into a file you're editing with a Unix text editor such as *vi*.

If you have material in your scroll buffer you want to find, use ⌘-F (or select Find → Find from the Edit menu) and enter the specific text. ⌘-G (Find → Find Next) lets you search down the scroll buffer for the next occurrence, and Shift-⌘-G (Find → Find Previous) lets you search up the scroll buffer for the previous occurrence. You can also search for material by highlighting a passage, entering ⌘-E (Find → Use Selection for Find), or jumping to the selected material with ⌘-J (Find → Jump to Selection). You can also save an entire Terminal session as a text file with File → Save Text As, and you can print the entire session with File → Print. It's also a good idea to study the key sequences shown in the Scrollback menu, as illustrated in Figure 2-14.

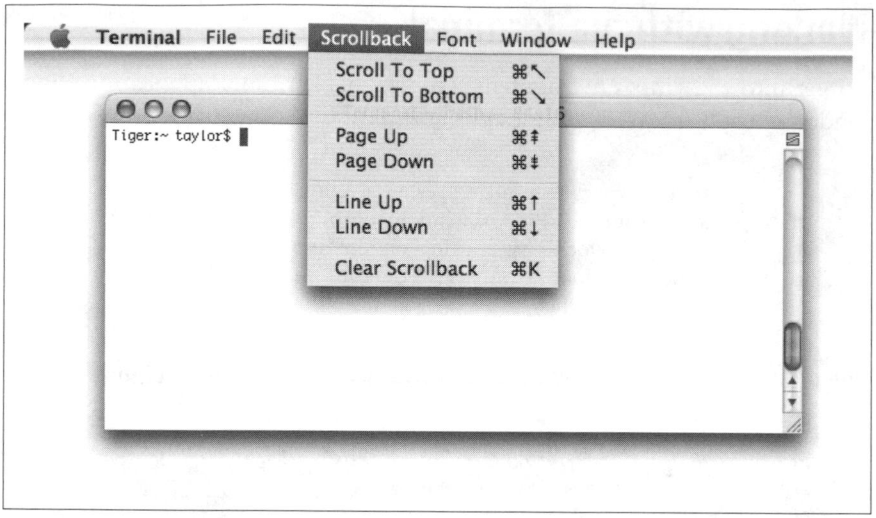

Figure 2-14. *Command sequences accessible from the Scrollback menu*

There are some symbols in the Scrollback menu you might not have seen before in your Mac OS X exploration: the upward facing diagonal arrow for Scroll to Top is the Top or Home key on your keyboard, and the downward facing diagonal arrow for Scroll to Bottom is the End key. You can move up a page with the Page Up key, and down a page with the Page Down key. To move up or down lines, use z–up arrow or z–down arrow, as needed.

Inside the Terminal window, you're working with a program called a *shell*. The shell interprets command lines you enter, runs programs you ask for, and generally coordinates what happens between you and the Unix operating system. The default shell on Mac OS X is called *bash* (it used to be *tcsh* in previous versions of Mac OS X). Other available shells include the Bourne shell (*sh*), the C shell (*csh*), the Korn shell (*ksh*), the Tabbed C shell (*tcsh*), and the Z shell (*zsh*). To change the shell that Terminal uses, see "Changing the Terminal's Preferences."

For a beginner, differences between shells are slight. If you plan to work with Unix a lot, though, you should learn more about your shell and its special commands.

To find out which shell you're using, run the command *echo $SHELL*. The answer, which will be something like */bin/bash*, is your shell's path and name.

The Shell Prompt

When the system is ready to run a command, the shell outputs a *prompt* to tell you that you can enter a command.

The default prompt in *bash* is the computer name (which might be something automatically generated, such as dhcp-254-108, or a name you've given your system), the current directory (which might be represented by ~, Unix's shorthand for your home directory), your login name, and a dollar sign. For example, the complete prompt might look like this: limbo:~ taylor$. The prompt can be customized, though, so your own shell prompt may be different. I show you how to customize your prompt later in this chapter.

A prompt that ends with a hash mark (#) usually means you're logged in as the *superuser*. The superuser doesn't have the protections for standard users that are built into the Unix system. If you don't know Unix well, you can inadvertently damage your system software when you are logged in as the superuser. In this case, I highly recommend that you stop work until you've found out how to access your personal Unix account.

The simplest solution is to open a new Terminal window (File → New Shell) and work in that window. If you've still got the superuser prompt, it means that you either logged into Mac OS X as the superuser or your shell prompt has been customized to end with a #, even when you're not the superuser. Try logging out of Mac OS X completely (→ Log Out, or Shift-⌘-Q) and logging back in as yourself.

Entering a Command

Entering a command line at the shell prompt tells the computer what to do. Each command line includes the name of a Unix program. When you press Return, the shell interprets your command line and executes the program.

The first word that you type at a shell prompt is always a Unix command (or program name). Like most things in Unix, program names are case sensitive; if the program name is lowercase (and most are), you must type it in lowercase. Some simple command lines have just one word, which is the program name.

date

An example of a single-word command is *date*. Entering the command *date* displays the current date and time:

```
$ date
Mon Jan  3 13:37:56 MST 2005
$
```

As you type a command line, the system simply collects your keyboard input. Pressing the Return key tells the shell that you've finished entering text, and it can run the program.

who

Another simple command is *who*. It displays a list of each logged-on user's username, terminal number, and login time. Try it now, if you'd like.

The *who* program can also tell you which account is currently using the Terminal application, in case you have multiple user accounts on your Mac. The command line for this is *who am i*. This command line consists of the command (*who*, the program's name) and arguments (*am i*). (Arguments are explained in "Syntax of a Unix Command" earlier in this chapter.) For example:

```
$ who am i
taylor    console  Jan 3 13:07
taylor    ttyp2    Jan 3 16:26
```

The response shown in this example says that:

- taylor is the username. The username is the same as the Short Name you define when you create a new user with System Preferences → Accounts → +.

- Both the console and terminal ttyp2 are in use. The console is the administrative window to the entire Mac OS X system and indicates when you booted up the computer. The cryptic ttyp2 syntax is a hold-over from the early days of Unix. All you need to know as a Unix beginner is that each time you open a new Terminal window, the number at the end of the name gets incremented by one. The first is ttyp1, the second ttyp2, and so on. The terminal ID also can also be included in the titlebar of the Terminal window, if desired.

- A new Terminal window was opened at 16:26 (or 4:26 p.m.) in the afternoon of January 3rd.

Recalling Previous Commands

Modern Unix shells remember commands you've typed previously. They can even remember commands from previous login sessions. This handy feature can save you a lot of retyping of common commands. As with many things in Unix, though, there are several different ways to do this; I don't have room to show and explain them all. You can get more information from sources listed in Chapter 11.

After you've typed and executed several commands, try pressing the up arrow key on your keyboard. You will see the previous command after your shell prompt, just as you typed it. Pressing the up arrow key again recalls the previous command, and so on. Also, as you'd expect, the down arrow key will recall more recent commands.

To execute one of these remembered commands, just press the Return key. (Your cursor doesn't even have to be at the end of the command line.)

Once you've recalled a command, you can edit it as necessary. If you don't want to execute any remembered commands, cancel the command shown either with the Mac-standard ⌘-. (Command-period) or with the Unix-standard, Control-C. The next section explains both of these.

Completing File and Directory Names

Most Unix shells can complete a partially typed file or directory name for you. If you're using the default shell in Mac OS X (i.e., *bash*), just type the first few letters of the name, then press Tab. (Different shells have different methods.) If the shell finds just one way to finish the name, it will; your cursor moves to the end of the new name, where you can type more Unix commands, or just press Return to run the command.

 You can also edit or erase the completed name by hitting the Delete key or moving the cursor back and forth with the left and right arrow keys.

What happens if more than one file or directory name matches what you've typed so far? The shell beeps at you to let you know that it couldn't find a unique match. To get a list of all possible completions, simply press the Tab key again and you will see a list of all names starting with the characters you've typed so far (you won't see anything if there are no matches). Here's an example from the *bash* shell:

```
$ cd /usr/bin
$ ma<Tab><Tab>
mach_init   machine   mail      mailq      mailstat   makedbm    makeinfo
man         manpath
$ ma
```

At this point, you could type another character or two—an **i**, for example—and then press Tab once more to list only the mail-related commands.

Running Multiple Commands on the Command Line

An extremely helpful technique for working with the Unix system is the ability to have more than one command specified on a single command line. Perhaps you want to run a command and find out how long it took to complete. This can be done by calling *date* before and after the command. If you hunt and peck out *date* each time, the timing is hardly going to be accurate. Much better is to put all three commands on the same line:

```
$ cd ; date ; du -s . ; date
Tue Feb  8 13:00:11 PST 2005
21551000        .
Tue Feb  8 13:00:19 PST 2005
```

This shows four different commands all strung together on a single command line, using the semicolon character (;) to separate each command.

- First, *cd* moves you into your home directory, then *date* shows the current date and time.

- Next, the *du -s* command figures out how much disk space is used by the current directory, as denoted by the period (.). A second *date* command shows the time after the *du* command has run.

Now you know it takes exactly eight seconds to calculate disk space used by your home directory, rather than knowing it takes 25 seconds for you to type the command, for *du* to run, and for you to type *date* again.

Correcting a Command

What if you make a mistake in a command line? Suppose you type *dare* instead of *date* and press the Return key before you realize your mistake. The shell displays the following error message:

```
$ dare
-bash: dare: command not found
$
```

Don't be too concerned about getting error messages. Sometimes you'll get an error even if it appears that you typed the command correctly. This can be caused by accidentally typing control characters that are invisible on the screen. Once the prompt returns, reenter your command.

 As I said earlier, you can recall previous commands and edit command lines. Use the up arrow key to recall a previous command.

To edit the command line, use the left and right arrow keys to move your cursor to the point where you want to make a change. You can use the Delete key to erase characters to the left of the cursor, and type in changes as needed.

If you have logged into your Macintosh remotely from another system (see Chapter 8), your keyboard may be different. The erase character differs between systems and accounts, and can be customized. The most common erase characters are:

- Delete or Del
- Control-H

Control-C (or ⌘-.) interrupts or cancels a command, and can be used in many (but not all) cases when you want to quit what you're doing.

Other common control characters are:

Control-U
> Erases the whole input line; you can start over.

Control-S
> Pauses output from a program that's writing to the screen. This can be confusing, so I don't recommend using Control-S.

Control-Q
> Restarts output after a Control-S pause.

Control-D
> Signals the end of input for some programs (such as *cat*, explained in "Putting Text into a File" in Chapter 6) and returns you to a shell prompt. If you type Control-D at a shell prompt, it quits your shell. Depending on your preferences, your Terminal window either closes or sits there, which is useless, until you manually close the window.

Ending Your Session

To end a Unix session, you must exit the shell. You should *not* end a session just by quitting the Terminal application or closing the terminal window. It's possible that you might have started a process running in the background (see Chapter 7), and closing the window could therefore interrupt the process so it won't complete. Instead, type **exit** at a shell prompt and hit Return. The window will either close or simply not display any sort of prompt; you can then safely quit the Terminal application. If you've started a background process, you'll instead get one of the messages described in the next section.

Problem Checklist

The first few times you use Mac OS X, you aren't likely to have the following problems. But you may encounter these problems later, as you do more advanced work.

You get another shell prompt, or the shell says "logout: not login shell."
> You've been using a subshell (a shell created by your original Terminal shell). To end each subshell, type **exit** (or just type Control-D) until the Terminal window closes.

The shell says "There are stopped jobs" or "There are running jobs."
> Mac OS X and many other Unix systems have a feature called *job control* that lets you suspend a program temporarily while it's running or keep it running separately in the "background." One or more programs you ran during your session has not ended but is stopped (paused) or in the background. Enter **fg** to bring each stopped job into the foreground, then quit the program normally. (See Chapter 7 for more information.)

The Terminal application refuses to quit, saying "Closing this window will terminate the following processes inside it:," followed by a list of programs.
> Terminal tries to help by not quitting when you're in the middle of running a command. Cancel the dialog box and make sure you don't have any commands running that you forgot about.

Customizing the Shell Environment

The Unix shell reads a number of configuration files when it starts up. These configuration files are really *shell programs*, so they are extraordinarily powerful. Shell programming is beyond the scope of this book.

But let's look at what you can customize without having to become a full-fledged Unix geek, shall we?

Picking a Login Shell

The default login shell for Tiger is the ever-popular *bash* shell, but many Unix fans prefer to use the Korn shell (*ksh*) instead. As mentioned earlier, Mac OS X offers a host of different shells, including */bin/bash*, */bin/csh*, */bin/ksh*, */bin/tcsh*, */bin/zsh*, and */bin/sh*.

To change your login shell, you can either use the Unix *chsh* command (enter *chsh* on the command line and you'll be asked which shell you'd like starting the next time you log in), or just change it within the Terminal Inspector's Shell pop-up screen, as shown earlier, in Figure 2-3.

Changing the Command Prompt

The easiest customization you can make to the shell is to change your *command prompt*. By default, *bash* on Mac OS X has a shell prompt made up of your computer hostname, your current working directory, your account name, and a dollar sign. For example:

```
Dave-Taylors-Computer:~ taylor$
```

If you'd rather have something shorter, like just the dollar sign ($), enter the following command:

```
Dave-Taylors-Computer:~ taylor$ PS1="$ "
$
```

This command gives you a simple, sparse $ prompt, and nothing else. It isn't necessary to use the dollar sign as your prompt; you could use a colon (:), a greater-than sign (>), or any character you like. Just remember to include a space after the character you've chosen to use as the prompt, because that helps you differentiate between the command prompt and the actual command you're typing in.

 You can also edit the *.bashrc* file, which is the file *bash* uses to store its "preferences." Use the *vi* editor to create a file called *.profile* in your home directory (*/Users/yourname*), and then add the following to the end of the file: **export PS1="$ "**. (You can read more about the *vi* editor in Chapter 4.)

Of course, if that's all you could do to your command prompt, it wouldn't be very interesting. There are a number of special character sequences that, when used to define the prompt, cause the shell to print out various bits of useful data. Table 2-2 shows a partial list of these special character sequences for fine-tuning your prompt.

Table 2-2. Favorite escape sequences for bash prompts

Value	Meaning
\w	The current working directory
\W	The trailing element of the current working directory, with ~ substitution
\!	The current command history number
\H	The full hostname
\h	The hostname up to the first dot
\@	Time of day in 12-hour (a.m./p.m.) format
\A	Time of day in 24-hour format
\u	The username
\$	A # if the effective user ID is zero (*root*), or a $ otherwise

Experiment and see what sort of interesting Unix prompt you can create. For many years, a popular Unix prompt was:

```
$ PS1="Yes, Master? "
```

It might be a bit obsequious, but on the other hand, how many people in your life call you "Master"?

One prompt sequence that I like is:

```
$ PS1="\W \! \$ "
```

This prompt sequence shows the current working directory, followed by a space and the current history number, and then a $ or # to remind the user that this is *bash* and whether they're currently running as root. (The # is for when you're running as root, the administrator account, and the $ is for when you aren't root). For example, the prompt might read:

```
/Users/taylor 55 $
```

This tells you immediately that */Users/taylor* is the current directory, and that this will be the 55th command you'll execute. Because you can use the up or down arrow keys to scroll back or forward, respectively, to previous commands, as described in "Recalling Previous Commands," this is no longer as important, but there is a very powerful command history syntax built into *bash* that allows you to recall a previous command by number. If you're familiar with this syntax, making the command history number part of the prompt can be handy.

On multiuser systems, it's not a bad idea to put the username into the prompt as well. That way, you'll always know who the system thinks you are. And if you routinely use more than one computer system, you should also consider including the hostname in the prompt so you'll always know which system it is you're logged into.

Advanced Shell Customization

There's not much more you can do with the Terminal application than what's shown in this chapter, but there's an infinite amount of customization possible with the *bash* shell (or any other shell you might have picked). Here are a few directions to get you started.

Shell Configuration Settings

Because Unix is a multiuser system, there are two possible locations for the configuration files: one applies to all users of the system and another to each individual user.

The system-wide setup files that are read by *bash*, the default shell for Mac OS X, are found in */etc* (*profile* and *bashrc*). You only have permission to change these system-wide files if you use *sudo* (see "Superuser Privileges with sudo in Chapter 3). However, you can create another file called *.profile* in your home directory that will add additional commands to be executed whenever you start a new Terminal window. (If you configure Terminal to use another shell, such as the Bourne shell, the C shell, or the Z shell, you'll need to set up different configuration files. See the manpage for your selected shell to learn necessary details. To learn more about *csh*, for example, type *man csh*.)

The system-wide setup files are read first, then the user-specific ones, so commands in your *.profile* file can override those in the system-wide files. The system-wide *profile* and *bashrc* files are succinct:

```
$ cat /etc/profile
# System-wide .profile for sh(1)

PATH="/bin:/sbin:/usr/bin:/usr/sbin"
export PATH

if [ "${BASH-no}" != "no" ]; then
  [ -r /etc/bashrc ] && . /etc/bashrc
fi

$ cat /etc/bashrc
# System-wide .bashrc file for interactive bash(1) shells.
```

```
if [ -n "$PS1" ]; then PS1='\h:\w \u\$ '; fi
# Make bash check it's window size after a process completes
shopt -s checkwinsize
$
```

If you want to change the PATH for all users, perhaps to add */usr/local/bin* (see Chapter 4 for details on what you can find in that directory), modify the */etc/profile* contents as follows:

```
PATH="/bin:/sbin:/usr/bin:/usr/sbin:/usr/local/bin"
```

The *.profile* file can contain any shell command that you want to run automatically whenever you create a new Terminal. Some typical examples include changing the shell prompt, setting environment variables (values that control the operation of other Unix utilities), setting aliases, or adding to the search path (where the shell searches for programs to be run). A *.profile* file could look like this:

```
export PS1="\w (\!) : "
export LESS="eMq"
alias desktop="cd ~/Desktop"
date
```

This sample *.profile* file issues the following commands:

- The line that changes the value of PS1 tells the shell to use a different prompt than the standard one. I explained the details of prompt setting in "Customizing the Shell Environment" earlier in this chapter.

- The line with export LESS sets a shell variable that the *less* program recognizes to change its default behavior. In this case, it's identical to typing in **less -eMq** each time you use the command. Not all commands recognize environment variables, but for those that do, this type of environment variable setting saves you the trouble of typing the options on every command line.

- The line that begins with alias defines a new, custom command that your shell will recognize just as if it were a built-in Unix command. Aliases are a great way to save shorthand names for long, complicated Unix command lines, or even to fix common mistakes you might make when typing command lines. This particular alias creates a command for going right to the Desktop directory. A brief tutorial on creating aliases can be found later in this chapter in "Creating Aliases."

- The date line simply runs the *date* command to print the time and date when you open a new Terminal window. You might not want to do this, but it's good for you to see that you can include any command that you could type at the shell prompt and have it automatically executed whenever a new shell starts up.

By default, the *.profile* file doesn't yet exist in your Home directory, and only the system-wide configuration files are read each time a Terminal window is opened. But if you create the file in your Home directory, it is read and its contents are executed the next time you start a shell. You can create or change these files with a text editor, such as *vi* (see Chapter 4).

Don't use a word processor like Microsoft Word that breaks long lines or puts special nontext codes into the file. TextEdit can work if you really insist, but you need to ensure that you chose Format → Make Plain Text (Shift-⌘-T) before you save the file to ensure that no additional formatting information is added by the application.

Any changes you make to these files will take effect when you open a new Terminal window. Unfortunately, it's not always easy to know which shell setup file you should change. And an editing mistake in your shell setup file can interfere with the normal startup of the Terminal window itself. It is recommended that beginners get help from experienced users before tweaking these files. Also, you shouldn't make changes to these files at all if you're about to do some critical work with your account, unless there's some reason you have to make the changes immediately.

You can execute any customization command discussed here from the command line as well. In this case, the changes are in effect only until you close that window or quit Terminal.

For example, to change the default options for *less* so it clears the Terminal window before showing each new page of text, you could add the -c option to the LESS environment variable. The command looks something like this:

```
$ export LESS='eMqc'
```

If you don't want some of the *less* options shown here, you could leave those other options out.

Unix has many other configuration commands to learn about; the books and Web sites listed in Chapter 11 can help you identify which modifications you can make and how they can help you produce an optimal computing environment for yourself.

Just as you can execute the setup commands from the command line, any command that you can execute from the command line can be executed automatically when you log in by placing it in your setup file. (Running interactive commands such as *vi* or *ftp* from your setup file isn't a good idea, though.)

Creating Aliases

The flexibility of Unix is simultaneously its greatest strength and downfall; the operating system can do just about anything you can imagine (the command-line interface is certainly far more flexible than the Finder!), but it's very difficult to remember every single option to every command. That's where shell aliases can be a real boon. A shell alias is a simple mechanism that lets you create your own command names that act exactly as you desire.

For example, I really like the -a and -F options to be included every time I list a directory with ls, so I created the following alias:

```
$ alias ls="/bin/ls -aF"
```

Now every time I enter *ls* in the shell, the command is run, and the -a and -F options are specified automatically. To have this available in your next session, make sure you remember to also add the alias to your .*profile* file.

You can also have aliases that let you jump quickly to common locations, a particularly helpful trick when in Mac OS X:

```
$ alias desktop="cd ~/Desktop"
```

With that alias in place, all you need to do is enter **desktop** at the command prompt, and you're taken to your Desktop directory. The shell looks at its .*profile* file, sees that *desktop* is an alias, and runs the commands found in the quotes (in this case, *cd ~/Desktop*).

Another set of useful aliases are to automatically set the *rm*, *cp*, and *mv* commands into interactive mode, using their -i option. (Chapter 4 describes the *cp*, *mv*, and *rm* commands, which copy, move, and remove files, respectively.) Each of these supports the -i option, which prompts you before overwriting or deleting a file. You can use aliases to always enable this option:

```
$ alias rm="rm -i"
$ alias cp="cp -i"
$ alias mv="mv -i"
```

You can list all active aliases by typing *alias* without any arguments:

```
$ alias
alias cp='cp -i'
alias desktop='cd ~/Desktop'
alias ls='/bin/ls -a'
alias m2u='tr '\''\015'\'' '\''\012'\'''
alias u2m='tr '\''\012'\'' '\''\015'\'''
```

Have an alias you want to get rid of? You can use the *unalias* command for that. For example, *unalias ls* removes the -aF options added earlier.

The Unresponsive Terminal

During your Unix session, your terminal may not respond when you type a command, or the display on your screen may stop at an unusual place. That's called a "hung" or "frozen" terminal or session. Note that most of the techniques in this section apply to a Terminal window, but not to non-Terminal windows, such as a web browser.

A session can hang for several reasons. For instance, your computer can get too busy; the Terminal application has to wait its turn. In that case, your session resumes after a few moments. You should *not* try to "un-hang" the session by entering extra commands, because those commands will all take effect after Terminal comes back to life.

 If your display becomes garbled, press Control-L. In the shell, this will clear the screen and display the prompt. In a full-screen program, such as a text editor, this keyboard shortcut redraws the screen.

If the system doesn't respond for quite a while (how long that is depends on your individual situation; ask other users about their experiences), the following solutions usually work. Try the following steps in the order shown until the system responds:

Press the Return key once
> You may have typed text at a prompt (for example, a command line at a shell prompt) but haven't yet pressed Return to say that you're done typing and your text should be interpreted.

Try job control (see Chapter 7); type Control-Z
> This control key sequence suspends a program that may be running and gives you a shell prompt. Now you can enter the *jobs* command to find the program's name, then restart the program with *fg* or terminate it with *kill*.

Press Control-C or ⌘-.
> This interrupts a program that may be running. (Unless the program is run in the background; as described in Chapter 7, the shell waits for a background program to finish before giving a new prompt. A long-running background program may thus appear to hang the Terminal.) If this doesn't work the first time, try it once more; doing it more than twice usually won't help.

Type Control-Q

If output has been stopped with Control-S, this restarts the previously paused process. Note that some systems automatically issue Control-S if they need to pause output; this character may not have been typed from the keyboard.

Type Control-D once at the beginning of a new line

Some programs (such as *mail*) expect text from the user. A program may be waiting for an end-of-input character from you to tell it that you've finished entering text. Typing Control-D may cause you to log out, so you should try this only as a last resort.

Otherwise, close your Terminal window (⌘-W) and open a new one.

## CHAPTER 3

Exploring the Filesystem

Once you launch the Terminal, you can use the many facilities that Mac OS X provides at the command line, an environment that's quite a bit more powerful than the graphical interface you may be used to viewing. As a user, you have an account that gives you:

- A place in the filesystem where you can store your files
- A username that identifies you and lets you control access to files
- An environment you can customize

In this chapter, you'll see how all the thousands of files on your Mac are organized, how to learn more details about any given file, and how to move around through Mac OS X's filesystem. You'll see that the Finder has been hiding quite a lot of information from you, entire directories with thousands of files that are invisible from the Finder but easily found and explored within the Terminal.

The Mac OS X Filesystem

A *file* is the unit of storage in Mac OS X. A file can hold anything: text (a report you're writing, a to-do list), a program, digitally encoded pictures or sound, and so on. All of those are just sequences of raw data until they're interpreted by the right program.

Files are organized into *directories* (more commonly referred to as *folders* on the Aqua side of the Mac). A directory is actually a special kind of file where the system stores information about other files. You can think of a directory as a place, so that files are said to be contained *in* directories, and you work *inside* a directory. It's important that you realize that *everything is a file in Unix*. Whether you're working with a directory (perhaps moving files around) or editing a document, Unix fundamentally looks at everything as the same sort of container of information.

A *filesystem* includes all the files and directories on a mounted volume, such as your system's hard disk or your .Mac account's iDisk (which you *mount* on your system with a little help from WebDAV). This section introduces Mac OS X's filesystem, showing you how all the files on your Mac are organized and how to use Unix commands to explore your Mac's filesystem. Later sections show how you can look in files and protect them. Chapter 4 has more information.

Your Home Directory

When you launch the Terminal, you're placed in a directory called your *home directory*. This directory, which can also be viewed in the Finder by clicking the Home icon, contains personal files, application preferences, and application data such as Safari's bookmarks. In your home directory, you can create your own files, create other subdirectories, and so on. Like folders in a file cabinet, directories offer a way for you to organize your files.

You can find out where your home directory is at any time by typing the following command:

```
$ echo $HOME
/Users/taylor
$
```

As you can see, this tells me that my home directory (*taylor*) is found within the Users directory (*/Users*). In Unix, a forward slash (*/*) is used to separate directory names, with just a single slash signifying the very bottom, or *root level*, of your Mac's filesystem. For example, to change directories to the root level of your hard drive, use the following command:

```
$ cd /
```

For more information on the filesystem's structure and the root directory, see "The Directory Tree," later in this section.

Your Working Directory

Your *working directory* (also called your current directory) is the directory in which you're currently working. Every time you open a new Terminal window, your home directory is your working directory. When you change to another directory, the directory you move to becomes your working directory, and so on.

Unless you specify otherwise, all commands that you enter apply to the files in your working directory. In the same way, when you create files, they're created in your working directory unless you specify another directory. For instance, if you type the command *vi report*, the *vi* editor starts, and a file named *report* is created in your working directory. (Unless, of course, a *report* file already exists there; in which case that file would be opened in *vi*.) But if you enter the following command:

```
$ vi /Users/john/Documents/report
```

A *report* file is created in your *Documents* directory—all without your having to change from your current working directory. You'll learn more about this when I cover *pathnames* later in this chapter.

If you have more than one Terminal window open, each shell has its own working directory. Changing the working directory in one shell doesn't affect other Terminal windows.

You can find out your working directory at any time by entering the *pwd* command:

```
$ pwd
/Users/taylor
$
```

The Directory Tree

All directories on Mac OS X are organized into a hierarchical structure that you can imagine as a family tree. The parent directory of the tree (the directory that contains all other directories) is known as the *root directory* and is written as a forward slash (/). The root directory is what you see if you open a new Finder window, click the Computer icon, and then open your hard disk.

The root directory contains several other directories. Figure 3-1 shows a visual representation of the top of Mac OS X's filesystem tree: the root directory and some directories under the root.

Applications, *Library*, *System*, and *Users* are some of the *subdirectories* (child directories) of the root directory. There are several other directories that are invisible in the Finder but visible at the shell prompt (you can see them if you use the *ls /* command). These subdirectories are standard Unix directories: *bin*, *dev*, *etc*, *sbin*, *tmp*, *usr*, and *var*; they contain Unix system files. For instance, *bin* contains many Unix programs.

In the previous section, the parent directory of *Users* (one level above) is the root directory. *Users* has two subdirectories (one level below), *john* and *carol*. On a Mac OS X system, each directory has only one parent directory, but it may have one or more subdirectories.[*]

---

[*] The root directory at the top of the tree is *its own* parent.

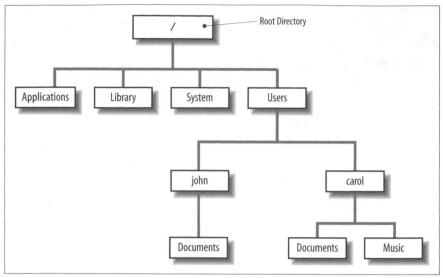

Figure 3-1. Example of a directory tree

A subdirectory (such as *carol*) can have its own subdirectories (such as *Documents* and *Music*).

To specify a file or directory location, write its *pathname*. A pathname is essentially the address of the directory or file in the filesystem. For more on pathnames, see "Absolute Pathnames" and "Relative Pathnames."

On a basic Mac OS X system, all files in the filesystem are stored on disks connected to your computer. Mac OS X has a way to access files on other computers: a *networked filesystem*. Networked filesystems make a remote computer's files appear as if they're part of your computer's directory tree. For instance, when you mount your .Mac account's iDisk (from the Finder's menu bar, select Go → iDisk → My iDisk), Mac OS X mounts your iDisk on your Desktop and also makes it available as a directory under */Volumes*. You can also mount shared directories from other Macs, Windows machines, or even Unix and Linux servers (from the Finder's menu bar, select Go → Connect to Server). These also appear in the */Volumes* directory, as will other disks, including any external FireWire drives connected to your Mac.

Absolute Pathnames

As you saw earlier, the Unix filesystem organizes its files and directories in an inverted tree structure with the root directory at the top. An *absolute pathname* tells you the path of directories through which you must travel to get from the root to the directory or file you want. In a pathname, slashes (/) are used between the directory names.

For example, */Users/john* is an absolute pathname. It identifies one (*only one!*) directory. Here's how:

- The root directory is the first slash (/).
- The directory *Users* (a subdirectory of the root directory) is second.
- The directory *john* (a subdirectory of *Users*) is last.

 Be sure that you do not type spaces anywhere in the pathname. If there are spaces in one or more of the directories, you need to either quote the entire directory pathname, or preface each space with a backslash (\)to ensure that the shell understands that the spaces are part of the pathname itself. The backslash is known as an *escape character*; escape characters are discussed in "Changing Your Prompt" in Chapter 2.

In Figure 3-2, you'll see that the directory *john* has a subdirectory named *Documents*. Its absolute pathname is */Users/john/Documents*.

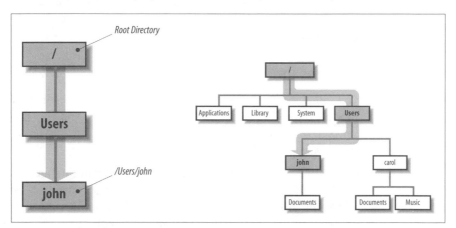

Figure 3-2. Absolute path of directory john

 The root directory is always indicated by the slash (/) at the start of the pathname. In other words, an absolute pathname always starts with a slash.

Relative Pathnames

You can also locate a file or directory with a *relative pathname*. A relative pathname gives the location relative to your working directory.

Unless you use an absolute pathname (a path that starts with a slash), Unix assumes that you're using a relative pathname. Like absolute pathnames, relative pathnames can go through more than one directory level by naming the directories along the path.

For example, if you're currently in the */Users* directory (see Figure 3-2), the relative pathname to the *carol* directory is simply *carol*:

```
MacTiger:/Users carol$ cd carol
MacTiger:~ carol$
```

If *carol* wanted to move from her home directory to the *Music* directory, the relative pathname to the *Music* directory would be as follows:

```
MacTiger:~ carol$ cd Music
MacTiger:~/Music carol$
```

Or, she could just use the following command to get from */Users* to *carol/ Music*:

```
MacTiger:/Users carol$ cd carol/Music
MacTiger:~/Music carol$
```

In these examples, notice that none of the pathnames start with a slash. That's what makes them relative pathnames! Relative pathnames start at the working directory, not the root directory. Just remember, a relative pathname never starts with a slash.

Relative pathnames up

You can go up the tree with the Unix shorthand .. (two periods, commonly referred to in Unix lingo as "dot, dot") for the parent directory. As you saw earlier, you can also go down the tree by using subdirectory names. In either case (up or down), separate each level by a forward slash (/).

Figure 3-3 shows part of Figure 3-1. If your working directory in the figure is *Documents*, then there are two pathnames for the *Music* subdirectory of *carol*. You already know how to write the absolute pathname, */Users/carol/ Music*. You can also go up one level (with ..) to *carol*, then go down the tree to *Music*. Figure 3-3 illustrates this.

The relative pathname would be *../Music*. It would be wrong to give the relative address as *carol/Music*. Using *carol/Music* would say that *carol* is a subdirectory of your working directory instead of what it is in this case: the parent directory.

Absolute and relative pathnames are interchangeable. Unix programs simply follow whichever path you specify to wherever it leads. If you use an absolute pathname, the path starts from the root. If you use a relative pathname, the path starts from your current working directory. Choose whichever is easier at the moment.

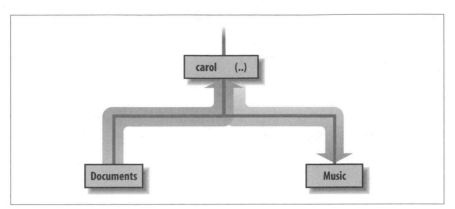

Figure 3-3. Relative pathname from Documents to Music

Pathname Puzzle

Here's a short but important question. The previous examples explain the relative pathname *carol/Music*. What do you think Unix would say about the pathname */carol/Music*? (Look again at Figure 3-2.)

Unix would say "No such file or directory." Why? (Please think about that a little bit; this is very important, and it's one of the most common mistakes made by Unix newbies.) Well, it's because the path starts with a slash, the pathname */carol/Music* is an absolute pathname that starts from the root. It says to look in the root directory (/) for a subdirectory named *carol*. But since there is no subdirectory named *carol*, the pathname is wrong. The only absolute pathname to the *Music* directory is */Users/carol/Music*.

Changing Your Working Directory

Once you know the absolute or relative pathname of a directory where you'd like to work, you can move up and down the Mac OS X filesystem to reach it. The following sections explain some helpful commands for navigating through a directory tree.

pwd

To find which directory you're currently in, use *pwd* (print working directory), which prints the absolute pathname of your working directory. The *pwd* command takes no arguments:

```
$ pwd
/Users/john
$
```

cd

You can change from your present working directory to any directory (including another user's directory, if you have permission) with the *cd* (change directory) command, which has the form:

```
cd pathname
```

The argument is an absolute or a relative pathname (whichever is easier) for the directory you want to change to:

```
$ cd /Users/carol
$ pwd
/Users/carol
$ cd Documents
$ pwd
/Users/carol/Documents
$
```

 The command *cd*, with no arguments, takes you to your home directory from wherever you are in the filesystem. It's identical to typing in *cd $HOME*.

Note that you can only change to another directory that you have permission to access. If you try to change to a directory that you're otherwise shut out of, you'll see an error:

```
$ cd /Users/john
-bash: cd: /Users/john: Permission denied
$
```

You also cannot *cd* to a filename. If you try, your shell (in this example, *bash*) gives you an error message:

```
$ cd /etc/manpath.config
-bash: cd: /etc/manpath.config:  Not a directory.
$
```

 If you're curious, */etc/manpath.config* is a file with information about the configuration of the *man* command.

One neat trick worth mentioning is that you can quickly give the Terminal a file's path by dragging a file or folder icon from the Finder onto the Terminal window. This is particularly helpful for those times when you'd have to type in an extra long pathname. For example, if you wanted to change directories to a song in your iTunes collection, you'd have to type in something like the following:

```
MacTiger:~ taylor$ cd /Users/taylor/Music/iTunes/iTunes\ Music/ .|
Dave\ Edmunds/Rockin\'\ -\ Best\ of\ Dave\ Edmunds
```

Sure, like you're going to remember that pathname off the top of your head!

To make this easier, you could just type *cd* followed by a space in a Terminal window, and then drag the folder in question from a Finder window onto the Terminal window, as shown in Figure 3-4. When you let go of the file or folder you're dragging into the Terminal window, the pathname gets added to the command prompt.

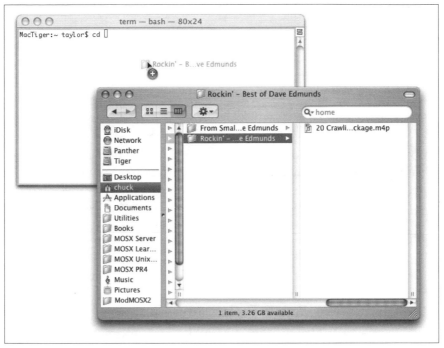

Figure 3-4. Dragging a folder from the Finder to a Terminal window saves you from having to type in long and complex paths

Files in the Directory Tree

A directory can hold subdirectories. And, of course, a directory can hold files. Figure 3-5 is a close-up of the filesystem around *john*'s home directory. There are six directories shown, along with the *mac-rocks* file created by using the *touch* command, as explained in the sidebar "Two Ways to Explore Your Filesystem."

Pathnames to files are constructed the same way as pathnames to directories. As with directories, files' pathnames can be absolute (starting from the root directory) or relative (starting from the working directory). For example, if your working directory is */Users*, the relative pathname to the

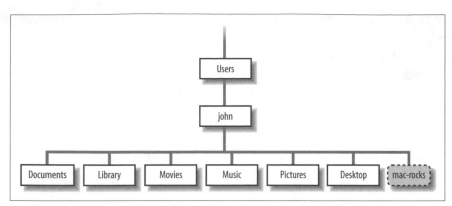

Figure 3-5. Files in the directory tree

Documents directory below would be *john/Documents*. The relative pathname to the *mac-rocks* file would be *john/mac-rocks*.

Unix filesystems can hold things that aren't directories or files, such as symbolic links (similar to aliases in Mac OS), devices (the */dev* directory contains entries for devices attached to the system), and sockets (network communication channels). You may see some of them as you explore the filesystem. These advanced topics aren't covered in this little book, however, because they're more complex, and overloading you with advanced stuff right now just wouldn't be fair.

Two Ways to Explore Your Filesystem

Every file and folder that you view from the Finder is also accessible from the Unix shell. Changes made in one environment are reflected (almost) immediately in the other. For example, the Desktop folder is also the Unix directory */Users/yourname/Desktop*.

Just for fun, open a Finder window, move to your Home folder, and keep it visible while you type these commands at the shell prompt:

```
$ cd
$ touch mac-rocks
```

Switch back to the Finder (you can click on the Desktop) and watch a file called *mac-rocks* appear magically. (The *touch* command creates an empty file with the name you specify.)

Now type:

```
$ rm mac-rocks
```

Return to the Finder, and watch the file disappear. The *rm* command removes the file.

Listing Files and Directories

To use the *cd* command, you must know which entries in a directory are subdirectories and which are files. The *ls* command lists entries in the directory tree and can also show you which is which.

The All-Powerful ls Command

When you enter the *ls* command, you get a list of the files and subdirectories contained in your working directory. The syntax is:

```
ls options directory-and-filenames
```

If you've just moved into an empty directory, entering *ls* without any arguments may seem to do nothing. This isn't surprising, because you haven't made any files in your working directory. If you have no files, nothing is displayed; you'll simply get a new shell prompt:

```
$ ls
$
```

But if you're in your home directory, *ls* displays the names of the files and directories in that directory. The output depends on what's in your directory. The screen should look something like this:

```
$ ls
Desktop      Library      Movies      Pictures      Sites
Documents    Mail         Music       Public        mac-rocks
$
```

Sometimes *ls* might display filenames in a single column. If yours does, you can make a multicolumn display with the -*C* option (multicolumn, sorted down) or the -*x* option (multicolumn, sorted across). *ls* has a lot of options that change the information and display format.

The -*a* option (for all) is guaranteed to show you some more files, as in the following example:

```
$ ls -a
.                     .bash_history     Desktop       Pictures
..                    .dvdcss           Documents     Public
.CFUserTextEncoding   .profile          Library       Sites
.DS_Store             .ssh              Mail          mac-rocks
.Trash                .sversionrc       Movies
.Xauthority           .viminfo          Music
$
```

When you use *ls -a*, you'll always see at least two entries named . (dot) and .. (dot, dot). As mentioned earlier, .. is always the relative pathname to the parent directory. A single . always stands for itself; believe it or not, this is useful with commands such as *cp* (see Chapter 4). There may also be other files, such as *.bashrc* or *.Trash*. Any entry whose name begins with a dot is hidden—it's listed only if you add the *-a* flag to the *ls* command.

Trying Out the ls Command

Since the *ls* command is such an important part of the Terminal, let's practice using some of the different commands.

Open the Terminal application, and then type along to see what your system shows you:

```
$ ls
Desktop       Library      Movies      Pictures     Sites
Documents     Mail         Music       Public       mac-rocks
$ ls -1
Desktop
Documents
Library
Mail
Movies
Music
Pictures
Public
Sites
mac-rocks
```

The *-1* option (that's the number one, not a lowercase L) causes *ls* to output the list of files in one-file-per-line format, which can be useful if you're going to paste the list into a Word document or other material.

One problem with *ls* is that unlike the Finder with its helpful icons, the output from *ls* doesn't let you differentiate between files and directories. That's where the helpful *-F* option comes in handy:

```
$ ls -F
Desktop/      Library/     Movies/     Pictures/    Sites/
Documents/    Mail/        Music/      Public/      mac-rocks
```

The *-F* option shows you which entries are directories by appending a forward slash (/) to the end of the name. If there were executable programs or scripts in this directory, *-F* would append an asterisk (*) after the filename; an at symbol (@) denotes symbolic links in this output.

The *-s* option indicates the size of each file, in units of 512 bytes. Why 512 bytes? Well, that's what Unix used all those years ago, and since then that's just what the *ls -s* command uses. If you really want to use *-s* but obviously aren't interested in 512-byte blocks, you can set the environment variable BLOCKSIZE to 1024 to make the resultant listings the more logical 1 kilobyte size:

```
$ ls -s
total 0
0 Desktop      0 Library    0 Movies    0 Pictures    0 Sites
0 Documents    0 Mail       0 Music     0 Public      0 mac-rocks
```

Directories and empty files are always shown as having zero blocks used (you need to use the *du*—disk usage—command, as discussed a bit later in this chapter, to find out the size of a directory), and the *mac-rocks* file is empty because I created it with the *touch* command.

A directory that has files that aren't empty is *Library/Preferences*:

```
$ ls -sF Library/Preferences/
 8 AddressBookMe.plist
 0 ByHost/
 0 Explorer/
 0 Macromedia/
 0 Microsoft/
 8 OfficeSync Prefs
 0 OpenOffice.org1.1.2/
24 QuickTime Preferences
 8 com.apple.AddressBook.plist
 8 com.apple.BezelServices.plist
 8 com.apple.Bluetooth.plist
...
40 com.apple.iTunes.eq.plist
40 com.apple.iTunes.plist
 8 com.apple.internetconfig.plist
...
 8 loginwindow.plist
 8 mdimportserver.plist
 8 org.OpenOffice.Start.plist
```

This is much more useful. You can see that the directories *ByHost*, *Explorer*, etc., are all zero size, as expected, but notice that some of the preference files, notably for QuickTime and iTunes, are bigger than the other files. The difference? Some applications have quite a bit of information that they store as preferences, while others save only preference settings that are different from the default configuration.

A more interesting place to look is your logfile directory, */var/log*:

```
$ ls -s /var/log
total 1416
 8 CDIS.custom        0 ipfw.log          0 ppp
 8 OSInstall.custom   8 ipfw.log.0.gz     0 sa
96 asl.log           32 lastlog           0 samba
 8 crashreporter.log  0 lookupd.log      16 secure.log
```

```
    0 cups            8 lookupd.log.0.gz    112 system.log
    8 daily.out       0 lpr.log              16 system.log.0.gz
    0 fax             8 lpr.log.0.gz          8 weekly.out
    0 ftp.log         8 mail.log            240 windowserver.log
    8 ftp.log.0.gz    8 mail.log.0.gz       144 windowserver_last.log
    0 httpd           8 monthly.out           8 wtmp
  616 install.log     0 netinfo.log           8 wtmp.0.gz
   24 install.log.0.gz 8 netinfo.log.0.gz
```

Notice that the first line of output with the -s option is always a sum of the size of all files in the specified directory. This shows that there are 1416 512-byte blocks, which you can easily divide by two to get kilobytes (708 Kb). The largest file in this directory is *install.log*, which was created after you installed Mac OS X.

Now let's see if there's a directory called *Library* in the current working directory:

```
$ ls Library
Application Support  Cookies         Internet Plug-Ins  Printers
Assistants           Documentation   Keyboard Layouts   Safari
Audio                Favorites       Keychains          Snapz Pro X
Autosave Information FontCollections Logs               Sounds
Caches               Fonts           Mail               Syndication
Classic              Icons           Metadata           Movie
ColorPickers         Indexes         Preferences        iTunes
```

This is a classic conundrum with the *ls* command; you want to see a folder, but you don't actually want to see what's inside the folder, just whether it exists or not. To accomplish this, you can't just specify the name of the folder because, as shown, you end up seeing what's inside. Instead, use the -d option to indicate that it's the directory information you want, not its contents:

```
$ ls -d Library
Library
$ ls -d
.
```

That second example is interesting because it confirms that the current directory is indeed the period (.) shorthand, as explained earlier.

Using the -l option

To get more information about each item that *ls* lists, add the -l option (that's a lowercase "L" for "long"). This option can be used alone, or in combination with -a, as shown in Figure 3-6.

```
  ⊖ ⊙ ⊙                          Terminal — bash — 112x27
Tiger:~ taylor$ ls -al
total 56
drwxr-xr-x   22 taylor   taylor    748 Jan  3 14:51 .
drwxrwxr-t    7 root     admin     238 Dec 14 16:10 ..
-rw-r--r--    1 taylor   taylor      3 Aug 27 15:14 .CFUserTextEncoding
-rw-r--r--    1 taylor   taylor   6148 Jan  3 14:02 .DS_Store
drwx------   10 taylor   taylor    340 Jan  3 14:09 .Trash
-rw-------    1 taylor   taylor      0 Aug 31 11:11 .Xauthority
-rw-------    1 taylor   taylor   3016 Jan  3 14:08 .bash_history
drwxr-xr-x    3 taylor   taylor    102 Sep  7 19:37 .dvdcss
-rw-r--r--    1 taylor   taylor     76 Jan  3 12:23 .profile.saved
drwx------    3 taylor   taylor    102 Aug 30 16:36 .ssh
-rw-r--r--    1 taylor   taylor     73 Aug 31 10:56 .sversionrc
-rw-------    1 taylor   taylor    632 Jan  3 12:23 .viminfo
drwx------   21 taylor   taylor    714 Jan  3 14:15 Desktop
drwx------    7 taylor   taylor    238 Oct  2 12:18 Documents
drwx------   31 taylor   taylor   1054 Jan  3 11:50 Library
drwx------    4 taylor   taylor    136 Aug 31 10:15 Mail
drwx------    3 taylor   taylor    102 Aug 27 15:14 Movies
drwx------    4 taylor   taylor    136 Aug 30 22:38 Music
drwx------    3 taylor   taylor    102 Aug 27 15:14 Pictures
drwxr-xr-x    4 taylor   taylor    136 Aug 27 15:14 Public
drwxr-xr-x    5 taylor   taylor    170 Aug 27 15:14 Sites
-rw-r--r--    1 taylor   taylor      0 Jan  3 14:51 mac-rocks
Tiger:~ taylor$ █
```

Figure 3-6. Output from ls -al

The long format provides the following information about each item:

Total n

> States the amount of storage space (*n*) used by everything in this direc-
> tory. This is measured in *blocks*. On Mac OS X, blocks are 1,024 bytes
> in size.

Type

> Tells whether the item is a directory (d) or a plain file (-). (There are
> other less common types as well.)

Access modes

> Specifies three types of users (yourself, your group, and all others) who
> are allowed to read (r), write (w), or execute (x) your files or directories.
> We'll talk more about access modes later. See the section, "File Permis-
> sions," later in this chapter.

Links

> Lists the number of files or directories linked to this directory. (This
> isn't the same as a web page link.)

Owner

> States the user who created or owns this file or directory.

Group

> Lists the group that owns the file or directory.

Size (in bytes)

States the size of the file or directory. (A directory is actually a special type of file. Here, the "size" of a directory is of the directory file itself, not the total of all the files in that directory.)

Modification date

States the date when the file was last modified or when the directory contents last changed (when something in the directory was added, renamed, or removed). If an entry was modified more than six months ago, *ls* shows the year instead of the time.

Name

Tells the name of the file or directory.

File Permissions

Notice especially the columns that list the owner and group of the files, and the access modes (also called *permissions*). The person who creates a file is its owner; if you've created any files, this column should show your short username. You also belong to a group. Files you create are marked either with the name of your group or, in some cases, the group that owns the directory.

The permissions indicate what type of file the item is (such as a directory or a regular file), as well as who can read, write, or execute the file or directory. The permissions have 10 characters, as shown in Figure 3-7. The first character shows the file type (d for directory or - for a plain file). The other characters come in groups of three.

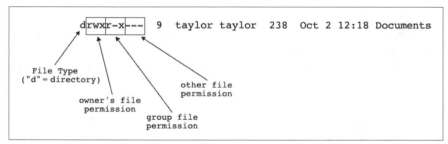

Figure 3-7. A detailed look at file permissions

The first group, characters 2 through 4, shows the permissions for the file's owner (which is you, if you created the file). The second group, characters 5 through 7, shows permissions for other members of the file's group, such as all people in the marketing team or everyone on Project Alpha in your firm. The third group, characters 8 through 10, shows permissions for all other users on the system.

The Finder shows directory permission in the Get Info dialog box. Figure 3-8 shows the Get Info permissions information for the *Documents* directory. Compare this to the *ls -l* output shown in Figure 3-7.

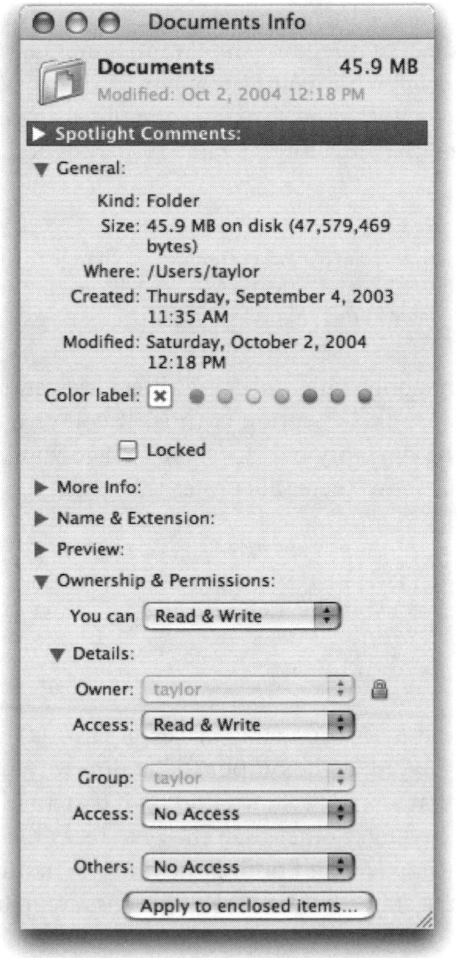

Figure 3-8. The Finder's Get Info window shows directory permissions much differently than how they appear in the Terminal

For example, the permissions for .*DS_Store* in Figure 3-6 are -rw-r--r--. The first hyphen, -, indicates that it's a plain file. The next three characters, rw-, mean that the owner, *john*, has both read (r) and write (w) permissions, but cannot execute the file, as noted by the hyphen following rw. The next two sets of permissions are both r--, which means that other users who belong to the file's group *john*, as well as all other users of the system, can only read the file; they don't have write or execute permissions, which means they can't make changes to the file, and if it's a program (such as a shell script), they can't execute it either.

In the case of directories, x means the permission to access the directory—for example, to run a command that reads a file there or to use a subdirectory. Notice that the first directory shown in Figure 3-6, *Desktop*, is executable (accessible) by *john*, but completely closed off to everyone else on the system. A directory with write (w) permission allows deleting, renaming, or adding files within the directory. Read (r) permission allows listing the directory with *ls*.

 You can use the *chmod* command to change the permissions of your files and directories (see "Protecting and Sharing Files" later in this chapter).

If you need to know only which files are directories and which are executable files, you can use the *-F* option with *ls*. If you give the pathname to a directory, *ls* lists the directory but does *not* change your working directory. The *pwd* command, shown here, illustrates this:

```
$ ls -F ~
$ ls -F
Desktop/        Library/        Music/          Public/         mac-rocks
Documents/      Movies/         Pictures/       Sites/
$ pwd
/Applications
$
```

As noted earlier, the *ls -F* command places a slash (/) at the end of each directory name displayed in the output. (The directory name doesn't really have a slash in it; that's just the shorthand *ls -F* uses to identify a directory.) In this example, every entry other than the *mac-rocks* file is a directory. You can verify this by using *ls -l* and noting the d in the first field of the output. Files with an execute status (x), such as programs, are marked with an asterisk (*).

The *ls -R* command (recursive), lists a directory and all its subdirectories. This gives you a very long list, especially when you list a directory near the root! (Piping the output of *ls* to a pager program—such as *more* or *less*—solves this problem. There's an example in Chapter 6.) You can combine other options with *-R*; for instance, *ls -RF* marks each directory and file type, while recursively listing files and directories.

Calculating File Size and Disk Space

You can find the size of a file with the *du* command (which stands for *disk usage*):

```
$ du Documents/Outline.doc
300     Documents/Outline.doc
```

The size is reported in kilobytes, so *Outline.doc* is 300 KB in size.

If you give *du* the name of a directory, it calculates the sizes of everything inside that directory, including any subdirectories and their contents:

```
$ du Library
8       Library/Application Support/AddressBook/Images
120     Library/Application Support/AddressBook
3776    Library/Application Support/Chess
...
```

This means that it's not a great idea to type *du /* unless you want to see a lot of information stream past your screen at a lightning pace!

If you want the total for the directory, use *-s* (summarize):

```
$ du -s Library
243768  Library
```

If you'd like separate totals for all directories and files, including hidden ones, use a wildcard pattern that ignores the current (.) and parent (..) directories as discussed earlier in this chapter:

```
$ du -s * .[^.]*
40      Desktop
2200    Documents
56120   Library
...
438048  .Trash
8       .bash_history
```

To gain information about the size of your default applications in Tiger, use the pattern */Applications/*.app*:

```
$ du -s /Applications/*app
45512   /Applications/Address Book.app
6176    /Applications/Automator.app
2424    /Applications/Calculator.app
7616    /Applications/Chess.app
9480    /Applications/DVD Player.app
152     /Applications/Dashboard.app
1832    /Applications/Dictionary.app
3144    /Applications/Font Book.app
4024    /Applications/Image Capture.app
2080    /Applications/Internet Connect.app
```

```
51736   /Applications/Mail.app
5920    /Applications/Preview.app
11328   /Applications/QuickTime Player.app
40616   /Applications/Safari.app
2648    /Applications/Sherlock.app
792     /Applications/Stickies.app
832     /Applications/System Preferences.app
1968    /Applications/TextEdit.app
55344   /Applications/iCal.app
42480   /Applications/iChat.app
13040   /Applications/iSync.app
60864   /Applications/iTunes.app
```

Notice that the output is in alphabetical order, but all the uppercase filenames are sorted before the lowercase filenames (that is, Safari appears before iChat in a case-sensitive sort).

One option that's worth keeping in mind when using *du -s* is *-h*, which produces more human-readable output:

```
$ du -sh /Library/*
  0B    /Library/Address Book Plug-Ins
 17M    /Library/Application Support
1.1M    /Library/Audio
7.4M    /Library/CFMSupport
 27M    /Library/Caches
152K    /Library/ColorSync
 24K    /Library/Colors
  0B    /Library/Components
 48K    /Library/Contextual Menu Items
 22M    /Library/Desktop Pictures
 86M    /Library/Dictionaries
116M    /Library/Documentation
  0B    /Library/Filesystems
140M    /Library/Fonts
 80K    /Library/Frameworks
  0B    /Library/Graphics
7.5M    /Library/Image Capture
2.9M    /Library/Internet Plug-Ins
4.0K    /Library/Java
  0B    /Library/Keyboard Layouts
 20K    /Library/Keychains
  0B    /Library/LaunchAgents
  0B    /Library/LaunchDaemons
6.6M    /Library/Logs
168K    /Library/MDImporters
 68K    /Library/Mail
1.8M    /Library/Modem Scripts
192K    /Library/Perl
112K    /Library/Preferences
1.2G    /Library/Printers
8.0K    /Library/Python
  0B    /Library/QuickTime
 57M    /Library/Receipts
```

```
  0B    /Library/Screen Savers
2.8M    /Library/Scripts
236K    /Library/Spotlight
256K    /Library/User Pictures
172K    /Library/WebServer
2.2M    /Library/Widgets
```

This is more readable in some sense, but the enormous */Library/Printers*, at 1.2 GB, doesn't jump out as it would if the *-h* flag weren't used and the output of 2619216 blocks was shown instead. Probably best to include the *-h* flag, but remember to scan the suffix letters to see if anything jumps out as ridiculously large.

Disk Space Available with df

You can calculate your system's free disk space with *df -h* (the *-h* produces more user-friendly output):

```
$ df -h
Filesystem              Size  Used  Avail Capacity  Mounted on
/dev/disk1s3            56G   33G    23G   59%      /
devfs                   103K  103K    0B   100%     /dev
fdesc                   1.0K  1.0K    0B   100%     /dev
<volfs>                 512K  512K    0B   100%     /.vol
/dev/disk0s8            49G   15G    34G   30%      /Volumes/Hello
automount -nsl [244]     0B    0B     0B   100%     /Network
automount -fstab [247]   0B    0B     0B   100%     /automount/Servers
automount -static [247]  0B    0B     0B   100%     /automount/static
```

Here's the breakdown for the output from the command:

- The first column (Filesystem) shows the Unix device name for the volume.

- The second column (Size) shows the total disk size, and it's followed by the amount of disk space used up (Used) and the amount that's available (Avail).

- The Capacity column shows the percentage of disk space used, followed by where the volume is hooked into the filesystem (Mounted on).

- The Mounted on column displays the paths for the volumes mounted on your computer. The / is the root of your filesystem (a volume that is named Macintosh HD by default). */dev* contains files that correspond to hardware devices, and */.vol* exposes some internals of the Mac OS X filesystem called *HFS+ file ids*.

Notice that I have two hard disks on my system, */dev/disk1s3* (which is 56 GB in size, of which 33 GB are used and 23 GB are still available) and */dev/disk0s8* (which is 49 GB in size, of which 15 GB are used and 34 GB are still available).

The *df* command has a second friendly output that uses the more common divide-by-10 rule for calculating sizes, rather than the more mathematically precise divide-by-two rule of the *-h* flag:

```
$ df -H
Filesystem               Size  Used  Avail Capacity  Mounted on
/dev/disk1s3              60G   35G    24G    59%     /
devfs                    105K  105K    0B   100%     /dev
fdesc                    1.0K  1.0K    0B   100%     /dev
<volfs>                  524K  524K    0B   100%     /.vol
/dev/disk0s8              53G   16G    37G    30%     /Volumes/Hello
automount -nsl [244]      0B    0B     0B   100%     /Network
automount -fstab [247]    0B    0B     0B   100%     /automount/Servers
automount -static [247]   0B    0B     0B   100%     /automount/static
```

These figures make more sense because I know that the hard disk mounted at */dev/disk1s3* is actually 60 GB in size. You might prefer the more accurate *-h* output, but many people prefer *-H* since disk sizes are shown consistent with expectations.

Yet another way to look at the data is to use the *-m* flag to have *df* show you 1 MB blocks, which rounds down all the tiny OS partitions like *devfs* and *.vol* to zero:

```
$ df -m
Filesystem           1M-blocks  Used Avail Capacity  Mounted on
/dev/disk1s3             57103 33548 23304    59%     /
devfs                       0     0     0   100%     /dev
fdesc                       0     0     0   100%     /dev
<volfs>                     0     0     0   100%     /.vol
/dev/disk0s8            50221 15066 35155    30%     /Volumes/Hello
automount -nsl [244]        0     0     0   100%     /Network
automount -fstab [247]      0     0     0   100%     /automount/Servers
automount -static [247]     0     0     0   100%     /automount/static
```

Finally, in addition to raw disk space, another factor to keep track of with your Mac OS X system is the number of inodes available. A given disk in Unix has a finite number of files and directories that can be created and even if there's additional disk space available, running out of inodes effectively stops the disk from being used. This unusual event can happen if you have lots and lots (I'm talking millions and millions) of tiny files.

The *-i* flag to *df* shows how you're doing with *inodes*, which are the fundamental disk blocks that are grafted together to make space for all the different size files in your filesystem. The details of how many inodes are allocated and available on each filesystem are shown in Figure 3-9.

Both disks have plenty of unused inodes, so there's nothing to worry about. Disk *2s3* has 4,834,748 available inodes, and disk *0s8* has 6,305,130 available inodes.

```
● ● ●                        /Users/taylor/Desktop — ssh — 103x11
$ df -i
Filesystem           512-blocks      Used    Avail Capacity iused    ifree %iused  Mounted on
/dev/disk2s3         116940016 77750032 38677984    67% 9783752 4834748   67%  /
devfs                      208       208        0   100%     622       0  100%  /dev
fdesc                        2         2        0   100%       4     253    2%  /dev
<volfs>                   1024      1024        0   100%       0       0  100%  /.vol
/dev/disk0s8         102854488 52413448 50441040    51% 6551679 6305130   51%  /Volumes/Hello
automount -nsl [154]         0         0        0   100%       0       0  100%  /Network
automount -fstab [158]       0         0        0   100%       0       0  100%  /automount/Servers
automount -static [158]      0         0        0   100%       0       0  100%  /automount/static
$ ▮
```

Figure 3-9. Output from df -i

Exercise: Exploring the Filesystem

Now that you're equipped with some basic commands, it's time to explore the filesystem with *cd*, *ls*, and *pwd*. Take a tour of the directory system, detailed in Table 3-1, hopping one or many levels at a time, with a mixture of *cd* and *pwd* commands.

Table 3-1. Take this guided tour of your filesystem; read each task (left column) and then enter the Unix command (right column) to see where you go

Task	Command
Go to your home directory.	*cd*
Find your working directory.	*pwd*
Change to new working directory with its absolute pathname.	*cd /bin*
List files in new working directory.	*ls*
Change directory to root and list it in one step. (Use the command separator: a semicolon.)	*cd /; ls*
Find your working directory.	*pwd*
Change to a subdirectory; use its relative pathname.	*cd usr*
Find your working directory.	*pwd*
Change to a subdirectory.	*cd lib*
Find your working directory.	*pwd*
Give a wrong pathname.	*cd xqk*
List files in another directory.	*ls /bin*
Find your working directory (notice that *ls* didn't change it).	*pwd*
Return to your home directory.	*cd*

Protecting and Sharing Files

Mac OS X makes it easy for users on the same system to share files and directories. For instance, all users in a group can read documents stored in one of their manager's directories without needing to make their own copies (if the manager has allowed such access). The advantage of this is that you wouldn't need to send around files via email as attachments. Instead, if everyone can access those files, they can do so with some help from the Unix filesystem.

Here's a brief introduction to file security and sharing. If you have critical security needs, or you just want more information, talk to your system staff, or see an up-to-date book on Unix security such as *Practical Unix and Internet Security*, by Simson Garfinkel, Gene Spafford, and Alan Schwartz (O'Reilly).

> Any user with admin privileges can use the *sudo* command (see "Superuser Privileges with sudo" later in this chapter) to do anything to any file at any time—regardless of what its permissions are. Access permissions won't keep your private information safe from *everyone*, although let's hope that you can trust the other folks who share your Macintosh! This is one reason that you want to be thoughtful about those to Directory Access Permissions

A directory's access permissions help to control access to the files and subdirectories in that directory:

- If a directory has read permission (r), a user can run *ls* to see what's in the directory and use wildcards to match files in it.
- A directory that has write permission (w) allows users to add, rename, and delete files in the directory.
- To access a directory (that is, to read or write the files in the directory or to run the files if they're programs), a user needs execute permission (x) on that directory. To access a directory, a user must *also* have execute permission to all its parent directories—all the way up to the root.

> Mac OS X includes a shared directory for all users: */Users/Shared*. Any user can create files in this directory and modify files you have put there. However, you cannot modify a file that's owned by another user. Instead, you'll have to copy that file from */Users/Shared* to another directory in which you have write permissions (such as your *Documents* directory).

In practice, there are three directory permissions you'll see in Unix:

- --- means that user cannot access the directory.
- r-x means that the user can access the directory with read-only permission, but cannot add, delete, or modify the directory.
- rwx means that the user has read, write, and access permission.

For example, here are the default permissions for a home directory, courtesy of *ls -l*:

```
$ ls -ld $HOME
drwxr-xr-x  66 taylor  staff  2244 27 Dec 11:07 /Users/taylor/
$
```

This shows that the owner, *taylor*, has read, write, and access permission for this directory, while the group, *staff*, and everyone else on the system are restricted to read-only access.

In contrast, the following example shows that user *taylor* has complete access, but everyone else is shut out from browsing the *Documents* directory:

```
$ ls -ld $HOME/Documents
drwx------  51 taylor  staff  1734 13 Dec 14:46 /Users/taylor/Documents/
$
```

The Finder shows directory permission in the Get Info dialog box. Figure 3-10 shows the Get Info permissions information for both *$HOME* and *$HOME/Documents*.

File Access Permissions

The access permissions on a file control what can be done to the file's *contents*. Likewise, the access permissions on the directory where the file is kept control whether the file can be renamed or removed. If this seems confusing, think of it this way: the directory is actually a list of files. Adding, renaming, or removing a file changes the contents of the directory. If the directory isn't writable, you can't change that list.

Read permission controls whether you can read a file's contents. Write permission lets you change a file's contents. A file shouldn't have execute permission unless it's a program or a script.

Let's have a look at a few file permissions on your system.

```
$ ls -l .viminfo
-rw-------  1 taylor  staff  2159 27 Dec 11:07 .viminfo
$
```

This permission allows user *taylor* to read from the file or write to the file, but everyone else is prevented from touching its contents.

```
$ ls -l /mach.sym
-r--r--r--  1 root  admin  576276  3 Jan 16:19 /mach.sym
```

This file, a part of the operating system core (known in Unix-geek circles as the *kernel*), is owned by *root* and has read-only permission for everyone,

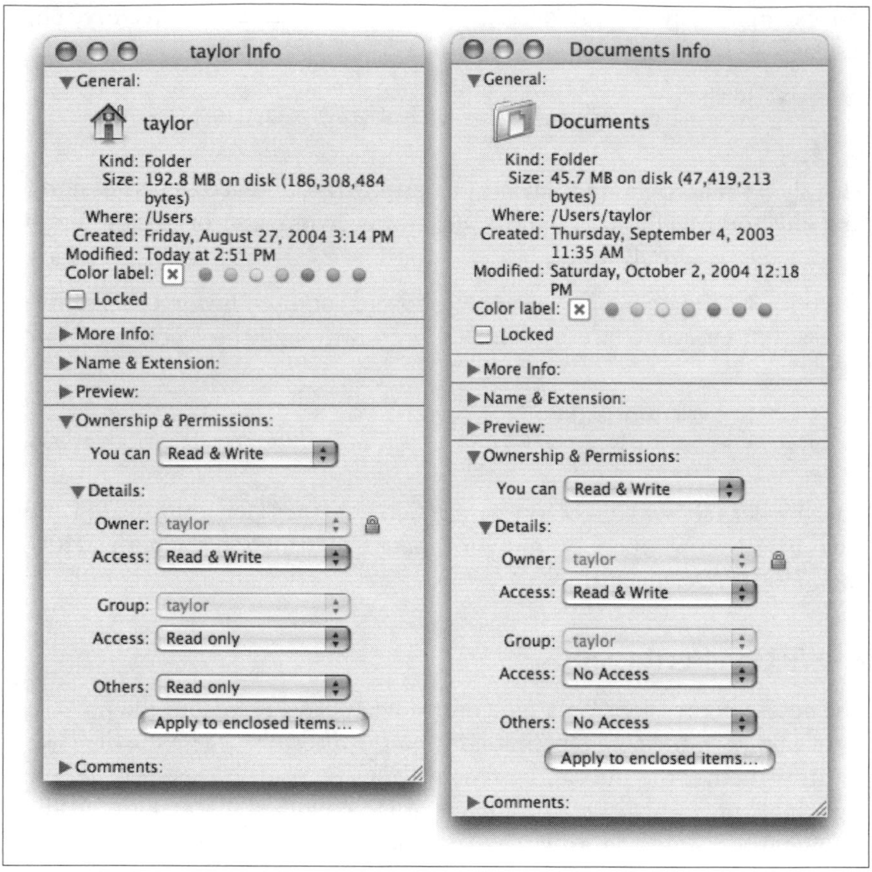

Figure 3-10. The Finder's Get Info window shows directory permissions differently

including *root* itself. Typically, this type of permission denotes an important system file that shouldn't be touched in any way.

```
$ ls -l /etc/authorization.cac
-rw-r----- 1 root admin 16541  2 Dec /etc/authorization.cac
```

Finally, this security database file that belongs to the operating system has read-write permission for the owner, *root*, read-only permission for anyone in the *admin* group, and is off-limits from anyone else on the computer.

Setting Permissions with chmod

Once you know what permissions a file or directory needs—and if you're the owner (listed in the third column of *ls -l* output)—you can change the permissions with the *chmod* program. If you select a file or folder in the Finder, and then choose File → Get Info (⌘-I), you can also change the permissions using the Ownership & Permissions section of the Get Info dialog (see Figure 3-10). One reason to use the Finder method is because changing the permission of files and directories *inside* the directory is easy to accomplish by clicking the "Apply to Enclosed Items..." button (this can be done on the command line, too, but it's a bit more advanced, and beyond the scope of this book).

There are two ways to change permissions: by specifying the permissions to add or delete, or by specifying the exact permissions. For instance, if a directory's permissions are almost correct, but you also need to make it writable by its group, tell *chmod* to add group-write permission. But if you need to make more than one change to the permissions—for instance, if you want to add read and execute permission but delete write permission—it's easier to set all permissions explicitly instead of changing them one by one. The syntax is:

```
chmod permissions file(s)
```

Let's start with the rules, followed by some examples a little later. The *permissions* argument has three parts, which you must give in order with no space between:

1. The category of permission you want to change. There are three: the owner's permission (which *chmod* calls "user," abbreviated *u*), the group's permission (*g*), or others' permission (*o*). To change more than one category, string the letters together, such as *go* for "group and others," or simply use *a* to mean "all" (same as *ugo*).

2. Whether you want to add (+) the permission, delete (-) it, or specify it exactly (=).

3. What permissions you want to affect: read (*r*), write (*w*), or execute (*x*). To change more than one permission, string the letters together—for example, *rw* for "read and write."

Some examples should make this clearer! In the following command lines, you can replace *dirname* or *filename* with the pathname (absolute or relative) of the directory or file. An easy way to change permissions on the working directory is by using its relative pathname, . (dot), as in *chmod o-w*.

You can combine two permission changes in the same *chmod* command by separating them with a comma (,), as shown in the final example:

- To protect a file from accidental editing, delete everyone's write permission with the command:
  ```
  chmod a-w filename
  ```
  On the other hand, if you own an unwritable file that you want to edit, but you don't want to change other peoples' write permissions, you can add "user" (owner) write permission with:
  ```
  chmod u+w filename
  ```

- To keep yourself from accidentally removing files (or adding or renaming files) in an important directory of yours, delete your own write permission with the command:

  ```
  chmod u-w dirname
  ```

- If other users have that permission, too, you could delete everyone's write permission with:

  ```
  chmod a-w dirname
  ```

- If you want you and your group to be able to read and write all the files in your working directory—but those files have various permissions now, so adding and deleting the permissions individually would be a pain—this is a good place to use the = operator to set the exact permissions you want. Use the filename wildcard *, which means "everything in this directory" (explained in "File and Directory Wildcards in Chapter 4) and type:

  ```
  chmod ug=rw *
  ```

- If your working directory has any subdirectories, though, that command would be wrong, because it takes away execute permission from the subdirectories, so the subdirectories couldn't be accessed anymore. In that case, you could try a more specific wildcard. Or, instead of a wildcard, you can simply list the filenames you want to change, separated by spaces, as in:

  ```
  chmod ug=rw afile bfile cfile
  ```

- To protect the files in a directory and all its subdirectories from everyone else on your system, but still keep the access permissions *you* have there, you could use:

  ```
  chmod go-rwx dirname
  ```

  to delete all "group" and "others" permission to read, write, and execute. A simpler way is to use the command:

  ```
  chmod go= dirname
  ```

  to set "group" and "others" permission to exactly nothing.

- You want full access to a directory. Other people on the system should be able to see what's in the directory (and read or edit the files if the file permissions allow it) but not rename, remove, or add files. To do that, give yourself all permissions, but give "group" and "others" only read and execute permission. Use the command:

  ```
  chmod u=rwx,go=rx dirname
  ```

After you change permissions, it's a good idea to check your work with *ls -l filename*, *ls -ld dirname* (without the *-d* option, *ls* lists the contents of the directory instead of its permissions and other information), or by using the Finder's Get Info window.

Problem checklist

Here are some problems you might encounter while working with *chmod*, along with some solutions:

I get the message "chmod: Not owner."

> Only the owner of a file or directory (or the superuser) can set its permissions. Use *ls -l* to find the owner or use superuser privileges (see "Superuser Privileges with sudo," later in this chapter).

A file is writable, but my program says it can't be written.

> First, check the file permissions with *ls -l* and be sure you're in the category (user, group, or others) that has write permission.

> The problem may also be in the permissions of the file's directory. Some programs need permission to write more files into the same directory (for example, temporary files) or to rename files (for instance, making a file into a backup) while editing. If it's safe to add write permission to the directory (if other files in the directory don't need protection from removal or renaming), try that. Otherwise, copy the file to a writable directory (with *cp*), edit it there, and then copy it back to the original directory.

Changing Group and Owner

Group ownership lets a certain group of users have access to a file or directory. You might need to let a different group have access. The *chgrp* program sets the group owner of a file or directory. You can set the group to any of the groups to which you belong. Because you're likely going to be administering your system, you can control the list of groups you're in. (In some situations, the system administrator controls the list of groups you're in.) The *groups* program lists your groups.

For example, if you're a designer creating a directory named *images* for several illustrators, the directory's original group owner might be *admin*. You'd like the illustrators, all of whom are in the group named *staff*, to access the directory; members of other groups should have no access. Use commands such as:

```
$ groups
gareth admin
$ mkdir images
$ ls -ld images
drwxr-xr-x   2 gareth  admin           68 Nov  6 09:53 images
$ chgrp staff images
$ chmod o= images
$ ls -ld images
drwxr-x---   2 gareth  staff           68 Nov  6 09:53 images
```

Mac OS X also lets you set a directory's group ownership so that any files you later create in that directory will be owned by the same group as the directory. Try the command *chmod g+s dirname*. The permissions listing from *ls -ld* now shows an s in place of the second x, such as drwxr-s---.

The *chown* program changes the owner of a file or directory. Only the superuser can use *chown* (see "Superuser Privileges with sudo," later in this chapter).[*]

```
$ chown eric images
chown: changing ownership of `images': Operation not permitted
$ sudo chown eric images
Password:
$
```

Changing Your Password

The ownership and permissions system described in this chapter depends on the security of your username and password. If others get your username and password, they can log into your account and do anything you can, and if you have admin privileges, that could be anything—including deleting all your files. They can read private information, corrupt or delete important files, send email messages as if they came from you, and more. If your computer is connected to a network—whether to the Internet or a local network inside your organization—intruders may also be able to log in without sitting at your keyboard! See "Remote Logins" in Chapter 8 for one way this can be done.

Anyone may be able to get your username—it's usually part of your email address, for instance, or shows up as a file's owner in a long directory listing. Your password is what keeps others from logging in as you. Don't leave your password anywhere around your computer. Don't give your password to anyone who asks you for it unless you're sure he'll preserve your account security. Also, don't send your password by email; it can be stored, unprotected, on other systems and on backup tapes, where other people may find it and then break into your account.

If you think that someone knows your password, you should probably change it right away—although if you suspect that a computer "cracker" (or "hacker") is using your account to break into your system, you should ask

---

[*] If you have permission to read another user's file, you can make a copy of it (with *cp*; see "Copying Files" in Chapter 4). You'll own the copy.

your system administrator for advice first, if possible. You should also change your password periodically. Every few months is recommended.

A password should be easy for you to remember but hard for other people (or password-guessing programs) to guess. Here are some guidelines. A password should be between six and eight characters long. It should not be a word in any language, a proper name, your phone number, your address, or anything anyone else might know or guess that you'd use as a password. It's best to mix upper- and lowercase letters, punctuation, and numbers. A good way to come up with a unique but memorable password is to think of a phrase that only you might know, and use the first letters of each word (and punctuation) to create the password. For example, consider the password *mlwsiF!* ("My laptop was stolen in Florence!").

To change your password, you can use → System Preferences → Accounts, but you can also change it from the command line using the *passwd* command. After you enter the command, you're prompted to enter your old password. If the password is correct, you're asked to enter a new password—twice, to be sure there is no typing mistake.

```
$ passwd
Changing password for taylor.
Old password:
New password:
Retype new password:
```

For security, neither the old nor the new passwords appear as you type them.

Superuser Privileges with sudo

Most Mac OS X user accounts run with restricted privileges; there are parts of the filesystem to which you don't have access, and there are certain activities that are prohibited until you supply a password. For example, when you run the Software Update utility from System Preferences, Mac OS X may ask you for your password before it proceeds. This extra authentication step allows Software Update to run installers with superuser privileges.

You can invoke these same privileges at the command line by prefixing a command with *sudo* (short for "superuser do"), a utility that prompts you for your password and executes the command as the superuser. You must be an administrative (or *admin*, for short) user to use *sudo*. The user you created when you first set up your Mac is an admin user. You can add new admin users or grant admin status to a user in System Preferences → Accounts, as shown in Figure 3-11.

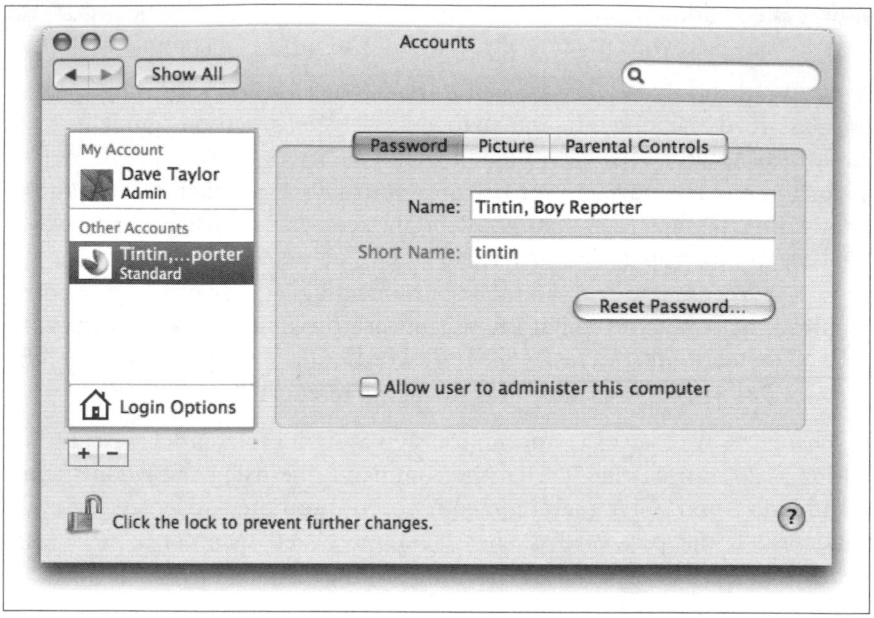

Figure 3-11. When checked, the "Allow user to administer this computer" option in the Accounts preference panel gives a user administrative privileges, which also lets her use the sudo command

You may need to use *sudo* when you install certain Unix utilities, or if you want to modify a file you don't own. Suppose you accidentally created a file in the */Users* directory while you were doing something else as the superuser. You won't be able to modify it with your normal privileges, so you'll need to use *sudo*:

```
$ ls -l logfile.out
-rw-r--r--    1 root     wheel      1784064 Nov  6 11:25 logfile.out
$ rm logfile.out
override rw-r--r--  root/wheel for logfile.out? y
rm: logfile.out: Permission denied
$ sudo rm logfile.out
Password:
$ ls -l logfile.out
ls: logfile.out: No such file or directory
```

If you use *sudo* again within five minutes, it won't ask for your password. Be careful using *sudo*, since it gives you the ability to modify protected files, all of which are protected to ensure the system runs properly.

I commonly find myself using *sudo* when I want to search across the entire filesystem without worry about disk permissions. For example, if *makewhatis* was once in */usr/sbin*, but looking in that directory reveals it has moved somewhere else. To find it, I search the entire filesystem using the *find* command (as discussed in Chapter 5) with *sudo*:

```
$ sudo find / -name makewhatis -print
Password:
/usr/bin/makewhatis
```

Without the use of *sudo*, I would see hundreds of error messages as the command tried to peek into directories that I as a regular user don't have permission to visit.

Exploring External Volumes

Earlier I mentioned that additional hard disks on your system and any network-based disks are all mounted onto the filesystem in the */Volumes* directory. Let's take a closer look to see how it works:

```
$ ls /Volumes
110GB           Extra 30        Tiger        X
$ ls -l /Volumes
total 8
drwxrwxrwx  29 taylor  staff      986 12 Jun 16:37 110GB
drwxrwxrwx  11 taylor  unknown    374  4 Jun 23:28 Extra 30
lrwxr-xr-x   1 root    admin        1 13 Jun 12:30 Tiger -> /
drwxrwxr-t  61 root    admin     2074 12 Jun 16:51 X
```

There are four disks available, one of which is actually the root (or boot) disk: Tiger. Notice that the entry for Tiger is different from the others, with the first character shown as l rather than a d. This means it's a link (see "Working with Links" in Chapter 4), which is confirmed by the fact that it's shown as Tiger in the regular *ls* output, while the value of the alias is shown in the long listing (you can see that Panther actually points to /).

If you insert a CD or DVD into the system, it also shows up in */Volumes*:

```
$ ls -l /Volumes
total 12
drwxrwxrwx  29 taylor  staff      986 22 Sep 16:37 110GB
dr-xr-xr-x   4 unknown nogroup    136 17 Aug  2001 CITIZEN_KANE
drwxrwxrwx  11 taylor  unknown    374  4 Sep 23:28 Extra 30
lrwxr-xr-x   1 root    admin        1 23 Sep 12:30 Tiger -> /
drwxrwxr-t  61 root    admin     2074 22 Sep 16:51 X
```

Plugging in an iPod and a digital camera proceeds as follows:

```
$ ls -l /Volumes
total 44
drwxrwxrwx  29 taylor  staff      986 22 Sep 16:37 110GB
dr-xr-xr-x   4 unknown nogroup    136 17 Aug  2001 CITIZEN_KANE
drwxrwxrwx  11 taylor  unknown    374  4 Sep 23:28 Extra 30
drwxrwxrwx   1 taylor  admin    16384 19 Aug 20:54 NIKON D100
```

```
lrwxr-xr-x    1 root    admin      1 23 Sep 12:30 Tiger -> /
drwxrwxr-t  61 root    admin    2074 22 Sep 16:51 X
drwxr-xr-x  15 taylor  unknown   510 27 Apr 09:37 Zephyr
```

Zephyr is the name of the iPod, and NIKON D100 is the camera.

Now, for a neat trick, let's use Unix commands to look at the files on the iPod Zephyr:

```
$ ls -F Zephyr
Calendars/              Icon?                   Norton FS Volume
Desktop DB              Norton FS Data          Norton FS Volume 2
Desktop DF              Norton FS Index         iPod_Control/
```

These are the files and directories on the iPod. Where's the music? Let's have a peek in *iPod_Control*:

```
$ cd Zephyr/iPod_Control/
$ ls -F
Device/        Music/         iPodPrefs*      iTunes/
$ ls -F iTunes
DeviceInfo*            iTunes Temp 3*          iTunesControl*
iTunesPrefs*
iTunes Temp*           iTunes Temp 4*          iTunesDB*
iTunes Temp 1*         iTunes Temp 5*          iTunesEQPresets*
iTunes Temp 2*         iTunes Temp 6*          iTunesPlaylists*
$ ls -F Music
F00/   F02/   F04/   F06/   F08/   F10/   F12/   F14/   F16/   F18/
F01/   F03/   F05/   F07/   F09/   F11/   F13/   F15/   F17/   F19/
$ ls -F Music/F00
A Thousand Years.mp3*                Moody_s Mood For Love.mp3*
African Ripples.mp3*                 My One And Only.mp3*
All The Pretty Little Ponie.mp3*     My Thanksgiving.mp3*
Apollo.mp3*                          Nucleus.mp3*
Arrival.mp3*                         Oh_ Yes_ Take Another Guess.mp3*
...
```

So you can see the disk structure the iPod uses, and it's completely Unix-friendly: music is stored in the *iPod_Control/Music* directory and split into directories called *F00* through *F19*.[*] Within each directory is a set of audio files (mp3, AIFF, AAC, etc.). You can even copy them using the commands we'll discuss in the next chapter. The iPod maintains a difficult-to-manipulate index of the audio files, so you can't add music to your iPod as easily. However, you can make directories in other areas of your iPod and copy files into them, using your iPod as a portable hard drive.

---

[*] Surprisingly, this disk structure is identical across iPods, regardless of size. It's a compromise between the slow seeks of a single directory for all data and the needless complexity of each album (or artist) having its own subdirectory.

## CHAPTER 4

File Management

The previous chapter introduced the Unix filesystem, including an extensive discussion of the directory structure, the *ls* command for seeing what files are on your system, and how to move around using *cd* and *pwd*. This chapter focuses on Unix filenaming schemes—which aren't the same as names you'd see in the Finder, as you'll see—and how to view, edit, rename, copy, and move files.

File and Directory Names

As Chapter 3 explained, both files and directories are identified by their names. A directory is really just a special kind of file, so the rules for naming directories are the same as the rules for naming files.

Filenames may contain any character except /, which is reserved as the separator between files and directories in a pathname. Filenames are usually made of upper- and lowercase letters, numbers, dots (.), and underscores (_). Other characters (including spaces) are legal in a filename, but they can be hard to use because the shell gives them special meanings or otherwise forces you to constantly be changing how you work with these filenames on the command line.

Spaces are a standard part of Macintosh file and folder names, so while I recommend using only letters, numbers, dots, and underscores for filenames, the reality is that you have to work with spaces in file and directory names, because that's what Mac people do. Rather than naming a file *myFile.txt* as a Unix person would, most Mac folks are used to adding spaces to filenames, such as *my file.txt*. The Finder, by contrast, dislikes colons (which older versions of Mac OS used as a directory separator, just as Unix uses the forward slash). If you display a file called *test:me* in the Finder, the name is shown as *test/me* instead. (The reverse is also true: if you create a file in the Finder whose name contains a slash, it will appear as a colon in the Terminal.)

Though it's tempting to include spaces in filenames as you do in the Finder, if you're planning on doing any substantial amount of work on the Unix side, get used to using dashes or underscores in place of spaces in your filenames. It's 99 percent as legible, but considerably easier to work with.

Further, in the interest of having files correctly identified in both the Finder and Unix, you'd be wise to get into the habit of using the appropriate file extensions, too (i.e., *.doc* for Microsoft Word documents, *.txt* for text files, *.xls* for Excel spreadsheets, and so on). As an added bonus, this makes life easier for your less-fortunate (Windows-using) friends when you send them files.

If you have a file with a space in its name, that space confuses the shell if you enter it as part of the filename. That's because the shell breaks commands into separate words with spaces as delimiters, just as we do in English. To tell the shell not to break an argument at spaces, either put quotation marks around the filename that includes spaces (for example, *"my file.txt"*), or preface each space with a backslash (\).

For example, the *rm* program, covered later in this chapter, removes Unix files. To remove a file named *a confusing name*, the first *rm* command in the following snippet doesn't work, but the second does. Also note that you can *escape* spaces (that is, avoid having the shell interpret them inappropriately) by placing a backslash character before the space, as shown in the third example:

```
$ ls -l
total 2
-rw-r--r--  1 taylor  staff  324 Feb  4 23:07 a confusing name
-rw-r--r--  1 taylor  staff   64 Feb  4 23:07 another odd name
$ rm a confusing name
rm: a: no such file or directory
rm: confusing: no such file or directory
rm: name: no such file or directory
$ rm "a confusing name"
$ rm another\ odd\ name
$
```

You also need to escape any of the following characters with a backslash (\), because they have special meaning to the shell:

```
* # ` " ' \ $ | & ? ; ~ ( ) < > ! ^
```

Open a Terminal window and change directories to your *Library* directory. You'll see files that contain spaces, though the other punctuation characters are more unusual components of filenames:

```
$ cd Library
$ ls
```

```
Application Support     Documentation        Keychains          Snapz Pro X
Assistants              Favorites            Logs               Sounds
Audio                   FontCollections      Mail               Syndication
Autosave Information    Fonts                Metadata           iMovie
Caches                  Icons                Preferences        iTunes
Classic                 Indexes              Printers
ColorPickers            Internet Plug-Ins    Recent Servers
Cookies                 Keyboard Layouts     Safari
$ cd App<TAB>
$ cd Application\ Support/
$
```

The last example shows a useful trick: hitting the Tab key after entering a few characters of the filename invokes the shell's file completion feature. When you hit the Tab key, the shell automatically includes the backslash required to escape any spaces in file or directory names.

One place where you can find all sorts of peculiar filenames is within your iTunes library, because iTunes uses the song title as the filename for the corresponding MP3- or ACC-encoded file. Here are a few examples of filenames from my own library that would be incredibly difficult to work with on the command line:

```
The Beatles/Sgt. Pepper's /Being For The Benefit of Mr. Kite!.mp3
The Art of Noise/In No Sense? Nonsense!/How Rapid?.mp3
Joe Jackson/Look Sharp!/(Do The) Instant Mash.mp3
```

True Unix diehards are undoubtedly cringing at those filenames, which include specific wildcard characters and other elements that are important to the shell, all of which would have to be escaped. For example, you see how those filenames look now, just imagine them like this:

```
The\ Beatles/Sgt\.\ Pepper\'s\ /Being\ For\ The\ Benefit\ of\ Mr\.\ Kite\!\.
mp3
The\ Art\ of\ Noise/In\ No\ Sense\?\ Nonsense\!/How\ Rapid\?\.mp3
Joe\ Jackson/Look\ Sharp\!/\(Do\ The\)\ Instant\ Mash\.mp3
```

Not pretty.

One more thing: a filename must be unique inside its directory, but other directories can have files with the same name. For example, you may have files called *chap1.doc* and *chap2.doc* in the directory */Users/carol/Documents* and also have different files with the same names in */Users/carol/Desktop*.

This often causes great confusion for people who are used to just having all their files on their Desktop or in the topmost level of the Documents directory. In that situation, an attempt to save a file as *chap1.doc* would just generate a warning that the file already exists, but if you create different directories for different projects, it's quite feasible that you'll end up with a dozen or more files with the exact same name.

File and Directory Wildcards

When you have a number of files named in series (for example, *chap1.doc* to *chap12.doc*) or filenames with common characters (such as *aegis*, *aeon*, and *aerie*), you can use wildcards to save yourself lots of typing and match multiple files at the same time. These special characters are the asterisk (*), question mark (?), and square brackets ([ ]). When used in a file or directory name given as an argument on a command line, the characteristics detailed in Table 4-1 are true.

Table 4-1. Shell wildcards

Notation	Definition
*	An asterisk stands for any number of characters in a filename. For example, *ae** matches any filename that begins with "ae" (such as *aegis*, *aerie*, *aeon*, etc.) if those files are in the same directory. You can use this to save typing for a single filename (for example, *al** for *alphabet.txt*) or to choose many files at once (as in *ae**). A * by itself matches all file and subdirectory names in a directory, with the exception of any starting with a period. To match all your dot files, try *.??**.
?	A question mark stands for any single character (so *h?p* matches *hop* and *hip*, but not *hp* or *help*).
[ ]	Square brackets can surround a choice of single characters (i.e., one digit or one letter) you'd like to match. For example, *[Cc]hapter* would match either *Chapter* or *chapter*, but *chap[12]* would match *chap1* or *chap2*. Use a hyphen (-) to separate a range of consecutive characters. For example, *chap[1-3]* matches *chap1*, *chap2*, or *chap3*.
{ , }	A list of two or more subpatterns that are matched consecutively. The pattern *a{b,c,d}e* would match *abe*, *ace*, and *ade*, but not *aee* because the middle *e* isn't inside the curly braces. This is most commonly used to reference multiple files within a subdirectory, as in *Mail/{drafts,inbox}* which is functionally identical to typing both *Mail/drafts* and *Mail/inbox*.

The following examples show how to use wildcards. The first command lists all the entries in a directory, and the rest use wildcards to list just some of the entries. The second-to-last one is a little tricky; it matches files whose names contain two (or more) *a*'s.

```
$ ls
chap0.txt        chap2.txt        chap5.txt        cold.txt
chap1a.old.txt   chap3.old.txt    chap6.txt        haha.txt
chap1b.txt       chap4.txt        chap7.txt        oldjunk
$ ls chap?.txt
chap0.txt        chap4.txt        chap6.txt
chap2.txt        chap5.txt        chap7.txt
$ ls chap[3-7]*
chat3.old.txt    chap4.txt        chap5.txt        chap6.txt        chap7.txt
$ ls chap??.txt
chap1b.txt
$ ls *old*
chap1a.old.txt   chap3.old.txt    cold.txt         oldjunk
```

```
$ ls *a*a*
chap1a.old.txt    haha.txt
$ ls chap{3,6}.txt
chap3.txt         chap6.txt
$
```

Wildcards are useful for more than listing files. Most Unix programs accept more than one filename, and you can use wildcards to name multiple files on the command line. For example, both the *cat* and *less* programs display files on the screen. *cat* streams a file's contents until end of file, while *less* shows the file one screen at a time. By *screen*, I'm referring to what the *less* command actually shows inside the Terminal window. (This term stems from the early days of Unix when you didn't have any windows and had only one screen.) Let's say you want to display files *chap3.old.txt* and *chap1a.old.txt*. Instead of specifying these files individually, you could enter the command as:

```
$ less *.old.txt
```

Which is equivalent to:

```
$ less chap1a.old.txt chap3.old.txt
```

Wildcards match directory names, too. You can use them anywhere in a pathname—absolute or relative—though you still need to remember to separate directory levels with forward slashes (/). For example, let's say you have subdirectories named *Jan*, *Feb*, *Mar*, and so on. Each has a file named *summary*. You could read all the *summary* files by typing *less */summary*. That's almost equivalent to *less Jan/summary Feb/summary*. However, there's one important difference when you use *less */summary*: the names will be alphabetized, so *Apr/summary* would be first in the list, not January.

This can also be useful if you've got lots of files to match. A classic example of where the shell is way more powerful than the Finder is when it comes to moving a subset of files in a directory that match a specific pattern. If all the JPEG image files in a directory should be moved to a new subdirectory called *JPEG Images*, while the TIFF and PNG format images should remain in the current directory, the fast command-line solution is:

```
$ mv *.{jpg,JPG} JPEG\ Images
```

Versus a tedious one-by-one selection process in the Finder!

Looking Inside Files

By now, you're probably tired of looking at files from the outside. It's like visiting a bookstore and never getting to open the book and read what's inside. Fortunately, it doesn't have to be this way, so let's look at three different programs for looking inside text files.

Why the caveat "text files" rather than "all files"? Because since Unix treats everything as a file, it'll let you "look at" image data, executable programs, even the actual bits of the directory structure itself. None of those are useful, and while there's a program called *strings* that helps you snoop around in these datafiles, it's not at all commonly used in the world of Mac OS X and Terminal.

cat

The most rudimentary of the programs that let you look inside a file is called *cat*, not for any sort of feline, but because that's short for *concatenate*, a fancy word for "put a bunch of stuff together." The *cat* command is useful for peeking at short files, but because it doesn't care how long the file is or how big your Terminal window is set, using *cat* to view a long file results in the top lines scrolling right off before you can even read them.

At its most basic form, you list one or more files, and *cat* displays their contents to the screen:

```
$ cd /etc
$ cat notify.conf
#
# Notification Center configuration file
#

reserve com.apple.system. 0 0 rwr-r-
monitor com.apple.system.timezone /etc/localtime
$
```

In this case, I've moved to the */etc* administrative directory and used *cat* to display the contents of the *notify.conf* configuration file.

Using a wildcard pattern (shown earlier), I can look at a couple of different configuration files with a single invocation of *cat*:

```
$ cat {notify,ntp,xinetd}.conf
#
# Notification Center configuration file
#

reserve com.apple.system. 0 0 rwr-r-
monitor com.apple.system.timezone /etc/localtime
server time.apple.com minpoll 12 maxpoll 17
# man xinetd.conf for more information

defaults
{
        instances           = 60
        log_type            = SYSLOG daemon
```

```
                log_on_success          = HOST PID
                log_on_failure          = HOST
                cps                      = 25 30
        }

        includedir /etc/xinetd.d
        $
```

One serious drawback with using *cat* to view more than one file in this manner should be obvious: there's no indication of where one file ends and the next begins. The listing above is actually three different files all just dumped to the screen.

There are a couple of useful options for the *cat* command, most notably *-n* to add line numbers and *-v*, which ensures that everything displayed is printable (though not necessarily readable).

The split between files is more obvious when the *-n* option adds line numbers to the output, for example:

```
$ cat -n {notify,ntp,xinetd}.conf
     1  #
     2  # Notification Center configuration file
     3  #
     4
     5  reserve com.apple.system. 0 0 rwr-r-
     6  monitor com.apple.system.timezone /etc/localtime
     1  server time.apple.com minpoll 12 maxpoll 17
     1  # man xinetd.conf for more information
     2
     3  defaults
     4  {
     5          instances                = 60
     6          log_type                 = SYSLOG daemon
     7          log_on_success           = HOST PID
     8          log_on_failure           = HOST
     9          cps                      = 25 30
    10  }
    11
    12  includedir /etc/xinetd.d
```

Here, you can see that the line numbers for each file are printed to the left of the file's contents. So, to find out where a file begins, just look for the number 1, as that's the first line of a file. This output shows us that *notify.conf* is six lines long, *ntp.conf* only has one line, and *xinetd.conf* is 12 lines long.

less

If you want to "read" a long plain-text file in a Terminal window, you can use the *less* command to display one "page" (a Terminal window filled from top to bottom) of text at a time.

If you don't like *less*, you can use a program named *more*. In fact, the name *less* is a play on the name of *more*, which came first (but *less* has more features than *more*). Here's a Mac OS X secret, though: *more* is *less*. Really. The *more* utility is actually the very same program—just with a different name—which gives it a different default behavior. The *ls* command shows the truth:

```
$ ls -l /usr/bin/more /usr/bin/less
-rwxr-xr-x   2 root  wheel   119128 Dec  2 16:26 /usr/bin/less
-rwxr-xr-x   2 root  wheel   119128 Dec  2 16:26 /usr/bin/more
```

Rather than get confused between the two, I'll just stick with *less*. The syntax for *less* is:

```
less options files
```

less lets you move forward or backward in the files that you're viewing by any number of pages or lines; you can also move back and forth between two or more files specified on the command line. When you invoke *less*, the first "page" of the file appears. A prompt appears at the bottom of the Terminal window, as in the following example:

```
$ less ch03
A file is the unit of storage in Unix, as in most other systems.
A file can hold anything: text (a report you're writing,
  .
  .
  .
:
```

The basic *less* prompt is a colon (:); although, for the first screen, *less* displays the file's name as a prompt. The cursor sits to the right of this prompt as a signal for you to enter a *less* command to tell *less* what to do. To quit, type **q**.

Like almost everything about *less*, the prompt can be customized. For example, using the -M starting flag on the *less* command line makes the prompt show the filename and your position in the file (as a percentage) at the end of each page.

 If you want this to happen every time you use *less*, you can set the LESS environment variable to M (without a dash) in your shell setup file. See Chapter 2 for details.

You can set or unset most options temporarily from the *less* prompt. For instance, if you have the short *less* prompt (a colon), you can enter -M while *less* is running. *less* responds Long prompt (press Return), and for the rest of the session, *less* prompts with the filename, line number, and percentage of the file viewed.

To display the *less* commands and options available on your system, press **h** (for "help") while *less* is running. Table 4-2 lists some simple (but quite useful) commands.

Table 4-2. Useful less commands

Command	Description	Command	Description
Spacebar	Display next page	v	Starts the *vi* editor
Return	Display next line	Control-L	Redisplay current page
*n*f	Move forward *n* lines	h	Help
b	Move backward one page	:n	Go to next file on command line
*n*b	Move backward *n* lines	:p	Go back to previous file on command line
/*word*	Search forward for *word*	q	Quit *less*
?*word*	Search backward for *word*		

I quite commonly use the /*word* search notation, for instance, when using the *man* command, which uses *less* behind the scenes to display information one page at a time. For example, instead of flipping through *bash*'s manpage for information on file completion, typing **/file completion** at the colon prompt while reading the *bash* manpage lets you skip straight to what you seek. Gone too far? Use b to go back to the previous page.

grep

Instead of having the entire contents of the file dumped to your screen or having to step through a file one line at a time, you will undoubtedly find it useful to be able to search for specific patterns within a file or set of files. This is done with the oddly named *grep* command.

 grep gains its name from an old line-editor command, global/regular expression/print, which was used to list only the lines in the file being edited that matched a specified pattern. With the name *g/re/p*, it wasn't much of a stretch to end up with *grep*, and the programmer who created the command actually imagined it'd be mnemonic for his user community. Imagine!

grep uses a different pattern language than the filename patterns shown earlier in this chapter; it uses a more sophisticated pattern language, called *regular expressions*. Regular expressions are discussed in the next chapter, but for now, let's just use *grep* to find word fragments or specific words in a set of files.

Since we're already in the /etc directory, let's look to see if there's any mention of firewalls by using *grep*:

```
$ grep firewall *conf
named.conf:       * If there is a firewall between you and nameservers you
want
```

Within the set of configuration files, there was one match, as shown. In the output, the matching filename is shown, followed by a colon, followed by the actual matching line in the file.

You can search a lot more than just the configuration files, however, by changing the filename pattern. If you broaden this search, you'll inevitably have error messages about *grep* trying to search directory entries rather than files, "operation not permitted" errors. To sidestep this problem, *grep*'s -s option causes it to be quieter in its operation:

```
$ grep -s firewall *
grep: master.passwd: Permission denied
named.conf:       * If there is a firewall between you and nameservers you
want
named.conf.applesaved:   * If there is a firewall between you and
nameservers you want
named.conf.applesaved2:   * If there is a firewall between you and
nameservers you want
rc:if [ -f /Library/Preferences/com.apple.sharing.firewall.plist ]; then
services:csccfirewall   40843/udp   # CSCCFIREWALL
services:csccfirewall   40843/tcp   # CSCCFIREWALL
```

We'll look at *grep* in much greater detail in Chapter 5.

Creating and Editing Files

There are lots of ways to create and edit files when you're working on a Macintosh. You can use TextEdit, BBEdit, Microsoft Word, and any number of other applications within the Aqua graphical environment. If you'd like to stick to the command line, it turns out that there are a bunch of text-only, Terminal-friendly editors included with Mac OS X.

Chief among these options is an editor called *vi* that can be a bit tricky to learn but is powerful, fast, and available on a wide range of Unix and Linux systems, too. And because *vi* is so powerful, that's what we'll focus on in this section.

Text Editors and Word Processors

A text editor lets you add, change, and rearrange text easily. Three popular Unix editors included with Mac OS X are *vi* (pronounced "vee-eye"), *Pico*, ("pea-co"), and *Emacs* ("e-max"; no relation to Apple's eMac, either). By contrast, a word processor has all sorts of fancy layout and presentation capabilities, typically built around a "what you see is what you get" (WYSIWYG, or "wizzy-wig") model similar to Microsoft Word. They work great for lots of things but are useless for creating files within the Terminal.

You should choose an editor you're comfortable with. *vi* is probably the best choice, because all Unix systems have it, but Emacs is also widely available and seems to be preferred by developers because of the features it offers. If you'll be doing simple editing, though, Pico is a great choice. Although Pico is much less powerful than *vi* or Emacs, it's a lot easier to learn. For this book, however, I'll focus on the rudiments of *vi* since it's the most widely available Unix editor, and there's a terrific version included with Mac OS X called *vim*.

None of these plain-text editors has the same features as popular word-processing software, but *vi* and Emacs are sophisticated, extremely flexible editors for all kinds of plain-text files: programs, email messages, and so on. By "plain text," I mean a file with only letters, numbers, and punctuation characters, and no formatting such as point size, bold and italics, or embedded images. Unix systems use plain-text files in many places: in redirected input and output of Unix programs (see Chapter 6), as shell setup files (see Chapter 2), for shell scripts (see Chapter 11), for system configuration, and more.

 Of course, you can opt to use a graphical text editor such as BBEdit (*www.barebones.com*) or TextEdit (*/Applications*) with good results, too, if you'd rather just sidestep editing while within the Terminal application. If you do, try using the *open* command within the Terminal to launch the TextEdit with the proper file already loaded. For example, the following command opens the specified file in TextEdit:

```
open -e myfile.txt
```

It's critical that you select Format → Make Plain Text (Shift-⌘-T) within TextEdit to ensure that no extraneous formatting characters or information is included in the text file.

Text editors edit these plain-text files. When you use a word processor, though, the screen may look as if the file is only plain text, but the file inevitably has some hidden codes, too. That's often true even if you tell the word processor to "Save as plain text."

 One easy way to check for nontext characters in a file is by reading the file with *less*; look for characters in reversed colors, codes such as <36>, and so on.

Fixing Those Pesky Carriage Returns

Switching between Finder applications and Unix tools for editing can be a hassle because you might end up having to translate file formats along the way. Fortunately, this is easy with the Unix command line.

One of the more awkward things about Apple putting a Mac graphical environment on top of a Unix core is that the two systems use different end-of-line sequences. If you ever open up a file in a Finder application and see lots of little boxes at the end of each line, or if you try to edit a file within Unix and find that it's littered with ^M sequences, you've hit the end-of-line problem.

To fix it, create the following command aliases:

```
alias m2u="tr '\015' '\012' "
alias u2m="tr '\012' '\015' "
```

Now, whenever you're working with Unix editing tools and you need to fix a Mac-format file, simply use *m2u* (Mac to Unix), as in:

```
$ m2u < mac-format-file > unix-friendly-file
```

And if you find yourself in the opposite situation, where you're editing a Unix file in a Mac tool and it has some carriage-return weirdness, use the reverse (Unix to Mac) within Terminal before editing:

```
$ u2m < unix-friendly-file > mac-format-file
```

Worthy of note is the helpful *tr* command, which makes it easy to translate all occurrences of one character to another. Use *man tr* to learn more about this powerful utility.

You can add these aliases to your future login sessions by copying the two alias definition lines into your *.bashrc* file, if you're using *bash*, or to *.kshrc*, if you're using the Korn shell.

If you need to do word processing—making documents, envelopes, and so on—your best bet is to work with a program designed for that purpose. While TextEdit is surprisingly powerful (it can read and write Word files), you might want to opt for something more powerful, such as Pages (which comes with Apple's iWork, *www.apple.com/iwork*); Microsoft Office; or NeoOffice/J (*www.neooffice.org*), an open source suite of applications similar to Microsoft Office.

The vi Text Editor

The *vi* editor, originally written by Bill Joy at the University of California, Berkeley, is easy to use once you master the fundamental concept of a modal editor. Mac OS X actually includes a version of *vi* called *vim* that has many useful new features. In this section, we cover *vi*'s basic commands, but if you become a *vi* master, you'll enjoy *vim*'s powerful extensions.

To learn more about *vi*, I'd recommend picking up a copy of *Learning the vi Editor*, by Linda Lamb and Arnold Robbins (O'Reilly) or the *vi Editor Pocket Reference*, by Arnold Robbins (O'Reilly). These books are packed with useful information about *vi*, and the *Learning* book includes a handy quick-reference card of commands you can use with *vi*. Though focused on *vi*, they offer extensive information about *vim* as well, and will get you up to speed in no time. Or, if you have a Safari account (*safari.oreilly.com*), you can read the books online.

Before we talk about all the useful additions, however, let's talk about *modality*. Modes can be best explained by thinking about your car stereo. When you have a CD in, the "1" button does one task, but if you are listening to the radio, the very same button does something else (perhaps jump to preprogrammed station number 1). The *vi* editor is exactly the same: in *Command mode*, pressing the i key on the keyboard switches you into *Insert mode*, but in Insert mode, the very same keystroke inserts an "i" into the text itself. The handiest key on your keyboard while you're learning *vi* is unquestionably the Escape key (Esc), located at the upper-left corner of your keyboard. If you're in Insert mode, Esc switches you back to Command mode, and if you're in Command mode, it'll beep to let you know that all is well. Use Esc often, until you're completely comfortable keeping track of what mode you're in.

Jump start your learning by using Mac OS X's included *vimtutor*: just type in *vimtutor* on the command line for a guided tour of the *vi* editor.

Start *vi* by typing its name; the argument is the filename you want to create or edit. For instance, to edit your shell's *.profile* setup file, you would *cd* to your home directory and enter:

```
$ vi .profile
```

The Terminal fills with a copy of the file (and, because the file is short, some blank lines, too, as denoted by the ~ at the beginning of the line), as shown in Figure 4-1.

The bottom row of the window is the status line, which indicates what file you're editing: ".profile" 4L, 76C. This indicates that the file has four lines (4L) with a total of 76 characters (76C). Quit the program by typing :q and pressing Return while in Command mode.

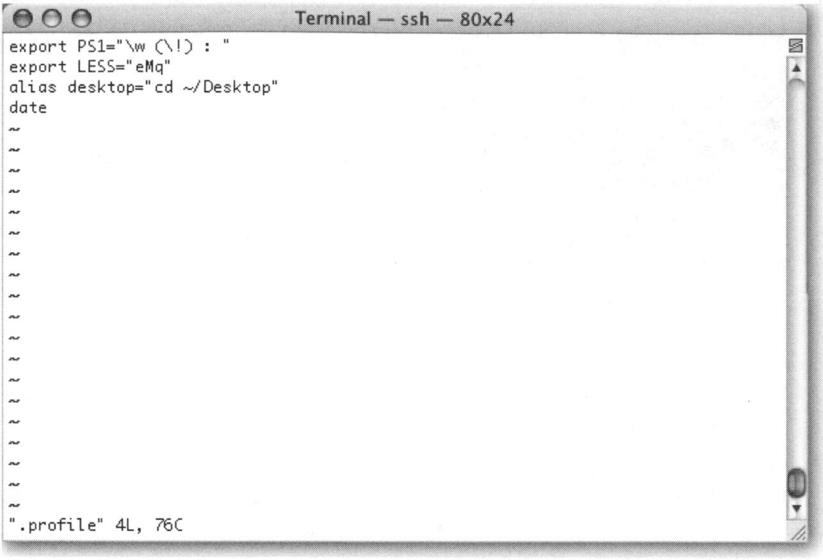

```
● ● ●                    Terminal — ssh — 80x24
export PS1="\w (\!) : "
export LESS="eMq"
alias desktop="cd ~/Desktop"
date
~
~
~
~
~
~
~
~
~
~
~
~
~
~
~
~
~
".profile" 4L, 76C
```

Figure 4-1. vi display while editing

vi Basics

Let's take a tour through *vi*. In this example, you'll create a new text file. You can call the file anything you want, but it's best to use only letters and numbers in the filename. For instance, to make a file named *sample*, enter the following command:

```
$ vi sample
```

Now, let's start the tour....

Your screen should look something like Figure 4-1, but the cursor should be on the top line and the rest of the lines will have the tilde character (~) to denote that the line is blank. The bottom status line indicates the following:

```
"sample" [New File]
```

To start entering text in the file, press **i** to switch from Command mode to Insert mode. Now type something. Make some lines too short (press Return before the line gets to the right margin). Make others too long; watch how *vi* wraps long lines. If you have another Terminal window open with some text in it, or if you have an application like Word or TextEdit open, you can use your mouse to copy text from another window and paste it into the Terminal window where you're working with *vi*. (Always make sure you're in Insert mode before you do this, however, or you could irrevocably mess up your file.) To get a lot of text quickly, paste the same text more than once.

Figure 4-2 shows how the *sample* file looks after I copied and pasted the previous paragraph into *vi*'s buffer.

```
● ● ●                    Terminal — ssh — 80x24
Enter some lines of text. Make some lines
too short
(press Return before the line gets to the right margin). Make others too long; w
atch how vi wraps long lines.
If you have another terminal window open with some text in it, or if
you have an Aqua application open, you can also use your mouse
to copy text from another window and paste it into the vi window.
(Always make sure you're in Insert mode before you do this, however,
or you could irrevocably mess up your file.) To get a lot of text
quickly, paste the same text more than
once.
~
~
~
~
~
~
~
~
~
~
~
~
/
```

Figure 4-2. vi with some text pasted into the buffer

To move the cursor around in the file, you'll need to leave Insert mode by pressing Esc once. Press it again and you'll hear a beep, reminding you that you are already in Command mode.

Tip: In Command mode, press Control-G to produce a useful status line that shows the filename, number of lines, and where the cursor is relative to the file buffer, as shown at the very bottom of Figure 4-2.

You can use the arrow keys on your keyboard to move around the file, but most vi users have taught themselves to move around with the h, j, k, and l motion keys (left, down, up, and right, respectively). They may seem unintuitive, but not having to move your hand off the main keyboard area can produce a dramatic increase in editing speed as you get more used to them.

You can also use the up, down, left, and right arrow keys on your keyboard to move *vi*'s cursor. Sometimes this is easier to remember than h (left arrow), l (right arrow), k (up arrow), and j (down arrow).

Unless you have enabled "Option click to position cursor" in Terminal's preferences (see Chapter 2), *vi* ignores your mouse if you try to use it to move the cursor.

If you've entered a lot of text, you can experiment with some additional movement commands: H to jump to the first line on the screen, G to jump to the very last line of the file. You should also try the w and b commands, to move forward and backward one word at a time (for example, to move forward three words, press the w key three times), and 0 (zero) jumps to the beginning of the line, while $ jumps to the end.

Searching in vi

While *vi* is proving to be a worthy text editor, you're probably thinking that it's lacking one feature that many graphical text editors have: the ability to use ⌘-F to search through the file for some text. Ah, but don't get too far ahead. You can search for text strings in *vi*; it's just a little different. *vi*'s search command is accessed by typing a forward slash (/) while in Command mode, followed by the desired pattern you want to search for. It's handy even on a short file, where it can be quicker to type / and a word than it is to use the cursor-moving commands. For example, if you wanted to search through a text file for the word "cheese," you would first press the Esc key twice (just to make sure you're out of Insert mode and in Command mode) and then type:

    /cheese

You'll see this string appear at the bottom of your Terminal window. When you hit Return, *vi* searches through the file for the word "cheese," and if it finds it, *vi* places the cursor at the beginning of the word. After the search finishes, you can press the n key to repeat the search. If *vi* finds another occurrence of that word, it moves the cursor to that word.

 Using the : to begin your *search* command is also a good example of how *vi* can move your cursor to the status line so you can enter more information.

Invoking external Unix commands

One fabulous feature of *vi* is that it's easy to invoke Unix commands and have their output included in the file you're editing. That said, *vi* also makes it easy to send some of the text in its buffer to a Unix command, ultimately replacing that text with the output of the command. Sound confusing? It's really not so bad.

For example, to include the current date in your file, type **o** in Command mode to open up a blank line immediately below the line that the cursor is sitting on, hit the Esc key to get out of Insert mode, and then enter **!!date**. As you type this, the cursor drops to the bottom of the screen and shows :.!date there. Press Return, and the blank line is replaced by the output from the *date* command.

Now justify a paragraph of text by feeding it to the external Unix *fmt* command. To do this, make sure you're in Command mode (hit Esc just to be safe), then use the arrow keys to move the cursor to the beginning of the paragraph and type **!}fmt**. (*vi*'s status line won't change until you press the } character.) Now the paragraph's lines should flow and fit neatly between the margins. Figure 4-3 shows what happened when I moved to the top of the file (using the H command) then typed in !}fmt to reflow the text in the document.

```
 ● ○ ○                   Terminal — ssh — 80x24
Enter some lines of text. Make some lines too short (press Return
before the line gets to the right margin). Make others too long;
watch how vi wraps long lines.  If you have another terminal window
open with some text in it, or if you have an Aqua application open,
you can also use your mouse to copy text from another window and
paste it into the vi window.  (Always make sure you're in Insert
mode before you do this, however, or you could irrevocably mess up
your file.) To get a lot of text quickly, paste the same text more
than once.
~
~
~
~
~
~
~
~
~
~
~
"sample" [Modified] line 1 of 9 --11%-- col 1
```

Figure 4-3. Reformatted text using the Unix fmt command

More powerful capabilities

Text can be deleted by using x to delete the character that's under the cursor, or the powerful d command:

dd

    Deletes lines

dw

    Deletes individual words

d$

Deletes to the end of the line

d0

Deletes to the beginning of the line

dG

Deletes to the end of the file (if you're seeing a pattern and thinking that it's d + *motion key*, you're absolutely correct)

To undo the deletion, press **u**.

You can also paste the deleted text with the p command, though truth be told, the copy and paste capability within *vim* is far weaker and more confusing than Mac OS X's standard Copy (⌘-C) and Paste (⌘-V) capabilities.

The first step to copying text is to position your cursor at the beginning of the word or line (or series of lines) you want to copy. In *vi*, you don't copy, you "yank" the text. The yw command copies ("yanks") one word, yy yanks the line, yy*n* yanks *n* lines (for example, yy5 yanks five lines), y1 yanks a single character, and y*n*w yanks *n* words (y5w yanks five words, for example). Move the cursor to the line you want to copy and press yy. After repositioning your cursor to where you'd like the text copied, press p to paste the text.

 Yank does not cut the text, it only copies it to *vi*'s paste buffer. If you want to move the text, you'll have to go back to the lines you've yanked (copied) and delete them.

As with any text editor, it's a good idea to save your work from *vi* every 5 or 10 minutes. That way, if something goes wrong on the computer or network, you'll be able to recover the edited buffer from the last time you saved it.

If the editor, Terminal, or the computer does crash, you can recover the saved temporary edit buffer by using the *-r* option when you next launch the program. If there is a file that can be recovered, *vi* shows specific information about it:

```
$ vi -r
Swap files found:
   In current directory:
1.     .sample.swp
            owned by: taylor    dated: Mon Jun  6 23:06:23 2005
         file name: ~taylor/sample
         modified: YES
         user name: taylor    host name: Tiger.local
        process ID: 8085
   In directory ~/tmp:
        -- none --
```

```
    In directory /var/tmp:
       -- none --
    In directory /tmp:
       -- none --
 $
```

To recover this file, just type **vi -r sample** and you'll move into the *vi* editor with the recovered version of the file.

In *vi*, to save your work to disk, you use the write command by typing **:w** followed by Return. The bottom of the display shows the filename saved and the number of lines and characters in the file.

For some reason, saving the edited file sometimes confuses *vi* beginners. It's really very simple: if you want to save the file with the same name it had when you started, just press **:w** and Return. That's all! If you'd rather use a different filename, type **:w** followed by the new filename. For example, :w new.sample. Press Return and it's saved.

Finally, if you try to exit with the usual :q command and the program beeps, warning you that the modified file has not been saved. If you want to override the warning and discard the changes that you've made since the last time the file was saved, type **:q!**. If you want to save the changes and don't need to rename the output file, you can use a shortcut: :wq writes out your changes and quits *vi*. In fact, there's a shortcut for that shortcut, too. Type ZZ and you'll write and quit if the file's been modified, or just quit without disturbing the file if it hasn't been changed. That's it!

There's a lot more you can learn about. In Table 4-3, you'll find a handy listing of some of the most common *vi* commands and their descriptions.

Table 4-3. Common vi editing commands

Command	Meaning
/pattern	Search forward for specified pattern. Repeat search with n.
:q	Quit the edit session.
:q!	Quit, discarding any changes.
:w	Write (save) any changes out to the file.
:wq or ZZ	Write out any changes, then quit (shortcut).
a	Move into Append mode (like Insert mode, but you enter information after the cursor, not before).
b	Move backward one word.
w	Move forward one word.
d1G	Delete from the current point back to the beginning of the file.
dd	Delete the current line.

Table 4-3. Common vi editing commands (continued)

Command	Meaning
dG	Delete through end of file.
dw	Delete the following word.
Esc	Move into Command mode.
h	Move backward one character.
l	Move forward one character.
i	Switch to Insert mode (Esc switches you back to Command mode).
j	Move down one line.
k	Move up one line.
O	Open up a line above the current line and switches to Insert mode.
o	Open up a line below the current line and switches to Insert mode.
P	Put (paste) deleted text before the cursor.
p	Put (paste) deleted text after the cursor.
X	Delete character to the left of the cursor.
x	Delete the character under the cursor.
yw	Yank (copy) from the cursor to the end of the current word. You can then paste it with p or P.
yy	Yank (copy) the current line. You can then paste it with p or P.

A Simpler vi Alternative: Pico

If the section on *vi* has left you longing for the safety and logic of the graphical world, you might want to explore the simple editing alternative of Pico. Originally written as part of a text-based email system called Pine (which itself was based on an email program called Elm that I wrote in the mid-1980s), Pico has taken on a life of its own and is included in many Unix distributions, including Mac OS X. Figure 4-4 shows the sample file from the earlier example in Pico.

Pico offers a menu-based approach to editing, with onscreen help. It's a lot friendlier than *vi*, whose primary way to tell you that you've done something wrong is to beep. Pico offers a comfortable middle-ground between text editors such as TextEdit and hardcore Unix text editors such as *vi*. It's a friendly editor that you can launch from the command line and never have to take your hands off the keyboard to use. To learn more about Pico, type Control-G while within the editor, or use *man pico* to read the manpage.

The GNU *nano* editor is actually included with Mac OS X Tiger as a fully functional open source version of Pico. You can type **nano** instead of *pico* if you'd like.

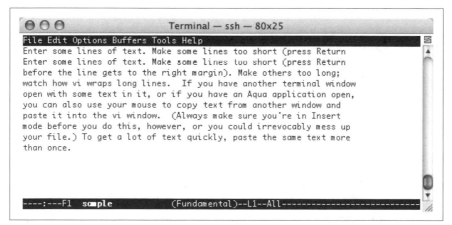

```
  ● ● ●                  Terminal — ssh — 80x25
  GNU nano 1.2.4 File: sample

  Enter some lines of text. Make some lines too short (press Return
  before the line gets to the right margin). Make others too long;
  watch how vi wraps long lines.  If you have another terminal window
  open with some text in it, or if you have an Aqua application open,
  you can also use your mouse to copy text from another window and
  paste it into the vi window.  (Always make sure you're in Insert
  mode before you do this, however, or you could irrevocably mess up
  your file.) To get a lot of text quickly, paste the same text more
  than once.



                        [ Read 9 lines ]
  ^G Get Help  ^O WriteOut  ^R Read File  ^Y Prev Page  ^K Cut Text  ^C Cur Pos
  ^X Exit      ^J Justify   ^W Where Is   ^V Next Page  ^U UnCut Txt ^T To Spell
```

Figure 4-4. Pico, a simpler alternative to vi

The More Complex Option: Emacs

If Pico is the simpler alternative to *vi*, then Emacs is the more complex alternative. Originally written as part of an artificial intelligence environment and including its own powerful programming language built atop LISP, Emacs is one of the most powerful editors available on any computer system. Indeed, hardcore Emacs users never leave the editor, and there are Emacs extensions for browsing the Web (albeit in text-only mode), reading and responding to email, chatting via instant message system, and more. Figure 4-5 shows Emacs with the sample file in the edit buffer.

```
  ● ● ●                  Terminal — ssh — 80x25
  File Edit Options Buffers Tools Help
  Enter some lines of text. Make some lines too short (press Return
  Enter some lines of text. Make some lines too short (press Return
  before the line gets to the right margin). Make others too long;
  watch how vi wraps long lines.  If you have another terminal window
  open with some text in it, or if you have an Aqua application open,
  you can also use your mouse to copy text from another window and
  paste it into the vi window.  (Always make sure you're in Insert
  mode before you do this, however, or you could irrevocably mess up
  your file.) To get a lot of text quickly, paste the same text more
  than once.



  ----:---F1  sample          (Fundamental)--L1--All------------------------
```

Figure 4-5. Emacs is the Ferrari of Unix text editors

But with great power comes great complexity, and Emacs is not only built upon a completely different paradigm—it's a *nonmodal* editor—but it requires you to memorize dozens of different control, meta, and option key sequences.

 If you are interested in trying out the Emacs editor, there's an X11-based version available at *http://mindlube.com/products/emacs/*. There's no better place to start learning more about Emacs than the book *Learning GNU Emacs* by Debra Cameron, James Elliott, and Marc Loy (O'Reilly).

Managing Files

The tree structure of the Unix filesystem makes it easy to organize your files. After you make and edit some files, you may want to copy or move files from one directory to another, or rename files to distinguish different versions of a file. You may even want to create new directories each time you start a different project. If you copy a file, it's worth learning about the subtle sophistication of the *cp* command: if you copy a file to a directory, it automatically reuses the original filename and copies the file to the new location. This can save lots of typing!

More than just saving typing, however, the command line is much more precise, offering greater control than the Finder's drag-and-drop interface. For example, if you want to create a new folder in the Finder, you need to mouse up to the File menu and choose New Folder or use a non-mnemonic keystroke combination. On the command line, it's just *mkdir* to create a new directory. Even more to the point, if you have a folder full of hundreds of files and want to just move those that have *temp* in their filenames into the Trash, that's a tedious and error-prone Finder task, while the command-line equivalent is the simple *rm *temp**.

A directory tree can get cluttered with old files you don't need. If you don't need a file or a directory, delete it to free storage space on the disk. The following sections explain how to make and remove directories and files.

Creating Directories with mkdir

It's handy to group related files in the same directory. If you were writing a spy novel and reviewed restaurants for a local newspaper, for example, you probably wouldn't want your intriguing files mixed with restaurant listings. You could create two directories: one for all the chapters in your novel (*spy*, for example) and another for restaurants (*boston.dine*).

To create a new directory, use the *mkdir* program. The syntax is:

```
mkdir dirname(s)
```

dirname is the name of the new directory. To make several directories, put a space between each directory name. To continue this example, you would enter:

```
$ mkdir spy boston.dine
```

This means that if you want to create a directory with a space in the name, you'll need to escape the space just as you had to earlier when you referenced files with spaces in them. To create the directory *My Favorite Music*, you'd use:

```
$ mkdir "My Favorite Music"
```

Another trick is that you can create a new directory and include a bunch of subdirectories within that directory, all from one single command. For example, your spy novel most likely has a few chapters in it, and let's say that you need separate directories for each chapter for holding the chapter file, any illustrations you want to add, research notes, whatever. You could use the following command to create the spy novel's main directory and individual subdirectories for the various chapter directories:

```
$ mkdir -p spy/{ch{01,02,03,04,05,intro,toc,index,bio}}
```

The curly braces ({ }) are used to contain the string that starts out with *ch* for each directory, and then appends that with the comma-delimited items in the enclosed string, which gives you the chapter numbers. Run the following command to see the list of directories and subdirectories you've created:

```
$ ls -F spy
ch01/        ch03/        ch05/        chindex/        chtoc/
ch02/        ch04/        chbio/       chintro/
```

Try doing *that* in the Finder! You can't. To do that, you'd have to first create a folder named *spy*, open that, and then create and rename all those subfolders. Talk about time consuming! But here, the power of Unix goes into action and saves the day.

Copying Files

If you're about to edit a file, you may want to save a copy of it first. That makes it easy to get back the original version should the edit go haywire. To copy files, use the *cp* program.

The *cp* program can put a copy of a file into the same directory or into another directory. *cp* doesn't affect the original file, so it's a good way to keep an identical backup of a file.

To copy a file, use the command:

```
cp old new
```

Here, *old* is a pathname to the original file and *new* is the pathname you want for the copy. For example, to copy the */etc/passwd* file into a file called *password* in your home directory, you would enter:

```
$ cp /etc/passwd ~/password
$
```

You can also use the form:

```
cp old olddir
```

This puts a copy of the original file *old* into an existing directory *olddir*. The copy has the same filename as the original.

If there's already a file with the same name as the copy, *cp* replaces the old file with your new copy. This is handy when you want to replace an old copy of a file with a newer version, but it can cause trouble if you accidentally overwrite a copy you wanted to keep. To be safe, use *ls* to list the directory before you make a copy there.

Also, *cp* has an *-i* (interactive) option that asks you before overwriting an existing file. It works like this:

```
$ cp -i master existing-file.txt
overwrite existing-file.txt? no
$
```

(You have to either type **yes** or **no** to respond to the question; you can also just type **y** or **n** and hit Return.)

You can copy more than one file at a time to a single directory by listing the pathname of each file you want copied, with the destination directory at the end of the command line. You can use relative or absolute pathnames (see the sections "Absolute Pathnames" and "Relative Pathnames" in Chapter 3) as well as simple filenames. For example, let's say your working directory is */Users/carol* (from the filesystem diagram in Figure 3-1). To copy three files called *ch1*, *ch2*, and *ch3* from */Users/john* to a subdirectory called *Documents* (that's */Users/carol/ Documents*), enter:

```
$ cp ../john/ch1.doc ../john/ch2.doc ../john/ch3.doc Documents
```

Or you could use wildcards and let the shell find all the appropriate files. This time, let's add the *-i* option for safety:

```
$ cp -i ../john/ch[1-3].doc Documents
cp: overwrite work/ch2.doc ? n
```

This tells you that there is already a file named *ch2.doc* in the *Documents* directory. When *cp* asks, answer **n** to prevent copying *ch2.doc*. Answering **y** overwrites the old *ch2doc*. As you saw in Chapter 3, the shorthand form . (a single dot or period) refers to the working directory, and .. (dot, dot) refers to the parent directory. For example, the following puts the copies into the working directory:

```
$ cp ../john/ch[1-3].doc .
```

One more possibility: when you're working with home directories, you can use a convenient shorthand *~account* to represent John and Carol's home directory (and ~ by itself to represent your own). So here's yet another way to copy those three files:

```
$ cp ~john/ch[1-3.doc] Documents
```

cp can also copy entire directory trees with the help of the -R option, for "recursive." There are two arguments after the option: the pathname of the top-level directory from which you want to copy and the pathname of the place where you want the top level of the copy to be.

As an example, let's say that a new employee, Asha, has joined John and Carol. She needs a copy of John's *Documents/work* directory in her own home directory. (See the filesystem diagram in Figure 3-1.) Her home directory is */Users/asha*. If Asha's own *work* directory doesn't exist yet (important!), she could type the following commands:

```
$ cd /Users
$ cp -R john/Documents/work asha/work
```

Or, from her home directory, she could have used:

```
$ cp -R ~john/Documents/work work
```

Either way, Asha now has a new subdirectory */Users/asha/work* with a copy of all files and subdirectories from */Users/john/Documents/work*.

 If you give *cp* -R the wrong pathnames, it can copy a directory tree into itself—running forever until your filesystem fills up!

When *cp* copies a file, the new copy has its ownership changed to the user running the *cp* command, too, so not only does Asha have the new files, but they're also owned by her. Here's an example of how that works:

```
$ ls -l /etc/shells
-rw-r--r--    1 root      wheel   179 Nov 14 03:30 /etc/shells
$ cp /etc/shells ~
$ ls -l ~/shells
-rw-r--r--    1 taylor    taylor  179 Jan  4 07:59 /Users/taylor/shells
$
```

Notice that the ~ shortcut for the home directory can also be used as a target directory with a *cp* command. Very helpful!

Problem checklist

The following tips should help you diagnose any error messages *cp* throws your way:

The system says something like "cp: cannot copy file to itself."
  If the copy is in the same directory as the original, the filenames must be different.

The system says something like "cp: filename: no such file or directory."
  The system can't find the file you want to copy. Check for a typing mistake. If a file isn't in the working directory, be sure to use its pathname.

The system says something like "cp: permission denied."
  You may not have permission to copy a file created by someone else or to copy it into a directory that does not belong to you. Use *ls -l* to find the owner and the permissions for the file, or use *ls -ld* to check the directory. If you feel that you should be able to copy a file, ask the file's owner or use *sudo* (see "Superuser Privileges with sudo" in Chapter 3) to change its access modes.

Copying Mac files with resources

The *cp* program works on plain files and directories, but the Macintosh system stores applications in bundles that include various resources used by the application. These attributes are known as *resource forks* and are used extensively in Mac OS applications and documents. (You will also find them in various places on the Mac OS X filesystem.) If you're a Mac OS 9 veteran, you'll remember that the resources in the resource fork were editable only with ResEdit, and otherwise were hidden in the system. A file's resource fork, if it exists, can be seen by looking at a special file called *filename/rsrc*. For example, notice how the Calculator application is actually saved on disk:

```
$ cd /Applications
$ ls -ld Calculator.app
drwxrwxr-x   3 root  admin  102 Jun 22  2004 Calculator.app/
```

By contrast, look at Figure 4-6, where the applications in Mac OS X are shown in the Finder.

The Unix command output appears rather puzzling, actually. According to the Finder, the Calculator is an application, not a directory, and if you double-click on the icon, the program launches. If it were a directory you'd just move into the directory, right? But the Unix *ls* command suggests otherwise

Figure 4-6. Calculator shows up in the Terminal as a directory, but the Finder says it's an application; it's really a bundle

because in fact it's not even called *Calculator* but *Calculator.app* and it *is* a directory!

Your might try to use *cp -R* where you'd otherwise use *cp*, which, logically, should move the entire directory, including whatever resources are needed:

```
$ cp Calculator.app ~
cp: Calculator.app is a directory (not copied).
$ cp -R Calculator.app ~
$
```

A quick glimpse at the Finder in Figure 4-7 shows that it didn't actually work (the application icon got lost in transit).

There's a special version of *cp* that you need to use instead, a program called *CpMac* which is available on your system only if you installed the Xcode Tools from Tiger's installation DVD.

With the Xcode Tools installed, you can now copy the application without anything getting lost:

```
$ /Developer/Tools/CpMac /Applications/Calculator.app ~
$
```

Notice that the Xcode utilities are in a nonstandard directory path. You will need to either specify the path each time, as shown above, create an alias, or modify your PATH to include the */Developer/Tools* directory (Chapter 2 showed how to modify your PATH).

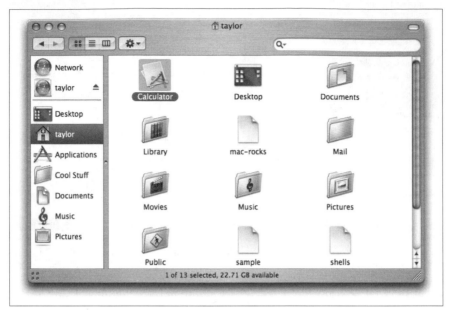

Figure 4-7. Our copy of Calculator lost its icon

Installing Xcode

If you're working with applications and other complex file structures in Mac OS X, you'll want to have access to *CpMac* and *MvMac*, both of which are available only after installing the Xcode Tools. Fortunately, Xcode is easy to get and install.

If you bought the boxed version of Mac OS X, Xcode is included in a separate folder on Tiger's install DVD. If you bought a new Macintosh that came with Mac OS X preinstalled, Xcode's installer should be in */Applications/Installers*.

The latest version of the Xcode Tools is also available from the Apple Developer Connection (ADC) web site (*http://connect.apple.com/*). Sign up for a free account, and you'll be able to download Xcode and install it yourself! Keep in mind, though, that the Xcode Tools is a pretty hefty download (almost 400 MB), so you shouldn't try downloading it if you don't have a broadband connection.

Renaming and Moving Files with mv

To rename a file, use *mv* (move). The *mv* program can also move a file from one directory to another.

The *mv* command has the same syntax as the *cp* command:

```
mv old new
```

Here, *old* is the old name of the file and *new* is the new name. *mv* writes over existing files, which is handy for updating old versions of a file. If you don't want to overwrite an old file, be sure that the new name is unique. Like *cp*, *mv* has an *-i* option for moving and renaming files interactively:

```
$ mv chap1.doc intro.doc
$ mv -i chap2.doc intro.doc
mv: overwrite `intro.doc'? n
$
```

The previous example changed the file named *chap1.doc* to *intro.doc*, and then tried to do the same with *chap2.doc* (answering **n** cancelled the last operation). If you list your files with *ls*, you'll see that the filename *chap1.doc* has disappeared, but *chap2.doc* and *intro.doc* are intact.

The *mv* command can also move a file from one directory to another. As with the *cp* command, if you want to keep the same filename, you need only give *mv* the name of the destination directory. For example, to move the *intro.doc* file from its present working directory to your Desktop, use the following command:

```
$ mv intro.doc ~/Desktop
```

If you need to move a directory (or an application or another Mac OS X file that's actually a directory with resource elements) you need to use *CpMac*'s cousin, the *MvMac* command:

```
$ alias MvMac="/Developer/Tools/MvMac"
$ MvMac ~/Calculator.app ~/MyApps/MyCalculator.app
$
```

The preceding command set up an alias for *MvMac* then used the alias to move the Calculator and all its resources into the *MyApps* subdirectory. To retain the alias on your next login, don't forget to add it to your *.profile* or *.cshrc* file, as appropriate for your login shell.

Removing Files and Directories

You may finish work on a file or directory and see no need to keep it, or the contents may be obsolete. Periodically removing unwanted files and directories frees storage space and saves you from getting confused when there are too many versions of files on your disk.

rm

The *rm* program removes files. One important thing to point out here, though, is that *rm* permanently removes the file from the filesystem. It doesn't move the file to the Trash, from which it can be recovered (at least until you select Empty the Trash from the Finder menu). Once you hit Return, that file is gone, so make darn sure that the file you're deleting with *rm* is something you really want to get rid of. Let me say that again: *rm* does *not* offer a way to recover deleted files.

The syntax is simple:

```
rm filename(s)
```

rm removes the named files, as the following example shows:

```
$ ls
chap10          chap2         chap5     cold
chap1a.old      chap3.old     chap6     haha
chap1b          chap4         chap7     oldjunk
$ rm *.old chap10
$ ls
chap1b    chap4    chap6    cold    oldjunk
chap2     chap5    chap7    haha
$ rm c*
$ ls
haha    oldjunk
$
```

When you use wildcards with *rm*, be sure you're deleting the right files! If you accidentally remove a file you need, you can't recover it unless you have a copy in another directory or in your backups.

Do not enter *rm* * carelessly. It deletes all the files in your working directory.

Here's another easy mistake to make: you want to enter a command such as *rm c** (remove all filenames starting with "c"), but instead enter *rm c ** (remove the file named *c* and all the other files in the current directory!)

It's good practice to list the files with *ls* before you remove them. Or, if you use *rm*'s *-i* (interactive) option, *rm* asks you whether you want to remove each file.

If you're security conscious, *rm*'s *-P* option might appeal to you: files are overwritten three times, with zeros, ones, and then zeros again, before they're removed. This makes it impossible for the data to be recovered— even by the most earnest malicious user. The flag doesn't produce any additional output or confirm that it's done a safe delete, however:

```
$ ls
haha    oldjunk
$ rm -P haha
$
```

rmdir

Just as you can create new directories with *mkdir*, you can remove them with the *rmdir* program. As a precaution, *rmdir* won't let you delete directories that contain any files or subdirectories; the directory must first be empty. (The *rm -r* command removes a directory and everything in it, but use the *-r* flag with caution: it can be dangerous for beginners.)

The syntax is:

```
rmdir dirname(s)
```

If you try to remove a directory that contains files, you'll get the following message:

```
rmdir: dirname not empty
```

To delete a directory that contains files or subdirectories:

1. Enter **cd *dirname*** to get into the directory you want to delete.
2. Enter **rm *** to remove all files in that directory.
3. Enter **cd ..** to go to the parent directory.
4. Enter **rmdir *dirname*** to remove the unwanted directory.

One such error you might encounter when using *rmdir* is that you might still get the *dirname* not empty message, even after you've deleted all the files inside. If this happens, use *ls -a* to check that there are no hidden files (names that start with a period) other than . and .. (the working directory and its parent). The following command is good for cleaning up hidden files (which aren't matched by a simple wildcard such as *). It matches all hidden files except for . (the current directory) and .. (the parent directory):

```
$ rm -i .[^.]*
```

Working with Links

If you've used the Mac for a while, you're familiar with *aliases*, empty files that point to other files on the system. A common use of aliases is to have a copy of an application on the Desktop, or to have a shortcut in your home directory. Within the graphical environment, you make aliases by Control-clicking on an item (a file, folder, application, whatever), and then choosing Make Alias from the context menu. This creates a file with a similar name in the same directory. The only difference is that the alias now has the word *alias* at the end of its filename. For example, if you were to look at this in Unix, you'd see the following:

```
$ ls -l *3*
-rw-r--r--  1 taylor  taylor  1546099 23 Sep 20:58 fig0403.pdf
-rw-r--r--  1 taylor  taylor        0 24 Sep 08:34 fig0403.pdf alias
```

In this case, the file *fig0403.pdf alias* is an alias pointing to the actual file *fig0403.pdf* in the same directory. But you wouldn't know it, because it appears to be an empty file: the size is shown as zero bytes.

 If you have a tendency to delete the *alias* part of a filename, as I do, then one quick technique for identifying if a file is an alias or not is to check out its file size: if it's size 0 but there's actually content when you look at it with *less*, it's an alias. Failing that, check out that directory in the Finder—use *open .* as a shortcut—and look for the telltale arrow on the icon.

Unix works with aliases differently; on the Unix side, we talk about *links*, not aliases. There are two types of links possible in Unix, *hard links* and *symbolic links*, and both are created with the *ln* command.

The syntax is:

```
ln [-s] source target
```

The *-s* option indicates that you're creating a symbolic link, so to create a second file that links to the file *fig0403.pdf*, the command would be:

```
$ ln -s fig0403.pdf neato-pic.pdf
```

and the results would be:

```
$ ls -l *pdf
-rw-r--r--  1 taylor  taylor  1532749 23 Sep 20:47 fig0401.pdf
-rw-r--r--  1 taylor  taylor  1539493 23 Sep 20:52 fig0402.pdf
-rw-r--r--  1 taylor  taylor  1546099 23 Sep 20:58 fig0403.pdf
lrwxr-xr-x  1 taylor  taylor       18 24 Sep 08:40 neato-pic.pdf@ ->
       fig0403.pdf
```

One way to think about symbolic links is that they're akin to a note saying "the info you want isn't here, it's in file X." This also implies a peculiar behavior of symbolic links (and Aqua aliases): move, rename, or remove the item being pointed to and you have an orphan link. The system doesn't automatically remove or update symbolic links.

The other type of link is a hard link, which essentially creates a second name entry for the exact same contents. That is, if you create a hard link to *fig0403.pdf*, you can then delete the original file, and its contents remain accessible through the second filename—even though the original file was deleted. Essentially, they're different doors into the same room (as opposed to a note taped on a door telling you to go to the second door, as would be the case with a symbolic link). Hard links are created with the *ln* command, except you omit the *-s* option:

```
$ ln mypic.pdf copy2.pdf
$ ls -l mypic.pdf copy2.pdf
```

```
-rw-r--r--  2 taylor  taylor  1546099 24 Sep 08:45 copy2.pdf
-rw-r--r--  2 taylor  taylor  1546099 24 Sep 08:45 mypic.pdf
$ rm mypic.pdf
$ ls -l copy2.pdf
-rw-r--r--  1 taylor  taylor  1546099 24 Sep 08:45 copy2.pdf
```

Notice that both files are exactly the same size when the hard link is created. This makes sense because they're both names to the same underlying set of data, so they should be identical. Then, when the original is deleted, the data survives with the second name now as its only name. The only difference is that the second field, the link count, shows 2 when there are two filenames pointing to the same data, but when the original is deleted, the link count of the second entry, *copy2.pdf*, goes back to 1.

Compressing and Archiving Files

Aqua users may commonly use StuffIt's *.sit* and *.hqx* formats for file archives or even the ZIP archive capability of Mac OS X itself (Control-click, choose Create Archive from the context menu, and your Mac promptly creates a *.zip* archive), but Unix users have many other options worth exploring.

Even though Mac OS X is far superior to Windows XP, we unfortunately live in a Windows world, which means you're going to occasionally send and receive email attachments with Windows users. It's also not uncommon to download shareware from a web or FTP site that's been zipped (a file with a *.zip* extension). Mac OS X gives you many ways to create your own ZIP archives (and to unzip the ones you receive, too). And if you're interacting with other Unix users (such as Linux, FreeBSD, or even Mac OS X), Mac OS X offers a suite of command-line utilities for batching and unbatching files.

There are three compression programs included with Mac OS X, though the most popular is *gzip* (the others are *compress* and *bzip2*; read their manpages to learn more about how they differ). There's also a very common Unix archive format called *tar* that I'll cover briefly.

gzip

Though it may initially confuse you into thinking that it's part of the ZIP archive toolset, *gzip* has nothing to do with the ZIP archive files created by Mac OS X's Make Archive capability. Instead, *gzip* is actually a compression program that does a very good job of shrinking down individual files for storage and transmission. If you're sending a file to someone with a dial-up connection, for example, running the file through *gzip* can significantly reduce its size and make it much more portable. Just as importantly, it can help save space on your disk by letting you compress files you want to keep but aren't using currently. *gzip* works particularly well with *tar*, too, as you'll see.

The syntax is:

```
gzip [-v] file(s)
```

The *-v* flag offers verbose output, letting the program indicate how much space it saved by compressing the file. Very useful information, as you may expect!

```
$ ls -l ch06.doc
-rwxr-xr-x  1 taylor   taylor  138240 24 Sep 08:52 ch06.doc
$ gzip -v ch06.doc
ch06.doc:                  75.2% -- replaced with ch06.doc.gz
$ ls -l ch06.doc.gz
-rwxr-xr-x  1 taylor   taylor  34206 24 Sep 08:52 ch06.doc.gz
```

You can see that *gzip* did a great job compressing the file, saving over 75 percent. Notice that it's automatically appended a *.gz* filename suffix to indicate that the file is now compressed. To uncompress the file, just use *gunzip*:

```
$ gunzip ch06.doc.gz
$ ls -l ch06.doc
-rwxr-xr-x  1 taylor   taylor  138240 24 Sep 08:52 ch06.doc
```

The amount of space saved by compression varies significantly based on the format of the original data in the file. Some file formats lend themselves to compression, but others end up being just as big as the original file:

```
$ ls -l 10*.m4a
-rw-r--r--  1 taylor   taylor  4645048 Jan  3 21:29 10 Serpentine Lane.m4a
$ gzip -v 10*.m4a
10 Serpentine Lane.m4a:   0.9% -- replaced with 10 Serpentine Lane.m4a.gz
$ ls -l 10*
-rw-r--r--  1 taylor   taylor  4603044 Jan  3 21:29 10 Serpentine Lane.m4a.gz
$
```

This example resulted in a space savings of less than 1 percent of the file size.

tar

In the old days, Unix system backups were done to streaming tape devices (today you can only see these units in cheesy 60s Sci-Fi films, the huge round tape units that randomly spin as data is accessed). The tool of choice for creating backups from Unix systems onto these streaming tape devices was *tar*, the *tape archiver*. Fast-forward to Mac OS X, and *tar* continues its long tradition as a useful utility, but now it's used to create files that contain directories and other files within, as an archive. It's similar to the ZIP format, but differs from *gzip* because its job is to create a file that contains multiple files and directories. *gzip*, by contrast, makes an existing file shrink as much as possible through compression.

The *tar* program is particularly helpful when combined with *gzip*, actually, because it makes creating archive copies of directories simple and effective. Even better, if you use the *-z* flag to *tar*, it automatically invokes *gzip* to compress its output without any further work. Here's a fun bit of jargon, too: compressed *tar* archives are known in the Unix community as *tarballs*.

The syntax is:

```
tar [c|t|x] [flags] files and directories to archive
```

The *tar* program is too complex to fully explain here, but in a nutshell, *tar -c* creates archives, *tar -t* shows what's in an existing archive, and *tar -x* extracts files and directories from an archive. The *-f file* flag is used to specify the archive name, and the *-v* flag offers verbose output to let you see what's going on. As always, *man tar* produces lots more information about *tar*'s options.

```
$ du -s Masters\ Thesis
6704    Masters Thesis
$ tar -czvf masters.thesis.tgz "Masters Thesis"
Masters Thesis/
Masters Thesis/.DS_Store
Masters Thesis/analysis.doc
...
Masters Thesis/Web Survey Results.doc
Masters Thesis/web usage by section.doc
$ ls -l masters.thesis.tgz
-rw-r--r--  1 taylor  staff  853574 24 Sep 09:20 masters.thesis.tgz
```

 Notice that we gave *tar* the directory name, rather than a list of files. This ensures that when the directory is unpacked, the files are placed in a new directory (*Masters Thesis*), rather than filling the current directory. This is a good habit for people who make lots of archives.

In this example, the directory *Masters Thesis* is 6.7 MB in size, and hasn't been accessed in quite a while. This makes it a perfect candidate for a compressed *tar* archive. This is done by combining the following options: *-c* (create), *-z* (compress with *gzip*), *-v* (verbose), and *-f file* (output file; notice that we added the *.gz* suffix to avoid later confusion about the file type). In under 10 seconds, a new archive file is created, which is less than 1 MB in size, yet it contains all the files and directories in the original archive. To unpack the archive, use the following command:

```
$ tar -xvfz masters.thesis.tgz
```

Files on Other Operating Systems

Chapter 8 explains ways to transfer files across a network—possibly to non-Unix operating systems. Mac OS X has the capability of connecting to a variety of different filesystems remotely, including Microsoft Windows, other Unix systems, and even web-based filesystems.

If the Windows-format filesystem is mounted with your other filesystems, you'll be able to use its files by typing a Unix-like pathname. If you've mounted a remote Windows system's *C:* drive over a share named *winc*, you can access the Windows file *C:\WORD\REPORT.DOC* through the pathname */Volumes/winc/word/report.doc*. Indeed, most external volumes are automatically mounted within the */Volumes* directory.

## CHAPTER 5

Finding Files and Information

One of the fundamental challenges with modern computers is finding files and information. Whether you're highly organized and use wonderfully mnemonic names for every file or directory created, or whether you have lots of *letter1*, *letter2*, and *work* directories scattered around your filesystem, there will undoubtedly come a time when you need to find something on your computer based on its contents, filename, or similar attribute.

It turns out that there are four different ways in Unix to search for—and hopefully find—what you seek. To look inside files, you need to use the *grep* command, as introduced briefly in the previous chapter. To find files by filename, the fastest solution is the *locate* command. A more sophisticated filename and attribute search can be done with the Unix power-user's *find* command. And finally, Tiger introduces an entirely new search system called Spotlight that has a powerful command-line component worth exploring.

The Oddly Named grep Command

The *grep* program searches the contents of files for lines that have a certain pattern. The syntax is:

```
grep pattern file(s)
```

The simplest use of *grep* is to search for files that contain a particular word by feeding *grep* a pattern (in this case, the single word "Unix") and a list of files in which to search. For example, let's search all the files in the working directory for the word "Unix." We'll use the wildcard * to quickly give *grep* all filenames in the directory:

```
$ grep "Unix" *
ch01:Unix is a flexible and powerful operating system
ch01:When the Unix designers started work, little did
ch05:What can we do with Unix?
$
```

Note that *grep* understands plain text—and that's all. Feeding it nontext files can produce puzzling and peculiar results. For example, Word files (and those created by other WYSIWYG editors) contain characters that, when sent to the Terminal, mess up your display in strange and interesting ways.

 One way to search such files from the command line is to extract only the printable characters using the *strings* program (see *man strings* for details).

grep can be used in a *pipe*, which enables *grep* to scan the output of a different command. This makes it so only those lines of the input files containing a given string are sent to the standard output. Pipes are denoted with the | symbol (which can be found above the \ on a standard Apple keyboard layout) and are a method of joining the output of one command to the input of another (in the following example, the output of the *ls* command to the input of the *grep* command), flowing data between them just as a plastic pipe transports water from a water main to a sprinkler head in your garden.

When *grep* searches multiple files, it shows the filename where it finds each matching line of text. Alternatively, if you don't give *grep* a filename to read, it reads its standard input; that's the way all filter programs work (standard input and output are discussed in Chapter 6):

```
$ ls -l | grep "Jan"
drwx------    4 taylor   taylor   264  Jan 29 22:33 Movies/
drwx------    2 taylor   taylor   264  Jan 13 10:02 Music/
drwx------   95 taylor   taylor   3186 Jan 29 22:44 Pictures/
drwxr-xr-x    3 taylor   taylor   264  Jan 24 21:24 Public/
$
```

First, the example runs *ls -l* to list your directory. The standard output of *ls -l* is piped to *grep*, which outputs only lines that contain the string Jan (that is, files or directories that were last modified in January and any other lines that have the pattern "Jan" within). Because the standard output of *grep* isn't redirected, those lines go to the Terminal's screen.

Useful grep Options

Table 5-1 lists some of *grep*'s options, which you can use to modify your searches.

Table 5-1. Some grep options

Option	Description
-An	Show n lines after the matching line.
-Bn	Show n lines before the matching line.
-Cn	Show n lines before and after the matching line.
-v	Print all lines that do not match pattern.
-n	Print the matched line and its line number.
-l	Print only the names of files with matching lines (lowercase letter "L").
-c	Print only the count of matching lines.
-i	Match either upper- or lowercase.

In the previous search, a file named *jan-finances.xls* wouldn't have matched, because by default *grep* is case sensitive. That means your searches for "jan" wouldn't match "Jan", either. To make the search case insensitive, add *grep*'s *-i* option.

Though it may seem odd, being able to invert the search logic with the *-v* flag and show lines that don't match the given pattern can be quite useful. In particular, adding the *-l* option makes it so the *grep* command outputs only matching filenames (rather than the lines in those files that contain the search pattern). To find all the files in the current directory that *don't* mention Jane, for example, the command would be:

```
$ grep -lv Jane *
spread.xls        Mike Report.doc
$
```

This has the same potential case sensitivity, too, so an even better set of command flags would be *-lvi*, which then also matches "jane" in files, and therefore filters out even more files.

Matching context

When searching for specific lines in a file, you may actually want to also see a line or two above or below the matching line, rather than just the matching line. This can be accomplished in three ways, depending on whether you want lines above, lines below, or both, by using *-A*, *-B*, and *-C*, respectively.

To show one additional line above and below the matching line (and add line numbers by using the *-n* option, too):

```
$ grep -n -C1 Aqua sample
3-watch how vi wraps long lines.  If you have another terminal window
4:open with some text in it, or if you have an Aqua application open,
5-you can also use your mouse to copy text from another window and
```

Notice that the line that has a match has a colon after the line number, while the other context lines are preceded with a dash. Very subtle, but knowing what to look for helps you find your match instantly!

Matches in color

One great feature of Mac OS X's *grep* command is that it automatically shows you the matching passage in each line if you use the verbose *--color=always* option. Here's how it looks:

```
$ grep --color=always text sample
Enter some lines of text. Make some lines too short (press Return
open with some text in it, or if you have an Aqua application open,
you can also use your mouse to copy text from another window and
your file.) To get a lot of text quickly, paste the same text more
$
```

In the above command, you're searching for the word "text" within the *sample* file. Because you've added the *--color=always* option, any instances of the word "text" are highlighted in bold red text in the output. (Sorry, you can't see the true results here, but I think you get the picture.) In practice, this would be an excellent use for either a new *grep* alias that includes the *--color=always* option, or an environment variable set in your *.profile* or *.login* file, depending on your shell. If you use *bash*, add the following to your *.profile* file:

```
GREP_OPTIONS="--color=always";export GREP_OPTIONS
```

Now whenever you use *grep*, your results come back in blazing color.

 Wondering why you didn't get color output in Panther? Tiger's the first version of Mac OS X with built-in support for the newer, color-friendly *grep* command.

Counting matches rather than showing matching lines

When you're going through a large file and have a lot of matches, it's often quite useful to just get a report of how many lines matched rather than having all the output stream past your screen. This is accomplished with the *-c* option:

```
$ grep -c "hot key operating mode" windowserver.log
2457
```

You can also accomplish this result by piping the output to the *wc* command, as shown in Chapter 6, but this is considerably faster!

Working with Regular Expressions

You can use simple patterns with the *grep* program, patterns like "Jane" or "hot key", but *grep* actually has the ability to match incredibly complex and sophisticated patterns because it uses regular expressions, an entire language for specifying patterns. Let's spend some time talking about regular expressions so you can see how powerful they are.

 A word of warning, though: file matching patterns in the shell are not the same, and some patterns are interpreted quite differently in regular expressions than they are at the command line. This can be confusing when you have a command like grep *regexp* filematchpattern, with two different styles of pattern on the same line.

The fundamental building blocks of regular expressions are those that match a specific character. Fortunately, almost all characters automatically match themselves, so the pattern Jane is a regular expression that matches J, a, n, and e. To specify a range of characters, use brackets. [Jj]ane matches both Jane and jane, for example. You can also do ranges within brackets, so J[aeiou]ne and j[a-z]ne are both valid expressions, the first matches Jane, Jene, Jine, Jone, and June, and the second matches any occurrence of j followed by a lowercase letter, followed by ne.

Many classes of characters are already predefined, so [:alnum:], which is Unix shorthand for "alphanumeric," is equivalent to [a-zA-Z0-9] in English, [:digit:] is the same as [0-9], [:upper:] is the same as [A-Z], and so on. The important difference is that by using the named value, your expression can work in other languages in addition to English. Specifically, [a-z] won't include ñ, for example, but [:lower:] will, if the locale is set to Spanish. Table 5-2 lists the most important named character ranges.

Table 5-2. Named Character Ranges in Regular Expressions

Option	Description
[:alnum:]	Upper- and lowercase letters and numeric digit values (0-9)
[:alpha:]	Upper- and lowercase letters
[:digit:]	Numeric digit values (0–9)
[:lower:]	Lowercase letters
[:print:]	Printable (visible) characters
[:punct:]	Punctuation characters
[:space:]	The set of characters that can serve as a space, including the space, tab, and carriage return
[:upper:]	Uppercase letters
[:xdigit:]	Hexadecimal digit values (0–9, plus a–f and A–F)

Named character ranges are considered an element in a range expression, so the earlier pattern j[a-z]ne is correctly written as j[[:lower:]]ne. You can also negate the value of a range by prefacing it with the caret symbol (^), which you get with Shift-6. So, j[^aeiou]ne matches everything that has a j followed by any letter that *isn't a vowel*, followed by ne.

The period matches any single character, and the \w expression is synonymous with [[:alnum:]]. When not used in a character range, the ^ matches the beginning of the line, and the $ matches the end of the line. If you want to find blank lines that have no contents, the pattern ^$ does the trick. Lines that begin with a digit? Use ^[[:digit:]].

Each expression can be followed by what's called a repetition operator, which indicates how often the pattern can or should occur for a match to be found. For example:

- ? means that the preceding is optional and may be matched at most one time.
- * matches zero or more times.
- + matches one or more times.
- {n} is matched exactly *n* times.

To put these to the text, here's a pattern that matches exactly five digits followed by the letter M:

    [[:digit:]]{5}M

And here's a pattern that matches J, followed by any number of lowercase letters, followed by a period:

    J[[:lower:]]*\.

Notice you need to escape the period (.) so it's not seen as a request to match any single character.

The pattern jpe?g matches both jpeg and jpg, while jpe*g matches both of those words, also matching things like jpeeeg and jpeeeeeeeeeg.

You can list multiple patterns in an OR configuration by separating them with a pipe (|). This is almost always done by grouping the expression in parentheses. For example, (cat|dog)house matches both cathouse and doghouse, and [[:digit:]]+(am|pm) matches any one or more digit value followed by am or pm.

Quite a complex language, isn't it?

Next, let's use a few regular expressions to see how they work in practice. First, one that tells *grep* to find lines with root, followed by zero or more other characters (abbreviated in a regular expression as .*), then followed by Jan:

```
$ ls -l | grep "root.*Jan"
drwxr-xr-x  12 root    staff    364 Jan  9 20:24 NetInfo/
$
```

Next, let's look at the logfile for my tech Q&A web site, *www. AskDaveTaylor.com*. First off, visitors who enter data and submit questions on the site invoke what's called a POST action, which is differentiated from the GET of most page retrieval transactions. To find all the POST transactions is simple:

```
$ grep POST access_log
65.97.25.104 - - [04/Jan/2005:07:50:06 -0700] "POST /inject-query.cgi HTTP/
1.1" 200 7109 "http://www.askdavetaylor.com/ask.html" "Mozilla/4.0
(compatible; MSIE 6.0; Windows NT 5.1; SV1)"
64.12.116.73 - - [04/Jan/2005:11:22:13 -0700] "POST /inject-query.cgi HTTP/
1.1" 200 7109 "http://www.askdavetaylor.com/ask.html" "Mozilla/4.0
(compatible; MSIE 6.0; AOL 9.0; Windows NT 5.1; SV1; .NET CLR 1.0.3705)"
24.70.210.151 - - [04/Jan/2005:12:12:34 -0700] "POST /inject-query.cgi HTTP/
1.1" 200 7109 "http://www.askdavetaylor.com/ask.html" "Mozilla/5.0 (Windows;
U; Windows NT 5.1; en-US; rv:1.7.5) Gecko/20041107 Firefox/1.0"
67.173.253.115 - - [03/Jan/2005:23:57:32 -0700] "POST /mailman/admin/adt-
news HTTP/1.1" 200 13707 "http://www.askdavetaylor.com/mailman/admin/adt-
news" "Mozilla/5.0 (Macintosh; U; PPC Mac OS X; en-us) AppleWebKit/125.5.5
(KHTML, like Gecko) Safari/125.12"
```

If you look closely at that output, you'll see that an identification string from the actual browser that the visitor is using is included. The first match is Microsoft's Internet Explorer (MSIE), the second is the AOL version of MSIE, the third is Firefox, and the last is Safari.

grep can help identify those queries from only Firefox or Safari by using a sophisticated regular expression:

```
$ grep "POST.*(Safari|Firefox)" access_log
219.93.174.103 - - [12/Dec/2004:09:53:42 -0700] "POST /inject-query.cgi
HTTP/1.1" 200 7109 "http://www.askdavetaylor.com/ask.html" "Mozilla/5.0
(Windows; U; Windows NT 5.1; rv:1.7.3) Gecko/20041001 Firefox/0.10.1"
67.173.253.115 - - [19/Dec/2004:19:17:24 -0700] "POST /mailman/admin/adt-
news HTTP/1.1" 200 12475 "http://www.askdavetaylor.com/mailman/admin/adt-
news" "Mozilla/5.0 (Macintosh; U; PPC Mac OS X; en-us) AppleWebKit/125.5.5
(KHTML, like Gecko) Safari/125.12"
```

Coupled with a simple pipe and the *wc* word count program (both are discussed in more detail in Chapter 6), it's possible to figure out how many forms were submitted, and then break it down into MSIE and non-MSIE with just a few *grep* queries:

```
$ grep POST access_log | wc -l
      94
```

```
$ grep -E "POST.*MSIE" access_log | wc -l
     37
$ grep -E "POST.*(Firefox)" access_log | wc -l
     18
$ grep -E "POST.*(Safari)" access_log | wc -l
     31
```

This shows that of the 94 submissions, 37 were done with MSIE (Internet Explorer), 18 were done with Firefox, and 31 were done with Safari. Of course, having to enter all of those commands separately is fine if you're only doing this occasionally. But if you're going to need this sort of information more often, you should consider pulling them together in a shell script. That way, all you'll need to do is execute the shell script, and it would run the commands separately and provide you with an output that shows the results.

There's a lot more to regular expressions that I can fit into a page or two in this book. If you really want to become a regular expression maven, I suggest that you read the book *Mastering Regular Expressions*, by Jeffrey E. F. Friedl (O'Reilly).

If you'd like to learn more about shell scripts, start with my own book *Wicked Cool Shell Scripts* (No Starch).

Finding Files with locate

Sometimes, you'll create a file, save it someplace, and then forget about it. Of course, when you need that file two months later, you can't remember where you saved it. For situations like this, Mac OS X includes the *locate* program to help you find files quickly. You can use *locate* to search part or all of a filesystem for a file with a certain name. *locate* doesn't actually search the filesystem, however, it searches through a prebuilt listing of every single file and directory on the system. This is a good thing because the command doesn't have to traverse each and every directory in your filesystem, making *locate* very fast. However, it's also a potential problem because the *locate* database can get old and out of sync with the actual files on your system. The first step, therefore, is to build the locate database.

If you leave your Mac on most of the time, the *locate* database is automatically rebuilt weekly from a system *cron* job, so you won't need to worry about this administrative step.

Building the locate Database

First, you need to build the database of filenames. If you leave your computer on for days at a time, you might not need to do this step at all, but if you want to be as up to date as possible, use the *updatedb* command:

```
$ sudo /usr/libexec/locate.updatedb
```

It takes a while for this to complete, as it searches through all your directories looking for files and recording their names. (On my PowerBook, it took six minutes to rebuild the database.)

If you're like many Mac users and shut your system down completely when you're done each day, then you should use a different route to build the locate database, because your system has weekly tasks that aren't being run. Fortunately, you're on the command line, so it's all easy. Instead of *updatedb*, run this:

```
$ sudo periodic weekly
```

This runs the set of weekly administrative tasks—which shouldn't be run more than once a week, of course—that help keep your Mac running along smoothly.

 There are also daily and monthly tasks that should run on your computer, called *periodic daily* and *periodic monthly*. Working with those is beyond our scope, but with the Unix underpinnings, it's better to leave your Mac OS X system running as much as possible.

Using locate

Once you have the database updated, search it with the *locate* command. For instance, if you're looking for a file named *alpha-test*, *alphatest*, or something like that, try this:

```
$ locate alpha
/Users/alan/Desktop/alpha3
/usr/local/projects/mega/alphatest
/usr/share/man/man3/alphasort.3
/usr/share/man/man3/isalpha.3
/usr/share/man/man3/iswalpha.3
/Volumes/Hello/Applications/Cool Stuff/Mail.app/Contents/Resources/
alphaPixel.tiff
/Volumes/Hello/sw/fink/10.1/unstable/main/finkinfo/editors/emacs-alpha-21.1-
3.info
/Volumes/Hello/sw/share/doc/tar/README-alpha
/Volumes/Hello/usr/share/man/man3/alphasort.3
/Volumes/Hello/usr/share/man/man3/isalpha.3
/Volumes/Hello/usr/share/man/man3/iswalpha.3
```

You'll get the absolute pathnames of files and directories with *alpha* in their names. (If you get a lot of output, add a pipe to *less*. See "Pipes and Filters in Chapter 6.) *locate* may or may not list protected, private files.

Unfortunately, you can't specify regular expressions with *locate*; for example, the following command doesn't return any results:

```
$ locate "/man/.*alpha"
$
```

You instead need to use a series of *grep* commands to pick through the *locate* output. To accomplish the task of identifying which matches to the pattern *alpha* are from the */man/* directory, do this:

```
$ locate alpha | grep "/man/"
/Previous Systems/Previous System 1/usr/share/man/man3/alphasort.3
/Previous Systems/Previous System 1/usr/share/man/man3/isalpha.3
/Previous Systems/Previous System 1/usr/share/man/man3/iswalpha.3
/usr/share/man/man3/alphasort.3
/usr/share/man/man3/isalpha.3
/usr/share/man/man3/iswalpha.3
/Volumes/Hello/usr/share/man/man3/alphasort.3
/Volumes/Hello/usr/share/man/man3/isalpha.3
/Volumes/Hello/usr/share/man/man3/iswalpha.3
```

Using Find to Explore Your Filesystem

Reading about the limitations of the *locate* command undoubtedly caused you to wonder if there was a more powerful option, a command that could let you search through the actual, live filesystem to find what you seek. The *find* command not only lets you search for files by filename patterns, but a remarkable number of additional criteria, too.

find has a completely different syntax than any of the Unix commands examined to this point in the book, so the best place to start is with the *find* command syntax itself.

```
find flags pathname expression
```

Expressions are where the complexity shows up, because a typical expression is a "primary" followed by a relevant value, and there are dozens of different primaries that can be combined in thousands of different ways. An example is to match files that end with *.html*, you would use something like:

```
find -name "*.html"
```

To search for all HTML files on a Tiger system, here's how the command would look:

```
$ find . -name "*.html" -print
./Library/Preferences/Explorer/Favorites.html
./Sites/index.html
$
```

Notice that the pathname specified is the current working directory (.). Change this to the root directory (/), and the *find* command traverses the entire filesystem looking for matches. Rather than list all the matches, however, I'm going to feed the output of the command to the ever-helpful *wc* word count command to just get a count of matching entries:

```
$ find / -name "*.html" -print | wc -l
find: /.Metadata: Permission denied
find: /.Trashes: Permission denied
find: /private/var/backups: Permission denied
find: /private/var/cron: Permission denied
find: /Users/tintin: Permission denied
find: /Volumes/Hello/.Metadata: Permission denied
find: /Volumes/Hello/.TemporaryItems/0: Permission denied
find: /Volumes/Hello/.Trashes: Permission denied
133950
```

I've trimmed the output because hundreds of "Permission denied" errors were encountered. These are reassuring because as a regular user, I shouldn't be able to look in every single directory on the system. To search absolutely everything, I'd use *sudo* to temporarily become root. Notice that by starting at the / directory, the *find* command also searched through the Hello disk, which is an external 30 GB drive, mounted at */Volumes*.

Ignoring all the errors, there were a remarkable 133,950 files found on the Mac OS X system that match the filename pattern *.html*. That's a lot of web pages!

Matching by File Size

Another primary that can be tested is the file size, using *-size*. This is a typically complex *find* primary in that the default unit for specifying size is 512-byte blocks, so *-size 10* matches files that are 10*512 bytes or 5,120 bytes in size. To match a specific number of bytes, append a *c*; for example, *-size 10c* matches files that are exactly 10 bytes in size. But that's not really useful, and it turns out you can specify "more than" or "less than" by prefacing the number with a + or −, respectively. Now it starts to sound useful! To match only files that are greater than 5 Kb in size, I could use either *-size +10* or *-size +5120c* and to find files that are less than 100 bytes, I could use *-size -100c*.

Let's look at the HTML files again, but this time I'm going to constrain the search to just the */usr/X11R6* directory and list just those files that are greater than 35 Kb in size:

```
$ find /usr/X11R6 -name "*.html" -size +70 -print
/usr/X11R6/lib/X11/doc/html/bitmap.1.html
/usr/X11R6/lib/X11/doc/html/editres.1.html
```

```
/usr/X11R6/lib/X11/doc/html/fontconfig.3.html
/usr/X11R6/lib/X11/doc/html/glGet.3.html
/usr/X11R6/lib/X11/doc/html/manindex3.html
/usr/X11R6/lib/X11/doc/html/twm.1.html
/usr/X11R6/lib/X11/doc/html/X.7.html
/usr/X11R6/lib/X11/doc/html/XCreateGC.3.html
/usr/X11R6/lib/X11/doc/html/xdm.1.html
/usr/X11R6/lib/X11/doc/html/xmh.1.html
/usr/X11R6/lib/X11/doc/html/xterm.1.html
$
```

This is just the tip of the iceberg with *find* primaries, however, so let's have a closer look at the most useful primaries, listed in Table 5-3. This isn't an exhaustive list: if you want to know about every single possible primary, check the manpage for *find*.

Table 5-3. The most useful find primaries

Option	Description
-cmin *time*	True if the file has been changed within the last *time* minutes.
-ctime *time*	Same as *-cmin*, but for units of hours, not minutes.
-group *name*	True if file is owned by group *name*. Can be specified as group name or group ID.
-iname *pattern*	Identical to *-name* except tests are case insensitive.
-iregex *regex*	Identical to *-regex* but the regular expression is evaluated as case insensitive.
-ls	Produces *ls -l* output for matching files.
-name *pattern*	True if filename matches specified pattern.
-nouser	True if the file belongs to an unknown user (that is, a user ID that doesn't appear in either */etc/passwd* or NetInfo).
-perm *mode*	True if the file matches the specified permission. This complex primary is explained later in this chapter.
-print	Prints the full pathname of the current file.
-print0	Special version of *-print* that compensates for spaces and other nonstandard characters in filenames. An important addition for Mac OS X *find* usage.
-regex *regex*	Same as *-name* but allows full regular expressions rather than just simple filename pattern matches.
-size *n*	True if the file's size matches the specified size. Default unit is 512-byte blocks, append *c* for bytes, and prepend + for "more than" or - for "less than" tests.
-type *t*	True if the file is of the specified type. Common types are d for directories, and f for regular files
-user *name*	True if file is owned by the specified user. Can be a username or user ID number.

One of the more useful options listed in Table 5-3 that most Unix users ignore is *-ls*. Here's a more complex *find* command that uses this very primary, along with a test to ensure that the matching files are regular files, not symbolic links, etc:

```
$ cd /usr/X11R6/lib/X11/doc/html
$ find . -name "*.html" -size +100 -type f -ls
306579  152 -r--r--r--  1 root wheel 77053 May  8 2004 ./fontconfig.3.html
306704  136 -r--r--r--  1 root wheel 68835 May 8 2004  ./glGet.3.html
307132  304 -rw-r--r--  1 root wheel 153676 May 8 2004 ./manindex3.html
307173  152 -r--r--r--  1 root wheel 5513 May 8 2004   ./twm.1.html
307182  120 -r--r--r--  1 root wheel 61262 May 8 2004  ./X.7.html
307369  128 -r--r--r--  1 root wheel 63794 May 8 2004  ./xdm.1.html
307590  200 -r--r--r--  1 root wheel 100417 May 8 2004 ./xmh.1.html
307894  256 -r--r--r--  1 root wheel 130562 May 8 2004 ./xterm.1.html
$
```

This output is slightly different from a regular *ls -l* listing, but it does show the file permissions, owner and group information, file size, and date last modified.

Exploring find Permission Strings

find lets you search for files that match specific permission settings, but in a way that's one of the most confusing *find* elements for neophyte Unix folk. To try and avoid you sinking into the mire of this, let's just consider the symbolic permission notation that's shared with the *chmod* command (as discussed in Chapter 3).

In this model, permissions are specified as a sequence of:

who op perm

where *who* can be any of a (all), u (user), g (group), or o (other, that is, everyone who isn't the user or in the user's group). The *op* value for *find* permission strings can only be =, but in the *chmod* command itself there are other *op* possibilities. The possible values for *perm* are as shown in Table 5-4.

Table 5-4. Symbolic permission values for perm

Option	Description
r	Read permission
w	Write permission
x	Execute permission
s	Special set-user-ID-on-execution or set-group-ID-on-execution permission

Let's experiment with the *-perm* primary to get a better sense of how these different permission strings can be specified. To find all files in the */usr/bin* directory that start with the letter z, and that you have write permission for, use the following:

```
$ find /usr/bin -name "z*" -type f -perm +u=w -print
/usr/bin/zcat
/usr/bin/zcmp
/usr/bin/zdiff
/usr/bin/zforce
/usr/bin/zgrep
/usr/bin/zipgrep
/usr/bin/zipinfo
/usr/bin/zmore
/usr/bin/znew
$
```

What's going on here? We don't have write permission on any of these files:

```
$ ls -l /usr/bin/zcat
-rwxr-xr-x  4 root  wheel  65008 Dec  2 16:11 /usr/bin/zcat
$
```

The problem is that *find* takes the test literally: files that have write permission for *their owner*. When I said "that you have write permission for," I was misstating the test, in a way that's quite common for Unix folk. To tighten this *find* search to files to which you have write permission, you need to add a *-user* predicate. To make this as general as possible, you can use the $USER variable:

```
$ find /usr -type f -user $USER -perm +u=w
/usr/local/bin/dfont2res
/usr/local/bin/fondu
/usr/local/bin/frombin
/usr/local/bin/showfond
/usr/local/bin/tobin
/usr/local/bin/ufond
/usr/local/man/man1/dfont2res.1
/usr/local/man/man1/fondu.1
/usr/local/man/man1/frombin.1
/usr/local/man/man1/showfond.1
/usr/local/man/man1/tobin.1
/usr/local/man/man1/ufond.1
$
```

That's a weird result, too! Why, as a regular user, would you own files in the */usr* directory tree?

```
$ ls -l /usr/local/bin/tobin
-rwxr-xr-x  1 taylor  staff  34892 Dec 23  2002 /usr/local/bin/tobin
```

This incorrect ownership is probably the result of installing a package or two without being administrator. It's one reason that you should occasionally run the Disk Utility program(*/Applications/Utilities*) and choose Repair Disk Permissions. Making sure your disk permissions are in check keeps applications from telling you that you don't have permission to save a file, when you know darn well you do.

Using find to Identify Recently Changed Files

One of the most common uses of *find* is to identify files that have been changed within a certain amount of time. This is obviously quite useful for doing system backups, but it can also help ensure that files across multiple machines stay in sync, and it's just generally helpful to be able to list your files have been updated recently.

Just like the permissions test, the time tests in *find* behave quite differently depending on whether you specify an exact value, a value prefaced with a –, or a value prefaced with a +. Let's have a look:

```
$ find . -cmin 60 -print
$ find . -cmin -60 -print
./Library/Preferences
./Library/Preferences/com.apple.recentitems.plist
./mac-rocks
```

These first two tests are for files that have been changed *exactly* 60 minutes ago (no surprise, there aren't any) and files that have changed within the last 60 minutes (adding the – to the time), of which there are three. (Depending on how many files you've worked on in the last hour, the output from this command will differ.) One of the matches is the directory *./Library/Preferences*. You can easily remove that file from the list by using *-type f* as another primary if all you seek in your results is actual files (perhaps for backing up to a DVD).

What do you think will happen if you specify *-cmin +60*? If you're thinking that this command will give your Mac some level of clairvoyance and tell you which files you're going to work on in the next hour, think again. It'll list out all the files that have not been changed in the last 60 minutes which is, well, quite a few files:

```
$ find . -cmin +60 -print  | wc -l
    7262
```

To narrow that down to just plain files that haven't been changed, again I'll just add the *-type f* primary:

```
$ find . -cmin +60 -type f -print  | wc -l
    6124
```

The difference in these two values indicates that there are roughly 1,100 directories that are being matched in the first test. Quite a few!

This sort of time test can also be cast across the entire filesystem to see what's been changing. The following command identifies all the files owned by *root* that have been changed in the last 30 minutes:

```
$ sudo find / -cmin -30 -type f -user root -print
/.Metadata/.store.db
/.Metadata/ExportQueueLog
/.Metadata/ImportQueueLog
/.Metadata/ImportScanQueueLog
/.Metadata/store.db
...
/private/var/run/xinetd.pid
/private/var/slp.regfile
/private/var/vm/swapfile0
$
```

If you'd rather work with time units of a day rather than of minutes, just use *-ctime* instead of *-cmin*.

find's Faithful Sidekick: xarg

One primary that you might have immediately noticed is missing is a *-grep* or other primary that lets you look *inside* the files to find which have specific text within. It's missing because *find* doesn't know how to actually *open* any files: it can only test attributes.

If *grep* were smart enough to accept a list of filenames, then the solution to searching the contents of a set of files matched by *find* would be ridiculously easy: *find | grep*. Unfortunately that's not one of *grep*'s many skills. So, you're presented with a dilemma. You can generate a list of files to search, but there's no easy way to actually give that list to *grep* in a way that the program can understand.

The solution is to use *xargs*, a partner program to *find*, a program that turns a stream of filenames into iterative calls to whatever program is specified, with a subset of the filenames listed on the command line itself. This is confusing, so let me step you through a very simple example.

Let's say that the output of *find* is a list of four files, *one*, *two*, *three*, and *four*. Using *xargs*, these files could be given to *grep* two at a time by using:

```
find | xargs grep pattern
```

grep sees this with the following two invocations:

```
grep pattern one two
grep pattern three four
```

Make sense? Let's try it out so you can see how this tremendously powerful *find* partner program helps you become a real power command-line user!

```
$ find /var/log -not -name "*gz" -type f -size +0 -print
/var/log/asl.log
/var/log/CDIS.custom
/var/log/crashreporter.log
/var/log/cups/access_log
/var/log/cups/error_log
/var/log/daily.out
/var/log/install.log
/var/log/lastlog
/var/log/mail.log
/var/log/monthly.out
/var/log/OSInstall.custom
/var/log/secure.log
/var/log/system.log
/var/log/weekly.out
/var/log/windowserver.log
/var/log/windowserver_last.log
/var/log/wtmp
```

This is a delightfully complex *find* command, but we can step through it together, so I'm sure it'll make sense to you. First off, a sneak preview: you can reverse the logic of any *find* test by prefacing it with the *-not* primary, so the first test is to find all files whose names *do not* match the pattern **.gz*. That ensures we don't search in compressed (*gzip*'d) files.

Next, *-type f* matches just plain files, and *-size +0* matches files that aren't zero bytes in content. The end result can be summed up as "show me a list of all plain files in this directory that don't have a *.gz* file extension and are greater than zero bytes in size.

If you wanted to scan through all these files for any possible security warnings, your first attempt might be to do:

```
$ find /var/log -not -name "*gz" -type f -size +0 -print
| grep -i warning
$
```

But that won't work, of course, because it's scanning *the filename list itself* for the pattern, and there isn't anything available to match. To look inside the files, use *xargs* instead, and, since you're going to be looking inside these files, add a *sudo* invocation, too:

```
$ find /var/log -not -name "*gz" -type f -size +0 -print |
sudo xargs grep -i warning
/var/log/asl.log:[Time 2005.01.04 04:35:28 UTC] [Facility mail] [Sender
postfix/postqueue] [PID 5498] [Message warning: Mail system is down --
accessing queue directly] [Level 4] [UID -2] [GID -2] [Host Tiger]
/var/log/daily.out:  DUMP: WARNING: no file `/etc/dumpdates', making an
empty one
```

```
/var/log/daily.out:postqueue: warning: Mail system is down -- accessing
queue directly
/var/log/daily.out:postqueue: warning: Mail system is down -- accessing
queue directly
/var/log/daily.out:postqueue: warning: Mail system is down -- accessing
queue directly
/var/log/mail.log:Jan  4 03:15:02 Tiger postfix/postqueue[8262]: warning:
Mail system is down -- accessing queue directly
/var/log/system.log:Jan  7 16:28:28 Tiger sudo:   taylor : TTY=ttyp2 ; PWD=/
private/var/log ; USER=root ; COMMAND=/usr/bin/xargs grep -i warning
$
```

That's the general pattern that you'll use for searching inside lots of files matched by the *find* command, which might include shell scripts, plain text files, email message archives, and more.

 Because Mac OS X often adds spaces to filenames, there are times when the *find | xargs grep* command will fail with all sorts of scary "file not found" error messages. Not to worry, just switch from *-print* to *-print0* and then add a *-0* flag to *xargs*:

```
$ find $HOME -name "html" -print0 | xargs -0
grep -i intuitive.com
```

This finds all HTML files in my home directory, and searches through them all for references to the *intuitive.com* domain.

Further Refinements to find

You've already seen the *-not* primary that lets you switch the logic of a find primary, but there are a few more refinements that can help you create highly sophisticated filtering patterns. If you don't mind escaping the character, you can use ! as a substitute for *-not*, but if you don't use it as \! the shell inevitably interprets it and generates some screwy error messages.

You can also group one or more tests with parentheses, which is useful given that you can also specify an *-or* to allow logical OR tests, rather than the default AND test between each primary. This is particularly useful with filename matches, so you can find all files that end with either *.txt* or *.htm* with this find test:

```
$ find . -type f \( -name "*.txt" -or -name ".htm" \) -print
```

Again, notice that you must escape the parentheses so the shell doesn't try to interpret them and end up messing up your command completely.

Shining a Light on Spotlight

A completely new feature in Mac OS X Tiger is Spotlight, which indexes and stores metadata for all of the files on your system. This means that if you're looking for a file by name, you can use *locate* or *find*, but if you're looking for all images taken with a Nikon camera, or all PDF files that are more than 10 pages long, then Spotlight and its command-line tools are for you.

Spotlight builds what Apple calls a *metadata database* that has all the additional information about files on the system. Whenever you conduct a Spotlight search—either through the graphical interface or on the command line—this metadata is called to reveal information about the files on your system and offer up results. The two Spotlight commands that are analogous to the regular Unix commands *ls* and *find* are logically called *mdls* and *mdfind*.

Let's start with the *mdls* command—you're going to be quite impressed!

What's Metadata?

If you've been using computers for even a short time, you're used to certain data being associated with each file you create. The filename, file size, date of creation, those are all data that's familiar to you. But many files have additional, supplemental information.

For example, Microsoft Word records the name and address of the file creator, Adobe Photoshop remembers what version of Photoshop you last used to edit the image, and even digital cameras write out additional information for each image saved, including camera name, date and time the shot was taken, and often the film speed and lens focal length, all in EXIF information. This supplemental information is what Tiger calls metadata, and it's the heart of Spotlight.

Listing Spotlight Metadata with mdls

Some of the most interesting types of files to explore with *mdls* are the pictures you take with a digital camera. Here's what the *ls* command has to say about the JPEG file *Peanut.jpg*:

```
$ ls -l Peanut.jpg
-rw-r--r--  1 taylor  taylor  141515 Jan  7 20:18 Peanut.jpg
```

Not particularly useful in terms of what's actually *inside* the file. By comparison, here's what the *mdls* command reports:

```
$ mdls Peanut.jpg
Peanut.jpg -------------
kMDItemAcquisitionMake      = "NIKON CORPORATION"
```

```
kMDItemAcquisitionModel     = "NIKON D100 "
kMDItemAttributeChangeDate = 2005-01-07 20:24:59 -0700
kMDItemBitsPerSample        = 32
kMDItemColorSpace           = "RGB"
kMDItemContentType          = "public.jpeg"
kMDItemContentTypeTree      = ("public.jpeg", "public.image", "public.data",
"public.item", "public.content")
kMDItemDisplayName          = "Peanut.jpg"
kMDItemExposureMode         = 0
kMDItemExposureTimeSeconds = 0.01666667
kMDItemFlashOnOff           = 1
kMDItemFocalLength          = 35
kMDItemFSContentChangeDate = 2005-01-07 20:18:56 -0700
kMDItemFSCreationDate       = 2005-01-07 20:18:55 -0700
kMDItemFSCreatorCode        = 0
kMDItemFSFinderFlags        = 0
kMDItemFSInvisible          = 0
kMDItemFSLabel              = 0
kMDItemFSName               = "Peanut.jpg"
kMDItemFSNodeCount          = 0
kMDItemFSOwnerGroupID       = 501
kMDItemFSOwnerUserID        = 501
kMDItemFSSize               = 141515
kMDItemFSTypeCode           = 0
kMDItemHasAlphaChannel      = 0
kMDItemID                   = 715009
kMDItemKind                 = "JPEG Image"
kMDItemLastUsedDate         = 2005-01-07 20:18:56 -0700
kMDItemPixelHeight          = 531
kMDItemPixelWidth           = 800
kMDItemRedEyeOnOff          = 0
kMDItemResolutionHeightDPI = 300
kMDItemResolutionWidthDPI  = 300
kMDItemUsedDates            = (2005-01-07 20:18:56 -0700)
kMDItemWhiteBalance         = 0
```

Quite a bit more useful information thanks to Spotlight and its smart file parsing modules! Note that *mdls* offers the following details:

- The camera used (Nikon D100), as noted by kMDItemAcquisitionModel.
- The dimensions of the image (800 × 531), as noted by the kMDItemPixelWidth and kMDItemPixelHeight items, respectively.
- The resolution of the image (300 DPI), as noted by kMDItemResolutionHeightDPI and kMDItemResolutionWidthDPI.
- Various other digital photo data, including exposure time (kMDItemExposureTimeSeconds), focal length of the lens (kMDItemFocalLength), etc.

Here's another example of *mdls* output, this time with a PDF file:

```
$ mdls CH05.pdf
CH05.pdf -------------
kMDItemAttributeChangeDate = 2005-01-07 20:34:37 -0700
```

```
kMDItemContentType          = "com.adobe.pdf"
kMDItemContentTypeTree      = (
    "com.adobe.pdf",
    "public.data",
    "public.item",
    "public.composite-content",
    "public.content"
)
kMDItemDisplayName          = "CH05.pdf"
kMDItemEncodingApplications = ("Acrobat Distiller 4.0 for Macintosh")
kMDItemFSContentChangeDate  = 2002-01-24 13:13:36 -0700
kMDItemFSCreationDate       = 2002-01-24 13:13:36 -0700
kMDItemFSCreatorCode        = 0
kMDItemFSFinderFlags        = 256
kMDItemFSInvisible          = 0
kMDItemFSLabel              = 0
kMDItemFSName               = "CH05.pdf"
kMDItemFSNodeCount          = 0
kMDItemFSOwnerGroupID       = 99
kMDItemFSOwnerUserID        = 501
kMDItemFSSize               = 120017
kMDItemFSTypeCode           = 0
kMDItemID                   = 320122
kMDItemKind                 = "PDF Document"
kMDItemLastUsedDate         = 2002-01-24 13:13:36 -0700
kMDItemNumberOfPages        = 26
kMDItemPageHeight           = 657
kMDItemPageWidth            = 531
kMDItemUsedDates            = (2002-01-24 13:13:36 -0700)
kMDItemVersion              = "1.2"
```

On a PDF document, the information includes the number of pages (as noted with kMDItemNumberOfPages; this document has 26), the application used to encode the PDF (Acrobat Distiller 4.0 for Macintosh, as noted by kMDItemEncodingApplications), and the date and time that the PDF file was created (Jan 24, 2002 at 13:13:36, noted by kMDItemFSCreationDate).

Let's peek at one more file type before we explore what you can actually *do* with the Spotlight data, shall we? This time, it's an MP4 file from my iTunes library:

```
$ mdls 02\ Gigabyte.m4a
02 Gigabyte.m4a -------------
kMDItemAlbum                  = "Philly Style"
kMDItemAttributeChangeDate    = 2005-01-07 20:37:50 -0700
kMDItemAudioBitRate           = 127872
kMDItemAudioEncodingApplication = "iTunes v4.7, QuickTime 6.6"
kMDItemAudioTrackNumber       = 2
kMDItemAuthors                = ("Jeff Lorber")
kMDItemCodecs                 = (AAC)
kMDItemComposer               = "Jeff Lorber"
kMDItemContentType            = "public.mpeg-4-audio"
```

```
kMDItemContentTypeTree          = (
    "public.mpeg-4-audio",
    "public.audio",
    "public.audiovisual-content",
    "public.data",
    "public.item",
    "public.content"
)
kMDItemDisplayName              = "02 Gigabyte.m4a"
kMDItemDurationSeconds          = 233.7083333333333
kMDItemFSContentChangeDate      = 2005-01-03 21:25:38 -0700
kMDItemFSCreationDate           = 2005-01-03 21:24:21 -0700
kMDItemFSCreatorCode            = 1752133483
kMDItemFSFinderFlags            = 0
kMDItemFSInvisible              = 0
kMDItemFSLabel                  = 0
kMDItemFSName                   = "02 Gigabyte.m4a"
kMDItemFSNodeCount              = 0
kMDItemFSOwnerGroupID           = 501
kMDItemFSOwnerUserID            = 501
kMDItemFSSize                   = 3792517
kMDItemFSTypeCode               = 1295270176
kMDItemID                       = 626161
kMDItemKind                     = "MPEG-4 Audio File"
kMDItemLastUsedDate             = 2005-01-03 21:24:22 -0700
kMDItemMediaTypes               = (Sound)
kMDItemMusicalGenre             = "Jazz"
kMDItemStreamable               = 0
kMDItemTitle                    = "Gigabyte"
kMDItemTotalBitRate             = 127872
kMDItemUsedDates                = (2005-01-03 21:24:22 -0700)
$
```

Encoded in each audio file is the artist (kMDItemAuthors), album (kMDItemAlbum), song name (kMDItemTitle), genre (kMDItemMusicalGenre), length of track (kMDItemDurationSeconds), and much more, all accessible thanks to Spotlight and *mdls*.

Finding Files with mdfind

Knowing that there's so much useful and interesting information available through Spotlight, how do you actually do something useful with it? The answer is by using the *mdfind* command. However, while *find* has weird syntax, *mdfind* has an even weirder and more unfriendly command-line usage.

The *mdfind* command matches files in the filesystem that meet a specific criteria or set of criteria, specified as:

```
"metadata field name == 'pattern'"
```

For example, to find all photographs taken with a Nikon camera, you'd use the following:

```
$ mdfind "kMDItemAcquisitionModel == 'NIKON*'"
/Developer/Examples/Carbon/ScrollView/Car.jpg
/Users/taylor/Pictures/Ashley+Peanut2.jpg
/Users/taylor/Pictures/Dave-Smiling-200x300.jpg
/Users/taylor/Pictures/Dave-Smiling.jpg
/Users/taylor/Pictures/Linda-Taylor.jpg
/Users/taylor/Pictures/Little-Hand.jpg
/Users/taylor/Pictures/Mom-on-the-Phone.jpg
/Users/taylor/Pictures/Peanut.jpg
/Users/taylor/Pictures/Three-Kids-and-Linda.jpg
```

Want to constrain the search to a specific subdirectory? You might be tempted to specify the directly as you would in *find*, but that's not how it's done. Instead, you need to use a flag called *-onlyin* followed by a directory name. To find all the songs in your Jazz collection, use:

```
$ mdfind -onlyin ~/Music "kMDItemMusicalGenre == 'Jazz'"
```

You can also specify that you want a specific word anywhere in the metadata info by specifying just that word:

```
$ mdfind -onlyin ~ Jazz
/Users/taylor/Music/iTunes/iTunes Music/Jeff Lorber/Philly Style/01 Under
Wraps.m4a
/Users/taylor/Music/iTunes/iTunes Music/Jeff Lorber/Philly Style/02
Gigabyte.m4a
/Users/taylor/Music/iTunes/iTunes Music/Jeff Lorber/Philly Style/03
Regardless Of.m4a
...
/Users/taylor/Music/iTunes/iTunes Music/Jeff Lorber/Philly Style/09 Whe She
Smiles.m4a
/Users/taylor/Library/Syndication/Articles/iTunes 10 Just Added Albums/The
Pye Jazz Anthology Acker Bilk - Acker Bilk.newsarticle
/Users/taylor/Library/Syndication/Articles/iTunes 10 New Releases/Jazz In
Paris, Vol 74 Go-Go Goraguer - Alain Goraguer.newsarticle
JavaExamples/SwingSet2/tree.txt
$
```

This output is quite interesting because it matches not only files where the word Jazz is part of the Spotlight metadata (as in the iTunes files), but files that have Jazz in their name (the *Library/Syndication* directory) and even a plain text file where the word Jazz appears *in the text itself* (*tree.txt*). Pretty nifty, eh?

Making Spotlight Useful

Before leaving Spotlight, and certainly before we give up and assume that it's only useful on the command line, let's have a look at a couple of simple

Unix commands that can extract useful information from the *mdls* information stream.

Curious about the size of your JPEG files? You could quickly ascertain height and width by using *grep*:

```
$ mdls Peanut.jpg | grep -E '(PixelHeight|PixelWidth)'
kMDItemPixelHeight      = 531
kMDItemPixelWidth       = 800
```

You can identify the duration of an audio file without loading it into iTunes or any other audio player by using:

```
$ mdls "05 Soul Food.m4a" | grep Duration
kMDItemDurationSeconds      = 249.8916666666667
```

You can also use *find* and *xargs* to identify files by name and then extract specific characteristics:

```
$ find . -name "*jpg" -print0 | xargs -0 mdls | grep FocalLength
```

Or, you can actually use *mdfind* in the same manner (it does have a *-0* option that makes it possible to match filenames that have spaces without things breaking):

```
$ mdfind -0 "kMDItemFocalLength == '35'" | xargs -0 mdls |
grep -E '(PixelHeight|PixelWidth|DisplayName)'
kMDItemDisplayName      = "Little-Hand.jpg"
kMDItemPixelHeight      = 532
kMDItemPixelWidth       = 800
kMDItemDisplayName      = "Peanut.jpg"
kMDItemPixelHeight      = 531
kMDItemPixelWidth       = 800
```

This last search matches all pictures on the entire system with a focal length of 35 (meaning, they were taken with a 35mm lens), and then displays the name, height, and width of the images it finds.

These commands really beg for a simple shell script or two, where you could actually parse the output and reformat it as desired. We'll talk about writing shell scripts a bit later in the book, but here's just a sneak preview of what it could do:

```
$ photosize Peanut.jpg
800x531 at 300DPI
```

As you know, Spotlight is a new technology in Tiger, and the Spotlight commands accessible from the command line are new and haven't been refined quite yet. You can get started with the information shown here, but don't be surprised if a revision or two down the road turns the Spotlight commands into really powerful tools you can use.

## CHAPTER 6

Redirecting I/O

Many Unix programs read input (such as a file) and write output in a standard way that lets them work with each other. This exchange of information is commonly known in Unix circles as I/O (pronounced "eye-oh," which is short for input/output). In this chapter, we discuss some of these tools and learn how to connect programs and files in new and powerful ways.

This chapter generally *doesn't* apply to programs such as the *vi* editor, that take control of your entire Terminal window. (*less* does work in this way, however.) It also doesn't apply to graphical programs that open their own windows on your screen, such as iTunes or Safari. On the other hand, the vast majority of Unix commands that you use on the command line are line oriented, and they're exactly why I/O redirection is included in Mac OS X's Unix.

The difference between screen oriented and line oriented is a bit tricky to figure out when you're just starting. Think of it this way: if you can use arrow keys to move up and down lines, then it's a screen-oriented program. The *vi* editor is the classic example of a screen-oriented program. If the input or output is all shown line by line, as in the *ls* command's output, then it's a line-oriented command. Almost all Unix commands are line oriented, as you'll see in this chapter.

Standard Input and Standard Output

What happens if you don't give a filename argument on a command line? Most programs take their input from your keyboard instead (after you press Return to start the program running, that is). The keyboard you use to type commands into the Terminal is what's called the program's *standard input*. As soon as you hit that Return key, you're providing the shell with input.

As a program runs, the results are usually displayed on your Terminal screen. What you see displayed in the Terminal is the program's *standard output*. So, by default, each of these programs takes its information from the standard input and sends the results to the standard output. It turns out that where programs read their information and where their output goes can be changed depending on what you type on the command line. In Unix terminology, this is called *I/O redirection*.

If a program writes to its standard output, which is normally the screen, you can make it write to a file instead by using the greater-than symbol (>) operator followed by the name of the file to which the output should be saved. If you'd prefer connecting the output of one program to the input of another, as you saw in Chapter 5 when the output of *find* was given to the *wc* (word count) program to count the total number of output lines rather than just list them all, you can build a pipe. Command pipes are specified by using a pipe operator (|), which connects the standard output of one program to the standard input of another program.

If a program doesn't normally read from files, but reads from its standard input, you can give a filename by using the less-than symbol (<) operator followed by the name of the file.

Input/output redirection is one of the most powerful and flexible Unix features.

The *tr* (character translator) program allows us to demonstrate input redirection, because it expects its input to be from standard input, the keyboard. Here's how to use the input redirection operator to convert all vowels to x's in the *todo* file:

```
$ cat todo
1. Wake up
2. Look in mirror
3. Sigh
4. Go back to bed.
$ tr '[aeiou]' '[xxxxx]' < todo
1. Wxkx xp
2. Lxxk xn mxrrxr
3. Sxgh
4. Gx bxck tx bxd.
$$
```

Can you see what's happened here? The *tr* command has translated every vowel in the input file (*todo*, which replaced standard input because of the < notation) with a corresponding character in the second set, xs, displaying the output on standard output (the Terminal window).

Putting Text in a File

Instead of always letting a program's output come to the screen, you can redirect output to a file. This is useful when you'd like to save program output or when you put files together to make a bigger file.

cat

cat, which is short for "concatenate," reads files and outputs their contents one after another, without stopping. To display files on the standard output (your screen), use:

```
cat file(s)
```

For example, let's display the contents of the file */etc/bashrc*. This system file is the global login file for the *bash* shell:

```
$ cat /etc/bashrc
# System-wide .bashrc file for interactive bash(1) shells.
if [ -n "$PS1" ]; then PS1='\h:\w \u\$ '; fi
# Make bash check it's window size after a process completes
shopt -s checkwinsize
$
```

You cannot go back to view the previous screens, as you can when you use a pager program such as *less* (unless you're using a Terminal window with a sufficient scrollback buffer, that is). Because of this, *cat* is mainly used with redirection, as we'll see in a moment.

If you enter *cat* without a filename you might be wondering what's happening. Nothing's broken, however: *cat* simply reads from the keyboard (as we mentioned earlier) until the end-of-file character is sent. You can get out by pressing Control-D, which ends the input file for the program.

When you add > *filename* to the end of a command line, the program's output is diverted from the standard output to a file. The > symbol is called the *output redirection operator*.

For example, let's use *cat* with the output redirection operator. The file contents that you'd normally see on the screen (from the standard output) are diverted into another file, which we'll then read by using *cat* again, this time without any redirection:

```
$ cat /etc/bashrc > mybashrc
$ cat mybashrc
# System-wide .bashrc file for interactive bash(1) shells.
if [ -n "$PS1" ]; then PS1='\h:\w \u\$ '; fi
# Make bash check its window size after a process completes
shopt -s checkwinsize
$
```

An earlier example showed how *cat /etc/bashrc* displays the file */etc/bashrc* onscreen. The example here adds the > operator, so the output of *cat* goes to a file called *mybashrc* in the working directory. Displaying the *mybashrc* file shows that its contents are the same as the file */etc/bashrc* (in this simple case, the effect is the same as the copy command *cp /etc/bashrc mybashrc*).

You can use the > redirection operator with any program that sends text to its standard output—not just with *cat*. For example:

```
$ who > users
$ date > today
$ ls
mylogin    today    users    ...
```

We've sent the output of *who* to a file called *users* and the output of *date* to the file named *today*. Listing the directory shows the two new files. Let's look at the output from the *who* and *date* programs by reading these two files with *cat*:

```
$ cat users
taylor    console  Jan  9 19:18
taylor    ttyp1    Jan  9 19:25
taylor    ttyp2    Jan  9 20:08 (192.168.1.100)
$ cat today
Sun Jan  9 20:31:45 MST 2005
$
```

You can also use the *cat* program and the > operator to make a small text file. I told you earlier to type Control-D if you accidentally enter *cat* without a filename because the *cat* program alone takes whatever you type on the keyboard as input.

Thus, the following command takes input from the keyboard and redirects it to a file:

```
cat > filename
```

Try the following example:

```
$ cat > new-todo
Finish report by noon
Lunch with Xian
Swim at 5:30
^D
$
```

cat takes the text that you typed as input (in this example, the three lines that begin with Finish, Lunch, and Swim), and the > operator redirects it to a file called *new-todo*. Type Control-D *once*, on a new line by itself, to signal the end of the text. You should get a shell prompt.

You can also create a bigger file from smaller files with the *cat* command and the > operator. The form creates a file *newfile*, consisting of *file1* followed by *file2*:

```
cat file1 file2 > newfile
```

This highlights that the name cat comes from *concatenate*, meaning, "put a bunch of things together." Here's what I mean:

```
$ cat today todo > diary
$ cat diary
Sun Jan  9 20:31:45 MST 2005
1. Wake up
2. Look in mirror
3. Sigh
4. Go back to bed.
$
```

 You shouldn't use redirection to add a file to itself, along with other files. For example, you might hope that the following command would merge today's to-do list with tomorrow's, but this example isn't going to give you what you expect:

```
$ cat todo todo.tomorrow > todo.tomorrow
```

It works, but it runs for all eternity because it keeps copying the file over itself. If you cancel it with Control-C and use *ls* to examine the file, you'll see that it's gotten quite large:

```
^C
$ ls -sk to_do.tomorrow
81704 todo.tomorrow
```

ls -sk shows the size in kilobytes, so it grew to about 80 megabytes! The right way to do this is either to use a temporary file (as you'll see in a later example) or simply to use a text editor program.

You can add more text to the end of an existing file, instead of replacing its contents, by using the >> (append redirection) operator. Use it as you would the > (output redirection) operator. So, the following appends the contents of *file2* to the end of *file1*:

```
cat file2 >> file1
```

This doesn't affect the contents of *file2* since it is being read from, not written to.

For an example, let's append the contents of the file *users* and the current date and time to the file *diary*. Here's what it looks like:

```
$ cat users >> diary
$ date >> diary
$ cat diary
Sun Jan  9 20:31:45 MST 2005
1. Wake up
2. Look in mirror
3. Sigh
4. Go back to bed.
taylor    console  Jan  9 19:18
taylor    ttyp1    Jan  9 19:25
taylor    ttyp2    Jan  9 20:08 (192.168.1.100)
Sun Jan  9 21:39:55 MST 2005
$
```

Unix doesn't have a redirection operator that adds text to the beginning of a file but you can accomplish the same thing by renaming the old file, then rebuilding the contents of the file as needed. For example, maybe you'd like each day's entry to go at the beginning of your *diary* file. Simply rename *diary* to something like *temp*. Make a new *diary* file with today's entries, then append *temp* (with its old contents) to the new *diary*. For example:

```
$ mv diary older.diary
$ date > diary
$ cat users >> diary
$ cat older.diary >> diary
$ rm older.diary
```

This example could be shortened by combining the two *cat* commands into one, giving both filenames as arguments to a single *cat* command. That wouldn't work, though, if you were making a real diary with a command other than *cat users*.

Pipes and Filters

We've seen how to redirect input from a file and output to a file. You can also connect two programs *together* so the output from one program becomes the input of the next. Two or more programs connected in this way form a *pipe*. To make a pipe, place a vertical bar (|) on the command line between the two commands.

When a pipe is set up between two commands, the standard output of the command to the left of the pipe symbol becomes the standard input of the command to the right of the pipe symbol. Any two commands can form a pipe as long as the first program writes to standard output and the second program reads from standard input. For example:

```
$ ls -la | colrm 1 48
.
..
.CFUserTextEncoding
.DS_Store
.Trash
Desktop
Documents
Library
Movies
Music
Pictures
Public
Sites
$
```

This example combines *ls -la* (list all), and then uses the *colrm* (column remove) command to give you just a list of the contents of a directory. This shows the contents of a user's *Home* directory, including the hidden dot files.

> You could take this example one step further and redirect its output to a file; for example:
>
> ```
> $ ls -la | colrm 1 48 > homedirlist.txt
> ```
>
> That command line starts by listing the files, uses *colrm* to strip out everything that *ls -la* returns, and then redirects that information as the contents of a new file, named *homedirlist. txt*. Add another pipe, and you can open the file with TextEdit:
>
> ```
> $ ls -la | colrm 1 48 > homedirlist.txt |
> open homedirlist.txt
> ```
>
> You just can't do that in the Finder.

When a program takes its input from another program, performs some operation on that input, and writes the result to the standard output (which may be piped to yet another program), it is referred to as a *filter*. A common use of filters is to modify output. Just as a common filter culls unwanted items, Unix filters can restructure output.

Most Unix programs can be used to form pipes. Some programs that are commonly used as filters are described in the next sections. Note that these programs aren't used only as filters or parts of pipes. They're also useful on their own.

wc

The *wc* program is one of the most useful pipe programs, believe it or not. By default, the program counts characters, words, and lines in the input file or standard input, but you can constrain the output to just characters (-*c*), words (-*w*), or lines (-*l*). Counting lines turns out to be wonderfully useful.

Here's a classic example, identifying how many "core" files are in the filesystem.

 Core files are identified with the suffix *.core*, they're crashed program debugging datafiles and can be deleted to free up disk space as needed.

This is done with a call to *find* with the output piped to *wc*:

```
$ sudo find / -name "*.core" -print | wc -l
13
$
```

sudo helps sidestep any permissions problems here. A more common use of *find* and *wc* together is to count larger output streams. For example, wondering how many directories you have within your home directory? You might be surprised:

```
$ pwd
/Users/taylor
$ find . -type d -print | wc -l
    1122
```

You can see where having a single number displayed is far superior to having all 1,122 directory names stream past!

tr

Another simple and helpful program for command pipes is *tr*, the translator utility. The most common use for this command is to replace all occurrences of one character with another character. Here's how you would replace all occurrences of *x* with *y*:

```
tr "x" "y"
```

More usefully, *tr* can also work with sets of characters by either listing them all in a range or specifying a named range like *lower* or *alpha*, so it's an easy way to turn all lowercase text into uppercase:

```
tr "[:lower:]" "[:upper:]" < file1
```

For example:

```
$ tr "[:lower:]" "[:upper:]" < diary
SUN JAN  9 20:31:45 MST 2005
1. WAKE UP
2. LOOK IN MIRROR
3. SIGH
4. GO BACK TO BED.
TAYLOR    CONSOLE  JAN  9 19:18
TAYLOR    TTYP1    JAN  9 19:25
TAYLOR    TTYP2    JAN  9 20:08 (192.168.1.100)
SUN JAN  9 21:39:55 MST 2005
$
```

The *tr* command has a number of different options for power users, including *-c* to invert the specified pattern (that is, if you specify *tr -c "abc"* then the program matches anything other than a, b, or c), and *-d* deletes any characters from the first pattern specified.

To remove all vowels from the input, you could use:

```
$ tr -d "[aeiou]" < diary
Sn Jn  9 20:31:45 MST 2005
1. Wk p
2. Lk n mrrr
3. Sgh
4. G bck t bd.
tylr    cnsl  Jn  9 19:18
tylr    ttyp1 Jn  9 19:25
tylr    ttyp2 Jn  9 20:08 (192.168.1.100)
Sn Jn  9 21:39:55 MST 2005
```

The *tr* command can be quite useful in other situations, too. Wondering how many words appear in a large text file? *tr* can figure this out with a little help from the *-s* option, which tells it to output only one occurrence of a character if more than one is found:

```
$ tr -cs "[:alpha:]" "\n" < alice.in.wonderland.txt | wc -l
27339
```

 You can download Lewis Carroll's *Alice's Adventures in Wonderland* for yourself at *http://www.intuitive.com/wicked/ scripts/alice.txt.gz*.

As with the *wc* command, *tr* doesn't seem too useful by itself, but when you start building up more complex pipes, you'll be surprised how frequently it's useful to translate case and fix similar problems.

grep

As you learned in the previous chapter, *grep* searches the contents of files for lines that have a certain pattern. The syntax is:

```
grep "pattern" file(s)
```

Most of the earlier discussion, however, focused on how *grep* can help you search through files to find lines that match a specified pattern. In fact, *grep* is a tremendously useful command for pipes, too, because it can help you easily weed out the few lines you care about from hundreds or thousands of lines of information.

As an example, let's use the *mdfind* command to identify files on the system that reference the word "ipod" (*mdfind*, a part of Spotlight, is discussed in Chapter 5). The default command reveals that there are 39 matches, by using *wc*:

```
$ mdfind ipod | wc -l
   39
```

It turns out that many of these are RSS syndication information files that are part of Safari's news tracking system. They're easily identified by their *.newsarticle* file extension, however, so *grep*, with its useful -v option (everything but lines that match this pattern) helps us identify how many files *other than* RSS syndication feed articles match:

```
$ mdfind ipod | grep -v "newsarticle" | wc -l
   14
```

Of those 14, how many are within my home directory area?

```
$ mdfind ipod | grep -v "newsarticle" | grep "/taylor/" | wc -l
    6
```

Notice here that you can build pipes that are two, three, four, or even 10 or 20 commands long. Unix has no limit on how complex your pipes can be, and I commonly work with pipes that are six or seven commands long.

head and tail

When you have output of hundreds or thousands of lines, being able to peek in and see the first few or last few lines is critically important, and those two tasks are enabled by the helpful *head* and *tail* commands. With both commands, the default action is to show the 10 matching lines (the first 10 for *head*, last 10 for *tail*). You can change this by specifying -n where n is the desired number of lines. To see just the first three lines, use *head -3*, and to see the last 15, use *tail -15*.

For example, the last 15 words of *Alice in Wonderland* are:

```
$ tr -cs "[:alpha:]" "\n" < alice.in.wonderland.txt | tail -15
in
all
their
simple
joys
remembering
her
own
child
life
and
the
happy
summer
days
$
```

Don't forget that you can use *head* and *tail* to view the beginning or end of files, or with a little bit of fancy footwork, any range of lines in a file. Want to see lines 130–134? You could use:

```
$ head -134 alice.in.wonderland.txt | tail -4
Alice opened the door and found that it led into a small passage,
not much larger than a rat-hole: she knelt down and looked along
the passage into the loveliest garden you ever saw. How she longed
to get out of that dark hall, and wander about among those beds of
$
```

This could also be accomplished by using other Unix commands, and that's part of the power of Unix: there's usually more than one way to solve a problem at the command line.

sort

The *sort* program arranges lines of text alphabetically or numerically. The following example alphabetically sorts the lines in the *food* file (from Chapter 5). *sort* doesn't modify the file itself; it just reads the file and displays the result on standard output (in this case, the Terminal).

```
$ sort food
Afghani Cuisine
Bangkok Wok
Big Apple Deli
Isle of Java
Mandalay
Sushi and Sashimi
Sweet Tooth
Tio Pepe's Peppers
```

By default, *sort* arranges lines of text alphabetically. Many options control the sorting, and Table 6-1 lists some of them.

Table 6-1. Some sort options

Option	Description
-n	Sort numerically (for example, 10 sorts after 2); ignore blanks and tabs.
-r	Reverse the sorting order.
-f	Sort upper- and lowercase together.
+x	Ignore first *x* fields when sorting.

Don't forget that more than two commands may be linked together with a pipe. Taking a previous pipe example using *grep*, you can further sort the files modified in January by order of size. The following pipe uses the commands *ls*, *grep*, and *sort*:

```
$ ls -l | grep "Jan" | sort +4n
drwx------   2  taylor taylor  264  Jan 13 10:02 Music/
drwx------   4  taylor taylor  264  Jan 29 22:33 Movies/
drwxr-xr-x   3  taylor taylor  264  Jan 24 21:24 Public/
drwx------  95  taylor taylor 3186  Jan 29 22:44 Pictures/
$
```

Both *grep* and *sort* are used here as filters to modify the output of the *ls -l* command. This pipe sorts all files in your directory modified in January by order of size, and prints them to the Terminal screen. The *sort* option *+4n* skips four fields (fields are separated by blanks), then sorts the lines in numeric order. So, the output of *ls*, filtered by *grep*, is sorted by the file size (this is the fifth column, starting with 264).

sort is also a powerful tool for identifying the extremes of a list. A common use is to identify the largest files on the system, which can be done by using *find* and *xargs* to generate a list of all files, one per line, including their size in 512-byte blocks, then feeding that to sort *-rn* (reverse, numeric) and looking at the top few:

```
$ find . -type f -print0 | xargs -0 ls -s1 | sort -rn | head
37872 ./Library/Fonts/PMingLiU.ttf
36968 ./Documents/Microsoft User Data/Office 2004 Identities/Main
Identity/Database
18864 ./Library/Fonts/Batang.ttf
18008 ./.Trash/SnapzProX2.dmg
16648 ./Library/Fonts/MS Mincho.ttf
16208 ./.Trash/Recovered files/com.apple.SoftwareUpdate/iTunes4.pkg/
Contents/Archive.pax.gz
15064 ./Library/Fonts/MS PMincho.ttf
14072 ./Library/Fonts/MS Gothic.ttf
13720 ./Library/Fonts/SimSun.ttf
13544 ./Library/Fonts/Gulim.ttf
```

Coupled with the power of *find*, you should be able to see how you can not only identify the largest files, but also the largest files owned by a particular user (hint: use *-user XX* to match all files owned by that user).

uniq

Another command that's quite useful in pipes is the oddly named *uniq* command, which would be easier to remember if it were spelled correctly: *unique*. Give *uniq* a stream of input, however, and it silently eliminates duplicate lines. Add the *-c* flag and *uniq* not only removes duplicate lines but lists a count of how frequently each line occurs.

If you're thinking that *sort* and *uniq* are a good pair, you're absolutely correct! For example, to figure out how many unique words occur in the book *Alice's Adventures in Wonderland* is a simple task:

```
$ tr -cs "[:alpha:]" "\n" < alice.in.wonderland.txt | uniq | wc -l
  27313
```

Or is it? That's not correct, because in this situation, *uniq* needs to have the input sorted. Add that step and the number changes dramatically:

```
$ tr -cs "[:alpha:]" "\n" < alice.in.wonderland.txt | sort | uniq |
wc -l
  2868
```

It turns out that we should also ensure that all the letters are lowercase so that "Hello" and "hello," for example, are counted as one word, not two. This can be done by slipping in the *tr* program:

```
$ tr -cs "[:alpha:]" "\n" < alice.in.wonderland.txt |
tr "[:upper:]" "[:lower:]" | sort | uniq | wc -l
  2577
```

So now you know. The entire novel is written using only 2,577 different words.

Piping Output to a Pager

The *less* program, which you saw in Chapter 4, can also be used as a filter. A long output normally zips by you on the screen, but if you run text through *less*, the display stops after each page or a screen of text (that's why they're called *pagers*: they let you see the output page by page).

Let's assume that you have a long directory listing. (If you want to try this example and need a directory with lots of files, use *cd* first to change to a system directory such as */bin* or */usr/bin*.) To make it easier to read the sorted listing, pipe the output through *less*:

```
$ cd /bin
$ ls -l | sort +4n | less
total 8288
-r-xr-xr-x  1 root  wheel      9736 27 Aug 04:36 echo
-r-xr-xr-x  1 root  wheel     10256 27 Aug 04:44 sync
-r-xr-xr-x  1 root  wheel     10476 27 Aug 05:03 domainname
...
-r-sr-xr-x  1 root  wheel     25248 27 Aug 05:03 rcp
-r-xr-xr-x  1 root  wheel     27308 27 Aug 04:31 dd
```

less reads a screen of text from the pipe (consisting of lines sorted by order of file size), then prints a colon (:) prompt. At the prompt, you can type a *less* command to move through the sorted text. *less* reads more text from the pipe, shows it to you, and saves a copy of what it has read, so you can go backward to reread previous text if you want. (The simpler pager program *more* can't back up while reading from a pipe.) When you're done seeing the sorted text, type the **q** command at the colon prompt to quit *less*. Table 6-2 contains a list of useful commands to use along with *less*.

Table 6-2. Useful less commands to remember

Command	Meaning
d	Scroll down (forward) one half of the screen size
u	Scroll up (backward) one half the screen size
b	Scroll back one screen
f	Scroll forward one screen
/pat	Scroll forward until a line containing the specified pattern is found
?pat	Scroll back until a line containing the specified pattern is found
n	Repeat previous search
:n	Move to the next file in the file list (if more than one file was specified)
v	Open up the file in the *vi* editor
q	Quit

Printing

Sometimes there's no substitute for hardcopy, for information that's sent to your printer and printed on a piece of paper. You know, like this book. You can generate printouts from within the Terminal itself, of course, though you're constrained to just the text that's visible in the Terminal window itself. You can also select a portion of text then use File → Save Selected Text As, and then open that file in TextEdit and print it, but that's rather a hassle.

Instead, it turns out that you can print files directly from the Unix command line in Mac OS X, and there are two ways to do this. If you want the pure Unix solution, use the *lp* command series, but if you have an AppleTalk network and one or more printers accessible through AppleTalk, it turns out that you can queue up AppleTalk printouts from the command line, too.

The Unix Way

The command used for sending information to the printer is *lp*, and there are a set of *lp*-related commands that you'll need to become familiar with so you can actually print something. To start, you need to ensure that you have at least one printer configured in Mac OS X. If you haven't done so yet, use the Printer Setup Utility (Applications → Utilities → Printer Setup Utility) to add one to your system. Once you have at least one printer, you can identify it by name with the *lpstat* command.

lpstat

With the *-a* flag, *lpstat* shows everything about the known printers:

```
$ lpstat -a
_192.168.1.104 accepting requests since Jan 01 00:00
```

In this case, you can see that I have one IP-based printer and that it's online, known, and accepting print jobs. To see which of your possible printers is the default, use the *-d* option:

```
$ lpstat -d
system default destination: _192.168.1.104
```

 If you have printers hooked up through Bonjour, *lpstat* will see them too, which is particularly helpful!

If you really want to learn a lot about your printers, print queues, and more, use the *-t* option:

```
$ lpstat -t
scheduler is running
system default destination: _192.168.1.104
device for _192.168.1.104: socket://192.168.1.104:9100/?bidi
_192.168.1.104 accepting requests since Jan 01 00:00
printer _192.168.1.104 is idle.  enabled since Jan 01 00:00
        Ready to print.
```

Everything looks good!

```
$ lpstat -d
system default destination: DESKJET_895C@MacTiger.local
```

Which means it's picking up *.local* addresses as well. Very nice. And here's what I get with *lpstat -t*:

```
$ lpstat -t
scheduler is running
system default destination: DESKJET_895C@MacTiger2.local
device for DESKJET_895C@MacTiger2.local: ipp://MacTiger2.local:631/printers/
DESKJET_895C
DESKJET_895C@MacTiger2.local accepting requests since Jan 01 00:00
printer DESKJET_895C@MacTiger2.local is idle.  enabled since Jan 01 00:00
        Ready to print.
$
```

From looking at that output, you can see that Tiger conducts its printing using the Internet Printing Protocol (IPP) via CUPS (as noted by IPP's use of port 631).

lp

You actually add a job to the printer queue by using the *lp* command. To print the output of an *ls -l* command is easy:

```
$ ls -l | lp
request id is _192.168.1.104-460 (1 file(s))
```

The request ID is rather ugly, but unless you need to remove a job because you've changed your mind, you shouldn't need to pay attention to anything more than that the print job has been accepted.

A few seconds later, your printout should emerge from the printer.

The first time you print out more than a single page of content, you'll realize that *lp* is a crude printing tool without any capability to paginate, add any sort of header or footer, etc.

pr

The *pr* program does minor formatting of files on the Terminal or for a printer. For example, if you have a long list of names in a file, you can format it onscreen into two or more columns.

The syntax is:

```
pr option(s) filename(s)
```

pr changes the format of the file only on the screen or on the printed copy; it doesn't modify the original file. Table 6-3 lists some *pr* options.

Table 6-3. Some pr options

Option	Description
-*n*	Produces *n* columns of output
-d	Double-spaces the output
-h *header*	Prints *header* at top of each page
-t	Eliminates printing of header and top/bottom margins

Other options allow you to specify the width of columns, set the page length, etc. For a complete list of options, see the manpage, *man pr*.

Before using *pr*, here are the contents of a sample file named *food*:

```
$ cat food
Sweet Tooth
Bangkok Wok
Mandalay
Afghani Cuisine
Isle of Java
Big Apple Deli
Sushi and Sashimi
Tio Pepe's Peppers
$
```

Let's use *pr* options to make a two-column report with the header "Restaurants":

```
$ pr -2 -h "Restaurants" food

Sep 24 12:41 2003 Restaurants Page 1
Sweet Tooth                Isle of Java
Bangkok Wok                Big Apple Deli
Mandalay                   Sushi and Sashimi
Afghani Cuisine            Tio Pepe's Peppers.
  .
  .
$
```

The text is output in two-column pages. The top of each page has the date and time, header (or name of the file, if a header is not supplied), and page number. To send this output to the default Mac OS X printer instead of to the Terminal screen, create a pipe to the *lpr* printer program:

```
$ pr -2 -h "Restaurants" food | lpr
```

But even with *pr* involved, it's possible that your printer will complain because it might accept only full PostScript jobs. If so, you need to use *enscript*.

enscript

One reason for the success of the Macintosh is its integrated support of Post-Script for printing. Allowing sophisticated imaging and high-quality text, PostScript printers are the norm in the Mac world. However, this proves a bit of a problem from the Unix perspective, because Unix commands are used to working with regular text without any special PostScript formatting included.

Translating plain text into PostScript is the job of *enscript*. The *enscript* program has a remarkable number of different command flags, allowing you access to all the layout and configuration options you're familiar with from the Page Setup and Print dialog boxes in Aqua.

The most helpful command flags are summarized in Table 6-4 (you can learn about all the many options to *enscript* by reading its manpage). A typical usage is to send the file to a printer:

```
$ enscript -p - Sample.txt | atprint
[ 1 pages * 1 copy ] left in -
$
```

enscript can also produce PostScript output files for distribution in electronic form. The following translates *sample.txt* into PostScript and saves the resultant output to the file *sample.eps*:

```
$ enscript -psample.eps sample.txt
```

Table 6-4. Useful enscript options

Option	Description
-B	Do not print page headers.
-f *font*	Print body text using *font* (the default is Courier10).
-j	Print borders around columns (you can turn on multicolumn output with *-1* or *-2*).
-p *file*	Send output to *file*. Use - to stream output to standard out (for pipes).
-r	Rotate printout 90 degrees, printing in landscape mode instead of portrait (the default).
-W *lang*	Output in the specified language. Default is PostScript, but *enscript* also supports HTML, over-strike, and RTF.

The AppleTalk Way

If you have an AppleTalk-based printer, or want to use a network printer that's accessible on your AppleTalk network, there is a set of easy-to-use AppleTalk-aware Unix commands included with Mac OS X. The most important of the commands is *atprint*, which lets you easily stream any Unix output to a printer.

atlookup

To start working with the AppleTalk tools, run *atlookup*, which lists all the AppleTalk devices recognized on the network (and that can be quite a few):

```
$ atlookup
Found 5 entries in zone *
ff01.04.08    LJ2100TN-via-AppleTalk:SNMP Agent
ff01.04.9d    LJ2100TN-via-AppleTalk:LaserWriter
ff01.04.9e    LJ2100TN-via-AppleTalk:LaserJet 2100
ff78.69.80    Tiger!:Darwin
ff78.69.81    Tiger!:AFPServer
```

You can see that the LJ2100TN printer (an HP LaserJet2100) appears with three different AppleTalk addresses. Fortunately, that can safely be ignored as well as the other AppleTalk devices that show up in the list. The important thing is that the *atlookup* command confirmed that there is indeed an AppleTalk printer online.

at_cho_prn

To select a specific AppleTalk printer as the default printer for the *atprint* command, run the oddly named *at_cho_prn* command:

```
$ at_cho_prn LaserWriter
Directory /etc/atalk is missing, re-run as root to create it
```

Oops! You need to be root to set the default printer. Let's try again, using *sudo*:

```
$ sudo at_cho_prn LaserWriter
Zone:*
ITEM NET-ADDR     OBJECT : TYPE
   1: ff01.04.9d LJ2100TN-via-AppleTalk:LaserWriter

ITEM number (0 to make no selection)? 1
Default printer is:LJ2100TN-via-AppleTalk:LaserWriter@*
status: idle
$
```

If you are on a multizone network, you'll be prompted to select a zone first.

atprint

Now, finally, the LaserJet 2100 printer is selected as the default AppleTalk printer, and all subsequent invocations of *atprint* are sent to that printer without having to remember its exact name.

```
$ ls -l | atprint
Looking for LJ2100TN-via-AppleTalk:LaserWriter@*.
Trying to connect to LJ2100TN-via-AppleTalk:LaserWriter@*.
atprint: printing on LJ2100TN-via-AppleTalk:LaserWriter@*.
$
```

If your printout doesn't work, then it's possible that you are sending a non-PostScript print job to a PostScript printer. This can be solved by using the *enscript* program, as discussed earlier in this chapter.

atstatus

To find out if your printout is queued up through AppleTalk and whether there are any other jobs in the print queue, use *atstatus*:

```
$ atstatus
Default printer is:LJ2100TN-via-AppleTalk:LaserWriter@*
status: busy; source: EIO (ATALK)
```

Wait a few seconds and *atstatus* reports that there's nothing in the queue because your information will be waiting for you on the printer.

## CHAPTER 7

Multitasking

Mac OS X can do many jobs at once, dividing the processor's time between running applications and system processes so quickly that it looks as if everything is running at the same pace. This is called *multitasking*. As new applications are launched, processes are started, and others go idle or shut down entirely, the system monitors each of these tasks and doles out memory and CPU resources on the fly to make sure everything is running smoothly.

For most users, we think of multitasking in the way Mac OS X handles applications like Adobe Photoshop, Microsoft Word, Mail, iChat, Safari, etc.—allowing you to have multiple applications open, each with its own windows. But on the Unix side, Mac OS X allows you to run multiple Unix programs and/or processes at the same time as well. These processes can be run and monitored all through one single Terminal window, with a little help from something called *job control*. Even if you're using a window system, you may want to use job control to do several things inside the same Terminal window. For instance, you may prefer to do most of your work from one Terminal window, instead of having multiple Terminal windows open when you really don't need to.

Why else would you want job control? Suppose you're running a Unix program that takes a long time to run. On a single-task operating system, you would enter the command and wait for job to finish, returning you to the command prompt, which is your indication that you're free to enter a new command. In Mac OS X, however, you can enter new commands in the "foreground" while one or more programs are running in the "background."

When you enter a command as a background process, the shell prompt reappears immediately so that you can enter a new command. The original program still runs in the background, but you can use the same Terminal window to do other things during that time. Depending on your system and your shell, you may even be able to close the Terminal window or even completely log off from Mac OS X while the background process runs to completion.

Running a Command in the Background

Running a program as a background process is most often done to free a Terminal when you know the program is going to take a long time to run. It's also used whenever you want to launch a new application from an existing Terminal window—so you can keep working in the existing Terminal, as well as within the new application.

To run a program in the background, all you need to do is add the & character at the end of the command line before pressing the Return key. The shell then assigns and displays a process ID number for the program:

```
$ sort bigfile > bigfile.sort &
[1] 372
$
```

Sorting is a good example, because it can take a while to sort huge files.

The process ID (or PID) for this program is 372. The PID is useful when you want to check the status of a background process, or if you need to cancel it. To check on the status of the process, use the *ps* command with the following two options: *-u* to have user-friendly output, and *-p* because you're specifying a process ID. The full command for this example is:

```
$ ps -up 372
USER    PID %CPU %MEM    VSZ   RSS TT STAT STARTED     TIME COMMAND
taylor  372  0.0  0.0  18208   340 std  S   10:56PM  0:00.04 sort
```

To cancel a process, use the *kill* command, followed by the PID of the process you want to cancel. In this instance, the command would look like:

```
$ kill 372
$
```

Fortunately, you don't need to remember the PID every time, because there are Unix commands (explained in the next section) to check on the processes you have running. Also, *bash* writes a status line to your screen when the background process finishes.

In *bash*, you can put an entire sequence of commands separated by semicolons (;) into the background by putting an ampersand (&) at the end of the entire command line. In other shells, enclose the command sequence in parentheses before adding the ampersand:

```
(command1; command2) &
```

Mac OS X's Unix shells also have a feature (mentioned earlier) called *job control*. You can use the *suspend character* (usually Control-Z) to suspend a program running in the foreground. The program pauses, and you get a new shell prompt. You can then do anything else you like, including putting the suspended program into the background using the *bg* command. The *fg* command brings a suspended or background process to the foreground.

For example, you might start *sort* running on a big file, and, after a minute, you might want to edit another file. You can stop *sort* with Control-Z, and then put it in the background with the *bg* command. The shell then gives you another shell prompt, at which you can start using *vi* while *sort* runs merrily in the background.

```
$ sort hugefile1 hugefile2 > sorted
...time goes by...
CTRL-Z
Stopped
$ bg
[1]    sort hugefile1 hugefile2 > sorted &
$ vi test.txt
```

Checking on a Process

If a background process seems to be taking forever to run, or if you change your mind and want to stop a process, you can check the status of the process and even cancel it.

ps

When you enter the *ps* command, you can see how long a process has been running, the process ID of the background process, and the Terminal from which it was run. The tty program shows the name of the Terminal where the command is running; this is especially helpful when you're logged into multiple machines, as the following code shows:

```
$ ps
  PID  TT  STAT     TIME COMMAND
  347  p1  S     0:00.17 -bash
  391  p2  S+    0:00.02 -bash
$ tty
/dev/ttyp1
```

In the output, p1 corresponds to the Terminal window for ttyp1 (which is the current window as the *tty* command shows), and p2 corresponds to the Terminal window for ttyp2. In its basic form, *ps* lists the following:

Process ID (PID)
    A unique number assigned by Unix to the process.

Terminal name (TT)

The Unix name for the terminal from which the process was started.

Runtime state (STAT)

The current state of each job. S is sleeping, R is runnable, T is stopped, and I is idle (sleeping for more than 20–30 seconds). Additionally, the state can include + to indicate it's part of the foreground group process, E to indicate the process is exiting, and W to mean it's swapped out.*

Runtime (TIME)

The amount of computer time (in minutes and seconds) that the process has used.

COMMAND

The name of the process.

In Unix, each Terminal window has its own name. The previous example shows processes running on two windows: p1 and p2. If you want to see the processes that a certain user is running, use the following construct:

```
ps -U username
```

Where *username* is the username of someone logged into the system.

To see all processes running on the system, use *ps -ax*. The *-a* option shows processes from all users, and the *-x* option shows processes that are not connected with a Terminal session; many of these processes are a core part of Mac OS X, while others may be graphical programs you are running, such as Safari.

```
$ ps -ax | head -20
  PID  TT  STAT      TIME COMMAND
    1  ??  S<s    0:07.80 /sbin/launchd
   31  ??  Ss     0:02.46 /usr/sbin/syslogd -m 0 -c 5
   37  ??  Ss     0:02.70 kextd
   41  ??  Ss     1:29.52 /usr/sbin/configd
   42  ??  Ss     0:00.38 /usr/sbin/coreaudiod
   43  ??  Ss     0:15.34 /usr/sbin/diskarbitrationd
   45  ??  Ss     0:04.01 /usr/sbin/securityd
   48  ??  Ss     0:05.26 /usr/sbin/notifyd
   49  ??  S      0:00.04 /usr/sbin/memberd
   50  ??  Ss     0:11.28 /usr/sbin/DirectoryService
   51  ??  Ss     0:11.68 /usr/sbin/distnoted
   53  ??  S      0:00.44 /usr/sbin/blued
   78  ??  Ss     0:15.10 /System/Library/CoreServices/coreservicesd
   91  ??  Ss     0:02.50 netinfod -s local
   93  ??  Ss     1:26.95 update
   96  ??  Ss     0:00.00 dynamic_pager -F /private/var/vm/swapfile
```

---

* The *ps* manpage has details on all possible states for a process. It's quite interesting reading.

```
  101 ?? Ss    1:35.03 /System/Library/CoreServices/loginwindow.app/
Contents/MacOS/loginwindow console
  104 ?? Ss    0:00.01 /usr/libexec/crashreporterd
  105 ?? Ss    0:01.90 /System/Library/Frameworks/ApplicationServices.
framework/Frameworks/ATS.framework/Supp
$
```

The output of *ps -ax* can be baffling since almost all of what you get are the low-level system tasks that are required for Mac OS X and Aqua to run happily on your system.

 In the above list, notice that the OS kernel extensions module *kextd*, the configuration management daemon *configd*, the audio utility *coreaudiod*, the low-level disk management program *diskarbitrationd*, the *coreservices*, *dynamic_pager*, etc. These are processes that a regular user shouldn't have to worry about. Just beware before you try killing one of these processes; doing so could cause your system to crash.

You can find out what processes are being run as *root* by using *-U* user and including a *-u* option to get user-oriented output (basically, more fields):

```
$ ps -aux -U root | head
USER    PID %CPU %MEM    VSZ    RSS TT  STAT STARTED      TIME COMMAND
root      1  0.0  0.0  29004    516 ??  S<s   6:27PM   0:07.81 /sbin/
launchd
root     31  0.0  0.0  27416    256 ??  Ss    6:27PM   0:02.46 /usr/sbin/
syslogd -m 0 -c 5
root     37  0.0  0.1  28348    844 ??  Ss    6:27PM   0:02.70 kextd
root     41  0.0  0.1  29356   1168 ??  Ss    6:28PM   1:29.91 /usr/sbin/
configd
root     42  0.0  0.2  31972   1888 ??  Ss    6:28PM   0:00.38 /usr/sbin/
coreaudiod
root     43  0.0  0.1  27920   1060 ??  Ss    6:28PM   0:15.34 /usr/sbin/
diskarbitrationd
root     45  0.0  0.2  29412   1792 ??  Ss    6:28PM   0:04.01 /usr/sbin/
securityd
root     48  0.0  0.0  27996    280 ??  Ss    6:28PM   0:05.27 /usr/sbin/
notifyd
root     49  0.0  0.0  28968    296 ??  S     6:28PM   0:00.04 /usr/sbin/
memberd
```

You can also change the output, of course, by specifying yourself as the account with the $LOGNAME environment variable:

```
$ ps -aux -U $LOGNAME | head
USER      PID %CPU %MEM     VSZ    RSS TT  STAT STARTED      TIME COMMAND
taylor   1645  0.3  0.1   31084    572 ??  S     8:08PM   0:02.18 /usr/
sbin/sshd -i
taylor    303  0.1  0.8  158400   7888 ??  S     7:18PM   1:36.28 /
Applications/Snapz Pro X/Snapz Pro X.app/Con
```

```
taylor   284   0.0  0.2    47044   1756  ??  Ss   7:18PM  0:00.80 /System/
Library/CoreServices/pbs
taylor   290   0.0  0.7   160220   7132  ??  S    7:18PM  0:05.53 /System/
Library/CoreServices/Dock.app/Content
taylor   293   0.0  0.9   165676   9740  ??  S    7:18PM  0:01.70 /System/
Library/CoreServices/Finder.app/Conte
taylor   302   0.0  0.2   117740   2008  ??  S    7:18PM  0:00.20 /
Applications/Microsoft AutoUpdate.app/Conten
taylor   304   0.0  0.7   176380   7188  ??  S    7:18PM  0:11.37 /System/
Library/CoreServices/SystemUIServer.a
taylor   311   0.0  1.3   186612  13788  ??  S    7:25PM  0:56.55 /
Applications/Utilities/Terminal.app/Contents
taylor   315   0.0  0.1    27948    876  p1  S+   7:25PM  0:00.05 -bash
```

This is particularly long and complex, but *ps* is loaded with different options, and sometimes just removing an option makes it easier to figure out what's going on:

```
$ ps -ax -U $LOGNAME | head
  PID  TT  STAT      TIME COMMAND
  101  ??  Ss     1:35.04 /System/Library/CoreServices/loginwindow.app/
Contents/MacOS/loginwindow console
  105  ??  Ss     0:01.90 /System/Library/Frameworks/ApplicationServices.
framework/Frameworks/ATS.framework/Supp
  284  ??  Ss     0:00.80 /System/Library/CoreServices/pbs
  290  ??  S      0:05.53 /System/Library/CoreServices/Dock.app/Contents/
MacOS/Dock -psn_0_524289
  293  ??  S      0:01.70 /System/Library/CoreServices/Finder.app/Contents/
MacOS/Finder -psn_0_786433
  302  ??  S      0:00.20 /Applications/Microsoft AutoUpdate.app/Contents/
MacOS/Microsoft AU Daemon.app/Contents
  303  ??  S      1:36.40 /Applications/Snapz Pro X/Snapz Pro X.app/
Contents/MacOS/Snapz Pro X -psn_0_1048577
  304  ??  S      0:11.38 /System/Library/CoreServices/SystemUIServer.app/
Contents/MacOS/SystemUIServer -psn_0_1
  311  ??  S      0:56.62 /Applications/Utilities/Terminal.app/Contents/
MacOS/Terminal -psn_0_1441793
```

When you're just learning how to interpret the oft-confusing output of the *ps* command, you might find it quite helpful to simultaneously run the Activity Monitor (*/Applications/Utilities*), shown in Figure 7-1.

It's useful to change the filter at the top of the Activity Monitor from the default of My Processes to All Processes, as shown in Figure 7-1. This gives you a much better sense of what's happening on your computer, and if you do have a runaway application or one that's locked, it often doesn't show up in the My Processes view anyway.

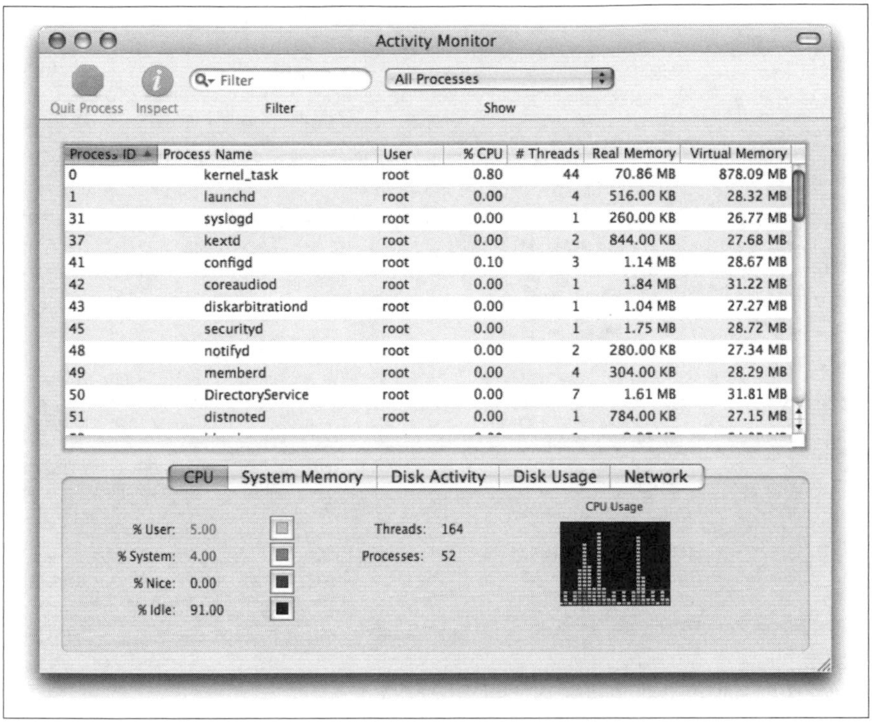

Figure 7-1. The Activity Monitor also shows running processes

top

A better way to see what applications are running and which are taking up the most resources is to use the helpful *top* command. Figure 7-2 shows *top* in action.

If you're curious what commands consume the most system resources, leave *top* running in a Terminal window while you work. However, do be aware that *top* itself consumes some system resources, so if you're not paying attention to its output, you can quit *top* by typing **q**. You can always start it up again if things seem to be oddly slow on your computer.

> You can run *top* as a background process (*top &*), but that doesn't really do you much good unless you're piping its output to another command for processing. The whole idea of using *top* is so you can quickly get a view of the processes on your system, and how they're taxing your system.

top packs a lot of information into its display, considerably more than we have space to explain here. However, look at the first few lines and you'll get

```
  ● ○ ○              Terminal — top — 80x25
Processes:  53 total, 2 running, 51 sleeping... 162 threads        10:34:27 ▤
Load Avg:  0.05, 0.11, 0.06     CPU usage:  14.5% user, 15.4% sys, 70.1% idle
SharedLibs: num =  118, resident = 37.0M code, 3.55M data, 13.0M LinkEdit
MemRegions: num =  7545, resident = 75.5M + 9.89M private, 82.1M shared
PhysMem:  88.8M wired, 117M active, 128M inactive, 334M used, 609M free
VM: 3.92G + 89.2M   295031(0) pageins, 147(0) pageouts

  PID COMMAND      %CPU   TIME   #TH #PRTS #MREGS RPRVT  RSHRD  RSIZE  VSIZE
 6250 top         12.8% 0:01.45  1   18    33   296K   600K   740K   27.1M
 6236 pmTool       4.1% 0:10.14  1   23    32   408K   544K   3.16M  27.2M
 6235 Activity M   7.8% 0:28.05  2   76   337   6.63M  24.1M  25.1M  199M
 4628 ipp          0.0% 0:04.84  1   14    25   220K   940K   768K   27.2M
 4576 slpd         0.0% 0:00.48  6   31    40   252K   1.19M  980K   30.5M
 4573 lookupd      0.0% 0:02.30  2   34    52   388K   1.16M  1.14M  28.6M
 4571 cupsd        0.0% 0:03.38  2   31    34   396K   1.41M  1.31M  28.0M
 3089 AppleSpell   0.0% 0:00.16  1   32    39   660K   2.19M  5.04M  36.7M
 3085 Safari       0.0% 0:08.93  7  133   358   7.19M  24.2M  36.3M  185M
 1647 bash         0.0% 0:00.88  1   14    21   256K   1.00M  900K   27.3M
 1645 sshd         0.0% 0:02.50  1   12    55   168K   1.93M  572K   30.4M
 1642 sshd         0.0% 0:00.75  1   15    52   112K   1.93M  1.36M  30.2M
  315 bash         0.0% 0:00.05  1   14    20   184K   1.07M  860K   27.3M
  313 login        0.0% 0:00.03  1   16    41   144K   696K   588K   27.0M
  311 Terminal     1.0% 0:58.87  6  100   482   5.32M+ 27.1M- 15.9M  193M    ▲
  304 SystemUISe   0.0% 0:11.52  2  208   273   3.11M  14.2M  6.96M  172M    ▼
  303 Snapz Pro    0.1% 1:39.08  2  145   234   8.61M  19.7M  18.6M  182M ▮
```

Figure 7-2. The top command shows processes running

some quick insight into how well your system configuration matches the
needs of the processes you're running. You can grab a snapshot of the first
six lines of output with this command (the flag used is a lowercase L followed by the digit one):

```
$ top -l 1 | head -6
Processes:  58 total, 2 running, 56 sleeping... 166 threads      10:55:19
Load Avg:  0.00, 0.00, 0.01  CPU usage:  0.0% user, 100.0% sys, 0.0% idle
SharedLibs: num =  118, resident = 37.0M code, 3.55M data, 13.0M LinkEdit
MemRegions: num =  7189, resident = 66.8M + 9.16M private, 73.6M shared
PhysMem:  82.6M wired,  113M active,  123M inactive, 319M used, 704M free
VM: 3.86G + 89.2M   295879(0) pageins, 155(0) pageouts
```

What you should look for here is high CPU usage (anything over about 25
percent is usually considered high unless you're running something like Photoshop or some other CPU-intensive task), too little free memory (here I
have 704M free—end of line 5—out of a 1GB RAM configuration, plenty of
space), or too many virtual memory pageouts (I have 155 pageouts, which is
quite low).

Swapping is based on the idea that the memory needed for an application can be broken into *pages*, as many as needed for the app at that particular moment. As multiple processes compete for the system memory, memory pages that haven't been accessed for a while are temporarily copied to a special place on the hard disk, then the page is given to the newer application. The process of swapping an older page for a newer one is called a *pageout*.

To display processes, sorted by CPU usage (rather than process ID), use:

```
$ top -o cpu
```

If you find this view to be more useful than *top*'s traditional view, you can add this as an alias to your *.profile* file:

```
alias top='/usr/bin/top -s 5 -o cpu'
```

This updates *top*'s display every five seconds rather than the default of every second, and sorts the results by highest CPU usage to lowest. For more information on *top*, visit its manpage (*man top*).

You can also specify PID values to *ps* to find out about specific jobs. If you know that Apple Mail is running as process 317, for example, then *ps -p 317* will give you information about that particular program.

If you haven't yet tried the *apropos* command, you should. It helps you find commands that are associated with a specific task or function. The only problem with *apropos* is that the database it uses needs to be created, and this task takes quite a while. This is a perfect opportunity to run that as a background job, and while it's running, you can check on its status with *ps*. Just follow these steps:

1. To rebuild the database, you need to use the *makewhatis* command (which isn't where the *apropos* documentation says it is). Instead, if you built the locate database (see "Finding Files with locate in Chapter 5), you can use *locate* to find it:

```
$ locate makewhatis
/usr/bin/makewhatis
/usr/libexec/makewhatis.local
/usr/share/man/man1/makewhatis.1.gz
/usr/share/man/man8/makewhatis.8
/usr/share/man/man8/makewhatis.local.8.gz
/Volumes/Hello/usr/libexec/makewhatis
/Volumes/Hello/usr/libexec/makewhatis.local
/Volumes/Hello/usr/share/man/man8/makewhatis.8
/Volumes/Hello/usr/share/man/man8/makewhatis.local.8
```

2. Now that you know where the command is (*/usr/bin*), it can be invoked as *root* with *sudo*:

```
$ sudo /usr/bin/makewhatis &
[1] 7536
```

3. Now, let's have a look at whether the program is still running by using the *ps* command, specifying the PID explicitly (don't forget: your PID will be different):

```
$ ps -p 7536
PID  TT  STAT      TIME COMMAND
 7536 p2  S       0:00.03 sudo /usr/bin/makewhatis
$ ps -up 7536
USER    PID %CPU %MEM      VSZ    RSS TT  STAT STARTED        TIME COMMAND
root   7536  0.0  0.1    27696    684 p2  S    11:38AM  0:00.03 sudo
/usr/bin/makewhatis
```

4. Since you know how to find out what process is associated with a specific PID, you can also use this technique to figure out what shell you're running:

```
$ ps -p $$
PID  TT  STAT      TIME COMMAND
 1647 p2  Ss      0:00.97 -bash
```

As the last command shows, you can easily ascertain what shell you're running at any time by using the $$ shortcut for the current shell's PID.

 You should be aware that there are two types of programs on Unix systems: *directly executable programs* and *interpreted programs*. Directly executable programs are written in a programming language such as C and have been compiled into a binary format that the system can execute directly. Interpreted programs, such as shell and Perl scripts, are sequences of commands that are read by an interpreter program. If you execute an interpreted program, you'll see an additional command (such as *perl*, *sh*, or *csh*) in the *ps* listing, as well as any Unix commands that the interpreter is executing currently.

Shells with job control have a command called *jobs* that lists background processes started from that shell:

```
$ jobs
[1]+  Running                 sudo /usr/bin/makewhatis &
```

As mentioned earlier, there are commands to change the foreground/background status of jobs (namely *bg* to put a job into background, and *fg* to bring a background job back into foreground). There are other job control commands as well. See the references in Chapter 11.

Canceling a Process

You may decide that you shouldn't have put a process in the background or the process is taking too long to execute. You can cancel a background process if you know its PID.

kill

The *kill* command terminates a process. This has the same result as using the Finder's Force Quit option. To *kill* a process, use the following format:

```
kill PID(s)
```

Mac OS X includes a very helpful utility called Force Quit, accessible from the Apple menu (⌘ → Force Quit, or Option-⌘-Esc), which can be quite useful when applications are stuck or nonresponsive. However, commands entered into the Terminal window can only be canceled from the command line—they don't show up in the Force Quit window. Additionally, Force Quit doesn't show you administrative processes. To stop Unix programs and administrative processes, you must either use the command line or the Activity Monitor (*/Applications/Utilities*).

kill terminates the designated PIDs (shown under the PID heading in the *ps* listing). If you do not know the PID, you should first run *ps* to display the status of your processes.

In the following example, the *sleep n* command simply causes a process to "go to sleep" for *n* seconds. Here, you'll see how to enter two commands—*sleep* and *who*—on the same line, and designate those to run as a background process:

```
$ (sleep 60;who) &
[1] 472
$ ps
  PID  TT  STAT     TIME COMMAND
  347 std  S      0:00.36 -bash
  472 std  S      0:00.00 -bash
  473 std  S      0:00.01 sleep 60
$ kill 473
$ -bash: line 53:   473 Terminated               sleep 60
taylor   console Sep 24 22:38
taylor   ttyp1   Sep 24 22:40

[1]+  Done                  ( sleep 60; who )
$
```

We decided that 60 seconds was too long to wait for the output of *who*. The *ps* listing showed that *sleep* had the PID number 473, so we use this PID to *kill* the *sleep* process. You should see a message like "Terminated" or "Killed"; if you don't, use another *ps* command to make sure the process has been killed (or that you killed the right process).

Now *who* executes immediately—as it's no longer waiting on *sleep*—and displays a list of users logged into the system.

killall

If you'd rather not worry about finding the PID for a particular process, you can always use the *killall* command, which lets you kill processes by name instead. Since it's possible to inadvertently kill the wrong processes (like your Terminal application or your shell), I strongly recommend that you always start by using the *-s* option so *killall* shows you what it'll do without actually killing anything:

```
$ (sleep 60;who) &
[2] 8762
$ killall -s make
No matching processes belonging to you were found
$ killall -s who
No matching processes belonging to you were found
$ killall -s sleep
kill -TERM 8763
```

Did it surprise you that there's no match to *killall -s who* even though *sleep;who* is running in background? The reason it didn't match is because the *who* command itself isn't yet running, but the *sleep* command is; you can see that it's matched by the third instance of *killall*.

If you have eagle eyes, you'll notice that the *sleep* command's PID isn't the same as the PID given by the shell when the *sleep;who* command was dropped into the background. That's because when a job is put into background, the shell copies itself and then the *copy shell* (Unix folk call that the *subshell*) manages the commands. It's the subshell that has PID 8762, and *sleep* is a subprocess of that shell, so it gets a different PID: 8763. When *sleep* finishes and the *who* command runs, that'll have yet another PID (most likely 8764).

To kill the *sleep* process, simply remove the *-s* flag from the *killall* command, or, if you're curious, replace it with *-v* so you can see what the program does:

```
$ killall sleep
$ -bash: line 210:  8778 Terminated               sleep 60
taylor   console  Jan  9 19:18
taylor   ttyp1    Jan  9 19:25
taylor   ttyp2    Jan  9 20:08 (192.168.1.100)
taylor   ttyp3    Jan 10 11:31 (192.168.1.100)
$ killall -v sleep
No matching processes belonging to you were found
[2]+ Done                      ( sleep 60; who )
$
```

Notice that the first *killall* killed the *sleep* process, which immediately caused *who* to be run. When I tried to use *killall* again with the *-v* flag, it was too late and there was no longer a *sleep* command running.

> ## The Process Didn't Die When I Told It To
>
> Some processes can be hard to kill. If a normal *kill* of these processes is not working, try entering:
>
> ```
> kill -9 PID
> ```
>
> Or, if you're using *killall*, try:
>
> ```
> killall -9 name
> ```
>
> This is a sure kill, and can destroy almost anything, including the shell itself. Most Unix folk refer to the *-9* option as "terminate with extreme prejudice," a nod to the popular James Bond movie series.
>
> Also, if you've run an interpreted program (such as a shell script), you may not be able to kill all dependent processes by killing the interpreter process that got it all started. You may need to kill them individually; however, killing a process that is feeding data into a pipe generally kills any processes receiving that data.

Launching GUI Applications

One great feature of Mac OS X's Unix command line is that you can interact with the graphical applications in Aqua. For example:

- Drag a file or folder from the Finder onto a Terminal window and watch as its full pathname gets dropped in after the command prompt.
- Want to use *vi* to edit a text file that's on your Desktop? Just type *vi* on the command line, followed by a space, and then drag the file onto the Terminal window.
- When viewing a file in the Finder, you'll see what's known as a proxy icon in the Finder's titlebar that shows you what directory you're in. Type *cd* followed by a space, then drag the proxy icon into the Terminal window and hit Return; you'll be taken to that same exact location, just in the Terminal.

If you can have the Finder interact with Terminal, it should be no surprise to you that you can also have Terminal interact with other graphical applications on the Mac. For this, Mac OS X offers the *open* command.

open

By default, the *open* command works identically to double-clicking an icon in the Finder. To open up a picture file in your default picture editor, use:

```
$ open peanut.jpg
$
```

If you don't have a graphic-editing application like Photoshop installed, the image opens in Preview (*/Applications*). If Preview is already running, the *peanut.jpg* image file opens in a new window.

The *open* command also lets you work at the command line with file matching since it accepts more than one filename at a time. For example, if you need to open up a bunch of Microsoft Word files in a directory, just use:

```
$ open *.doc
$
```

You can, however, get things a bit confused, because sometimes the system doesn't know what to do with certain files. For example, try issuing the following command:

```
$ open .profile
$
```

The default application that's used when there's no specific binding is TextEdit, which works in this instance, but look what happens when you try to open something it can't recognize:

```
$ open .sample.swp
2005-06-10 13:12:54.278 open[8836] LSOpenFromURLSpec() returned -10814 for
application (null) urls file://localhost/Users/taylor/.sample.swp.
```

In this case, *open* just couldn't figure out what to do with this temporary scratch file from the *vi* editor. That's because *open* uses a file's creator and/or type code to determine which application should be used to open a particular file. And since *vi*'s scratch files don't have a creator or type code, the command gets confused and ends up doing nothing.

Useful Starting Options for Use with open

The *open* command has a lot of power accessible through command options. For example, if you want to stream a bunch of input into a text file then open it in an Aqua file, you can do so by using the *-f* option:

```
$ mdfind NIKON | open -f
$
```

This quick call to Spotlight generates a list of all filenames that reference or include NIKON, producing the screenshot shown in Figure 7-3. It would be easy to generate a printout with TextEdit, too.

The most useful option for use with *open* is *-a*, which is used to specify an application to open. For example, you can launch iChat with the generic *open* command, but you need to know where it's located on your system:

```
$ open ichat
2005-01-10 13:58:53.118 open[10056] No such file: /Users/taylor/ichat
```

What Are Creator and Type Codes?

Unlike other operating systems, whenever you create and save a file with an application on the Mac, the application you use assigns its creator and type codes to the file. These codes are four characters in length, and can contain upper- and lowercase letters, numbers, and even spaces. Mac OS X uses these codes to figure out which icon gets assigned to certain files, but more importantly, to determine the default application for opening that file.

For example, in the Terminal, you can create a blank file on your Desktop with the following command:

```
$ touch myFile.txt
```

As you can see from the file extension (*.txt*), this is a plain text file. If you were to double-click on this file, and if you didn't have another graphical text editor on your system, the file would open in TextEdit.

If you rename that file and give it a *.doc* extension:

```
$ mv myFile.txt myFile.doc
```

You can trick the system into thinking that it's a Word file. Don't believe me, just try double-clicking the file and see which application opens it.

If you've installed the Xcode Tools on your Mac (see Chapter 4), you can use a couple special command-line utilities to peek inside a file to see its creator and type codes. For example, the following displays the output of the *GetFileInfo* command (located in */Developer/Tools*) when used on a Word file:

```
$ ./Developer/Tools/GetFileInfo lmut_ch07.doc
file: "lmut_ch07.doc"
type: "W8BN"
creator: "MSWD"
attributes: avbstclinmed
created: 02/01/2005 07:42:57
modified: 02/01/2005 07:42:57
$
```

Here you can see that the creator code is MSWD, short for Microsoft Word.

Add the *-a* option, though, and *open* knows that you're talking about an application, so it'll search in the */Applications* directory to find and launch it:

```
$ open -a ichat
```

Notice that *open* is smart enough to ignore case: the actually application is called iChat. You can also use the *open -a* command to open applications that are in a subdirectory of */Applications*. Want to launch the Console (located in */Applications/Utilities*)? Use *open -a console*. Ready to compare the output of Activity Monitor to the *ps* command, as discussed earlier in this chapter? Launch Activity Monitor with *open -a "activity monitor"*.

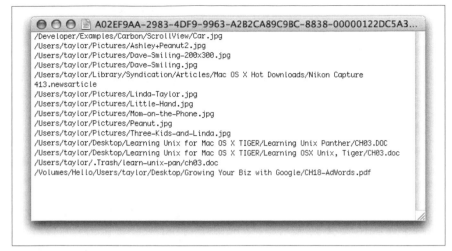

```
● ● ●  A02EF9AA-2983-4DF9-9963-A2B2CA89C9BC-8838-00000122DC5A3...
/Developer/Examples/Carbon/ScrollView/Car.jpg
/Users/taylor/Pictures/Ashley+Peanut2.jpg
/Users/taylor/Pictures/Dave-Smiling-200x300.jpg
/Users/taylor/Pictures/Dave-Smiling.jpg
/Users/taylor/Library/Syndication/Articles/Mac OS X Hot Downloads/Nikon Capture
413.newsarticle
/Users/taylor/Pictures/Linda-Taylor.jpg
/Users/taylor/Pictures/Little-Hand.jpg
/Users/taylor/Pictures/Mom-on-the-Phone.jpg
/Users/taylor/Pictures/Peanut.jpg
/Users/taylor/Pictures/Three-Kids-and-Linda.jpg
/Users/taylor/Desktop/Learning Unix for Mac OS X TIGER/Learning Unix Panther/CH03.DOC
/Users/taylor/Desktop/Learning Unix for Mac OS X TIGER/Learning OSX Unix, Tiger/CH03.doc
/Users/taylor/.Trash/learn-unix-pan/ch03.doc
/Volumes/Hello/Users/taylor/Desktop/Growing Your Biz with Google/CH18-AdWords.pdf
```

Figure 7-3. open lets us pour standard input into an Aqua application

If you want to open a file with TextEdit, there's another option to *open* that's worth knowing: use *open -e*, and whatever you specify will be opened with the TextEdit program, regardless of its type. For example, if you wanted to open an HTML file in TextEdit instead of with BBEdit, you could use the following:

```
$ open -e ~/Sites/someFile.html
```

After entering that command, the *open* command looks in your Sites folder for the file *someFile.html* and opens it in TextEdit.

Making open More Useful

open makes it a breeze to launch your favorite applications, but because it requires that you type in the full application name, a few aliases are in order:

```
alias word="open -a Microsoft\ Word"
alias excel="open -a Microsoft\ Excel"
alias gc="open -a GraphicConverter"
```

With these added to your *.profile*, you could then easily launch Graphic Converter by just entering *gc*, and launch Microsoft Excel with *excel*.

A more sophisticated approach would be to use a shell script wrapper that would give its arguments to *open* and if they failed, try to figure out what application you were talking about. It's an advanced topic, but here's how that script might look:

```
#!/bin/sh

# open2 - a smart wrapper for the cool Mac OS X 'open' command
```

```
#    to make it even more useful. By default, open launches the
#    appropriate application for a specified file or directory
#    based on the Aqua bindings, and has a limited ability to
#    launch applications if they're in the /Applications dir.

# first off, whatever argument we're given, try it directly:

open=/usr/bin/open

if ! $open "$@" >/dev/null 2>&1 ; then
  if ! $open -a "$@" >/dev/null 2>&1 ; then

    # More than one arg?  Don't know how to deal with it: quit
    if [ $# -gt 1 ] ; then
      echo "open: Can't figure out how to open or launch $@" >&2
      exit 1
    else
      case $(echo $1 | tr '[:upper:]' '[:lower:]') in
        acrobat      ) app="Acrobat Reader"           ;;
        adress*      ) app="Address Book"             ;;
        chat         ) app="iChat"                    ;;
        cpu          ) app="CPU Monitor"              ;;
        dvd          ) app="DVD Player"               ;;
        excel        ) app="Microsoft Excel"          ;;
        netinfo      ) app="NetInfo Manager"          ;;
        prefs        ) app="System Preferences"       ;;
        print        ) app="Print Center"             ;;
        profil*      ) app="Apple System Profiler"    ;;
        qt|quicktime ) app="QuickTime Player"         ;;
        sync         ) app="iSync"                    ;;
        word         ) app="Microsoft Word"           ;;
        * ) echo "open: Don't know what to do with $1" >&2
            exit 1
      esac
      echo "You asked for $1 but I think you mean $app." >&2
      $open -a "$app"
    fi
  fi
fi

exit 0
```

This script has a simple table of nicknames for common applications, allowing you to type *open2 qt* to launch QuickTime Player, for example.

 This script is from my book, *Wicked Cool Shell Scripts* (No Starch Press), which explains 101 powerful and interesting shell scripts. You can learn about the book, and download the above script for yourself, at *http://www.intuitive.com/wicked/*.

## CHAPTER 8

Taking Unix Online

A network lets computers communicate with each other, share files, send email, and much more. Unix systems have been networked for more than 25 years, and the Mac OS has had networking as an integral part of the system design from day one. In fact, AppleTalk was the first computer network that let computers connect directly together without needing a server in the middle.

This chapter introduces Unix networking: remotely accessing your Mac from other computers and copying files between computers. It also shows you how the Terminal's "Connect to Server" feature can make common connections a breeze once you've set them up the first time.

Remote Logins

There may be times when you need to access your Mac, but you can't get to the desk it's sitting on. If you're working on a different computer, you may not have the time or inclination to stop what you're doing, walk over to your Mac, and log in (laziness may not be the only reason for this: perhaps someone else is using your Mac when you need to get on it, or perhaps your Mac is miles away). Mac OS X's file sharing (System Preferences → Sharing → Services) lets you access your files, but there may be times you want to use the computer interactively, perhaps to move files around, search for a particular file, or perform a system maintenance task.

If you enable Remote Login (System Preferences → Sharing → Services), as shown in Figure 8-1, you can access your Mac's Unix shell from any networked computer that can run the Secure Shell, SSH.

The *ssh* client program is included with Mac OS X (access it from within Terminal) and all Unix and Linux systems. And just in case you need to

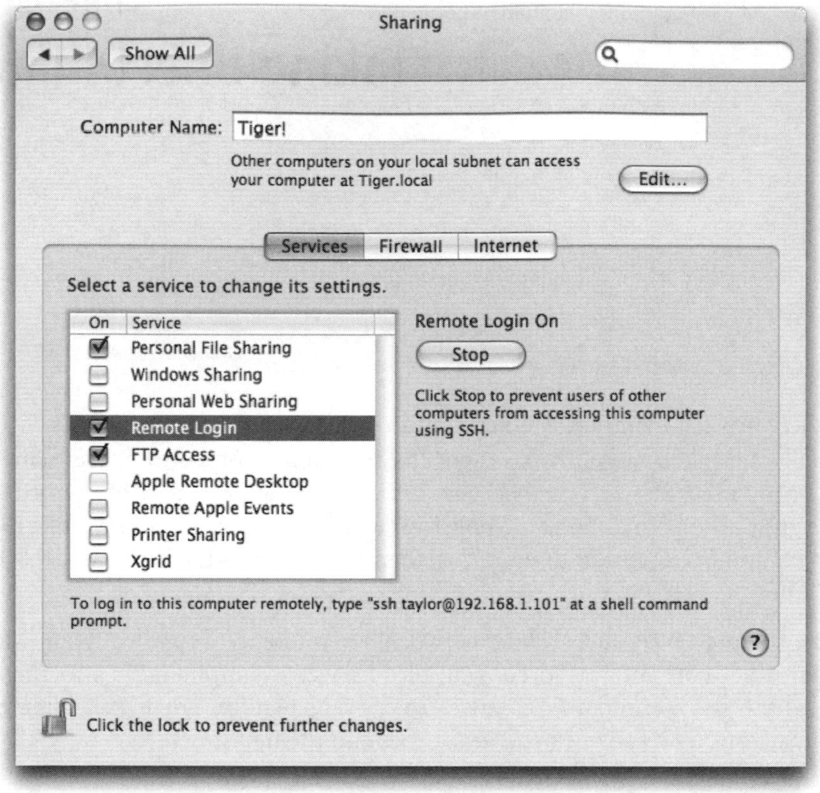

Figure 8-1. Enabling Remote Login in the Sharing preferences panel

access your Mac from a Windows system, there are a number of different *ssh* applications available, including:

- SSH (*www.ssh.com*)
- OpenSSH (*www.openssh.org*)
- PuTTY (*www.chiark.greenend.org.uk/~sgtatham/putty/*)

Figure 8-2 shows how remote login programs such as *ssh* work. In a local login, you interact directly with the shell with the Terminal application. In a remote login, you run a remote-access program (such as SSH) on your local system, and that program lets you interact with a shell program on the remote system. When you enable Remote Login, the Sharing panel displays instructions for logging into your Mac from another computer. This message is shown in Figure 8-1 near the bottom:

> To log in to this computer remotely, type "ssh taylor@192.168.1.101" at a shell command prompt.

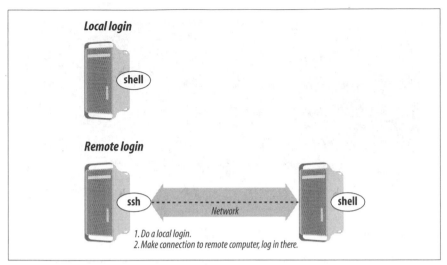

Figure 8-2. Local login, remote login

To log into your Mac from a remote Unix system, use the command displayed in the Sharing panel, as shown in the following sample session. Here, a user on a Red Hat Linux system is connecting to a Mac OS X computer (the first time you connect, you'll be asked to vouch for your Mac's authenticity):

```
Red Hat: taylor $ ssh taylor@192.168.1.101
The authenticity of host '192.168.1.101 (192.168.1.101)' can't be
established.
RSA key fingerprint is 86:f6:96:f9:22:50:ea:4c:02:0c:58:a7:e4:a8:10:67.
Are you sure you want to continue connecting (yes/no)? yes
Warning: Permanently added '192.168.1.101' (RSA) to the list of known hosts.
taylor@192.168.1.101's password:
Last login: Thu Sep 25 10:27:58 2003
Welcome to Darwin!
$
```

 If you have a firewall running, you need to open up a network port to allow remote connections. You can learn more about how to do this by starting with Apple's Tiger Help system. In the Finder, use Command-? to launch Help Viewer, then search for "firewall".

To log into your Mac from a Windows machine using PuTTY, launch the PuTTY application, specify SSH (the default is to use the Telnet protocol described later), and type in your Mac OS X system's IP address, as shown in the Mac's Sharing panel. PuTTY prompts you for your Mac OS X username and password. Figure 8-3 shows a sample PuTTY session.

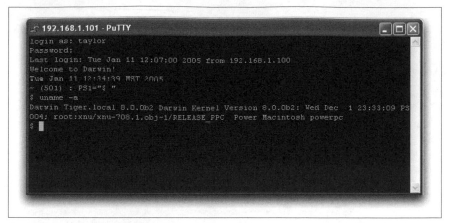

```
192.168.1.101 - PuTTY                                    _ □ ✕
login as: taylor
Password:
Last login: Tue Jan 11 12:07:00 2005 from 192.168.1.100
Welcome to Darwin!
Tue Jan 11 12:34:39 MST 2005
~ (501) : PS1="$ "
$ uname -a
Darwin Tiger.local 8.0.0b2 Darwin Kernel Version 8.0.0b2: Wed Dec  1 23:33:09 PS
004; root:xnu/xnu-708.1.obj~1/RELEASE_PPC  Power Macintosh powerpc
$ ▮
```

Figure 8-3. Connecting to Mac OS X with PuTTY

For the most part, being connected via *ssh* is identical to using the Terminal application itself. You can even use the *open* command (discussed in Chapter 7) to launch applications on the Macintosh system, which can surprise the heck out of anyone who might be watching the screen! Of course, you won't be able to use the applications if you're remote.

 Using Apple Remote Desktop or Virtual Network Computing (VNC) software, you can use Mac applications remotely. You can learn more about Apple Remote Desktop with the Help Viewer (launch Help Viewer with ⌘-? in the Finder, then search for "Remote Desktop") or Chicken of the VNC by starting at *http://sourceforge.net/projects/cotvnc/*. If these look like they'll meet your remote access needs, there's a lot more information on remote application access in *Mac OS X Tiger for Unix Geeks* (O'Reilly).

One of the very few differences is that the system records the Internet address of the system from which you're connected remotely, as shown in this *who* output:

```
$ who
taylor    console  Jan 13 16:56
taylor    ttyp1    Jan 13 17:00
taylor    ttyp2    Jan 13 17:10 (192.168.1.100)
```

The third entry is a remote connection by a user on a different computer.

Web and FTP Access

You can also use the Sharing preferences panel to enable your system's web and FTP server. To enable the Apache web server, you'll need to turn on Personal Web Sharing in the Services pane. Other users can access the main home page (located in */Library/WebServer/Documents*) using *http://address*, where *address* is your machine's IP address or hostname (see the sidebar "Remote Access and the Outside World" if you are using an AirPort Base Station (either Extreme or Express) or other router between your network and the Internet).

Remote Access and the Outside World

If your Macintosh has an IP address that was assigned by an AirPort Base Station, then it's probable that your machine is inaccessible to the outside world. Because of this, you will be able to connect to your Mac only from machines on your local network. You can allow remote users to connect by using the AirPort Admin Utility, and then follow these steps:

1. Select your Base Station.
2. Click the Configure button in the toolbar.
3. Select the Port Mapping tab.
4. Click the Add button to add a port that you want to map to an IP address on your local network.

For Remote Login via *ssh*, you must map port 22 to your Macintosh; use port 80 for Personal Web Sharing. Other SoHo (Small Office/Home Office) gateways may support this feature as well.

If you use this technique, the IP address shown in the Sharing preferences panel will be incorrect. You should use your AirPort Base Station's WAN address when you connect from a computer outside your local network.

To allow remote users FTP access to your Mac, you'll need to turn on the FTP Access option in the Sharing → Services panel. Once enabled, remote users can use your machine's IP address or hostname to connect to your Mac to download and upload files via FTP.

Later on in this chapter, I'll explain more about how to use the *ftp* program from the command line, but Figure 8-4 gives you a sneak preview of what it's like to connect from a Windows machine to a Mac OS X Tiger system using Firefox's built-in FTP capability. To learn more about Firefox and what it's capable of, visit the Mozilla Project page (*www.mozilla.org/*

products/firefox/central.html), or read *Don't Click on the Blue E: Switching to Firefox*, by Scott Granneman (O'Reilly).

Index of ftp://taylor@192.168.1.102/

Up to higher level directory

.DS_Store	7 KB	4/5/2005	3:11:00 PM
.ICEauthority		1/17/2005	9:34:00 PM
.Trash		4/5/2005	2:57:00 PM
.Xauthority	1 KB	4/5/2005	3:07:00 PM
.angband		1/17/2005	9:11:00 PM
.bash_history	9 KB	4/5/2005	3:24:00 PM
.gimp-1.2		1/17/2005	8:49:00 PM
.kde		1/17/2005	9:33:00 PM
.pine-debug1	11 KB	1/17/2005	9:08:00 PM
.pinerc	16 KB	1/17/2005	8:20:00 PM
.profile	1 KB	1/17/2005	12:04:00 PM
.qt		1/17/2005	9:33:00 PM
.ssh		8/30/2004	12:00:00 AM
.sversionrc	1 KB	1/15/2005	11:53:00 PM
.viminfo	6 KB	3/3/2005	1:48:00 PM
.xscrabble.save	1 KB	1/17/2005	3:50:00 PM
Desktop		4/5/2005	3:19:00 PM
Documents		10/2/2004	12:00:00 AM
Library		3/3/2005	3:29:00 PM

Figure 8-4. Connecting to Mac OS X FTP using Firefox in Windows

Remote Access to Other Unix Systems

You can also connect to other systems from Mac OS X. To do so, launch the Terminal application, and then start a program that connects to the remote computer. In addition to *ssh*, some typical programs for connecting over a computer network include *telnet*, *rsh* (remote shell), or *rlogin* (remote login). All of these are supported and included with Mac OS X Tiger. In any case, when you log off the remote computer, the remote login program quits and you get another shell prompt from your Mac in the Terminal window.

While you can use *ssh*, *telnet*, *rsh*, or *rlogin* to connect to a remote system, security experts highly discourage you using anything other than *ssh*, because none of the others are encrypted or secure. This means that when you type in your account and password information they're sent "in the clear" through the Internet to the remote system, exposing you to possible "sniffers" who would then be able to log in as if they were you. Better safe than sorry: insist that the remote system support *ssh* and use it exclusively.

The syntax for *ssh* is:

```
ssh remote-user@remote-hostname
```

For example, when Dr. Nelson wants to connect to the remote computer named *biolab.medu.edu*, her first step is to launch the Terminal. Next, she'll need to use the *ssh* program to reach the remote computer. Her session would look something like this:

```
Welcome to Darwin!

$ ssh nelson@biolab.medu.edu
nelson@biolab.medu.edu's password:

biolab$
.
.
.
biolab$ exit
Connection to biolab.medu.edu closed.
$
```

As you can see, the shell prompt from her account on the *biolab* server includes the hostname. This is helpful, because it reminds her when she's logged in remotely, and after exiting the remote system, she'll also know when she's back in her own territory. If you use more than one system but don't have the hostname in your prompt, see "Setting Your Prompt" in Chapter 2 to find out how to add it.

When you're logged on to a remote system, keep in mind that the commands you type take effect on the remote system, not on your local one! For instance, if you use *lpr* to print a file (see the section on printing in Chapter 6), the printer it comes out from won't be the one sitting under your desk, but quite possibly one that's far away.

The programs *rsh* (also called *rlogin*) and *ssh* generally don't give you a login: prompt. These programs assume that your remote username is the same as your local username. If they're different, you'll need to provide your remote username on the command line of the remote login program, as shown earlier for *ssh*.

You may be able to log in without typing your remote password or passphrase.* Otherwise, you'll be prompted after entering the command line.

Following are four sample *ssh* and *rsh* command lines. The first pair shows how to log into the remote system, *biolab.medu.edu*, when your username is

---

* In *ssh*, you can run an *agent* program, such as *ssh-agent*, that asks for your passphrase once, then handles authentication every time you run *ssh* or *scp* afterward.

the same on both the local and remote systems. The second pair shows how to log in if your remote username is different (in this case, *jdnelson*); note that the Mac OS X versions of *ssh* and *rsh* may support both syntaxes shown, depending on how the remote host is configured.

```
$ ssh biolab.medu.edu
$ rsh biolab.medu.edu
$ ssh jdnelson@biolab.medu.edu
$ rsh -l jdnelson biolab.medu.edu
```

About Security

Today's Internet and other public networks have users who try to break into computers and snoop on other network users. While the popular media calls these people *hackers*, the correct term to use is *crackers*. (Most hackers are self-respecting programmers who enjoy pushing the envelope of technology.)

Most remote login programs (and file transfer programs, which we cover later in this chapter) were designed 20 years ago or more, when networks were friendly places with cooperative users. Those programs (many versions of *telnet* and *rsh*, for instance) make a cracker's job easy. They transmit your data, including your password, across the network in a way that allows even the most inexperienced cracker to read it. Worse, some of these utilities can be configured to allow access without passwords.

SSH is different; it was designed with security in mind. It sends your password (and everything else transmitted or received during your SSH session) in a secure way. For more details on SSH, I'd recommend the book, *SSH, The Secure Shell: The Definitive Guide*, by Daniel J. Barrett and Richard Silverman (O'Reilly).

Transferring Files

You may need to copy files between computers. For instance, you can put a backup copy of an important file you're editing onto an account at a computer in another building or another city. Or, Dr. Nelson could copy a file from her local computer onto a central computer, where her colleagues can access it. Or you might want to download 20 files from an FTP server, but don't want to go through the tedious process of clicking on them one by one in a web browser.

If you need to do this sort of thing often, you may be able to set up a networked filesystem connection; then you'll be able to use the Finder or local programs such as *cp* and *mv* to help you move files around on your own system. But Unix systems also have command-line tools such as *scp* and *rcp* for transferring files between computers. These often work more quickly than most graphical applications, and believe it or not, they're pretty easy to use, as we'll explore in this section.

scp and rcp

Mac OS X includes both *scp* (secure copy) and *rcp* (remote copy) programs for copying files between two computers. In general, you must have accounts on both computers to use these commands. The syntax of *scp* and *rcp* are similar to *cp*, but they also let you add the remote hostname to the start of a file or directory pathname. The syntax of each argument is:

    hostname:pathname

hostname is needed only for remote files. You can copy from a remote computer to the local computer, from the local computer to a remote computer, or between two remote computers.

The *scp* program is much more secure than *rcp*, so I suggest using *scp* to transfer private files over insecure networks such as the Internet. For privacy, *scp* encrypts the file and your passphrase during the transfer of the data.

For example, let's copy the files *report.may* and *report.june* from your home directory on the computer named *w2.intuitive.com* and put the copies into your working directory (.) on the machine you're presently logged into. If you haven't set up an SSH agent that lets you use *scp* without typing your passphrase, *scp* asks you:

    $ scp w2.intuitive.com:report.may w2.intuitive.com:report.june .
    Enter passphrase for RSA key 'taylor@mac':

To use wildcards in the remote filenames, put quotation marks (`"`*name*`"`) around each remote name.[*] You can use absolute or relative pathnames; if you use relative pathnames, they start from your home directory on the remote system. For example, to copy all files from your *food/lunch* subdirectory on your *w2* account into your working directory (.) on the local account, enter:

    $ scp "w2.intuitive.com:food/lunch/*" .

Unlike *cp*, the Mac OS X versions of *scp* and *rcp* don't have an *-i* safety option. If the files you're copying already exist on the destination system (in the previous example, that's your local machine), those files are overwritten.

---

[*] Quotes tell the local shell not to interpret special characters, such as wildcards, in the filename. The wildcards are passed, unquoted, to the remote shell, which interprets them *there*.

To be safe, always use *ls* to check what's in the destination directory before you copy files.

Two useful command options for use with *scp* are *-p*, which has the creation and modification dates of the file preserved in the copy, and *-r*, which lets you recursively opy folders and their contents to the remote system. For example, to copy everything in my *Pictures* directory to the *w2* server:

```
$ scp -r ~/Pictures w2.intuitive.com:.
$
```

If your system has *rcp*, your system administrator may not want you to use it for system security reasons. Another program, *ftp*, is more flexible and secure than *rcp* (but much less secure than *scp*).

FTP

The File Transfer Protocol, or FTP, is a standard way to transfer files between two computers. Many users of earlier Mac OS versions are familiar with Fetch (*www.fetchsoftworks.com*), a shareware graphical FTP client that runs on all versions of Mac OS. There are also a number of graphical FTP programs available from the Apple web site (go to "Mac OS X Software" from the Apple menu, and then click on Internet Utilities in the web page that opens). While Fetch offers an easy-to-use interface, it also comes with a price tag, which begs the question: why spend your hard-earned cash on Fetch when you get FTP services for free with Unix?

The Unix *ftp* program does FTP transfers from the command line. But since it's fast, easy, and portable, I'll cover the standard *ftp* program here.

To start FTP, identify yourself to the remote computer by giving the username and password for your account on that remote system.

 Sending your username and password over a public network with *ftp* means that snoopers might see them—and then use them to log into your account on that system. Instead, you should use *sftp*, because it uses SSH for an encrypted, secure FTP connection.

A special kind of FTP, *anonymous FTP*, happens if you log into the remote server with the username *anonymous*. The password is your email address, such as *taylor@intuitive.com*. (The password isn't usually required; it's a courtesy to the remote server.) Anonymous FTP lets anyone log into a remote system and download publicly accessible files to their local systems.

Here's how that might look:

```
$ ftp ftp.apple.com
Trying 17.254.16.10...
Connected to ftp.apple.com.
220 ProFTPD 1.2.9 Server (Apple Anonymous FTP Server) [ftp01.apple.com]
Name (ftp.apple.com:taylor): anonymous
331 Anonymous login ok, send your complete email address as your password.
Password:taylor@intuitive.com
230 Anonymous access granted, restrictions apply.
Remote system type is UNIX.
Using binary mode to transfer files.
ftp> dir
229 Entering Extended Passive Mode (|||49378|)
150 Opening ASCII mode data connection for file list
drwxrwxrwx    3 ftpprod  ftpprod       102 May  7  2003 Apple_Support_Area
drwxrwxr-x   20 ftpprod  ftpprod       680 Aug 28  2003 developer
drwxrwxr-x   37 ftpprod  ftpprod      1258 May 18  2004 emagic
drwxrwxr-x   11 ftpprod  ftpprod       374 Mar  9  2004 filemaker
drwxrwxrwx   10 ftpprod  ftpprod       340 Apr  7  2003 research
226 Transfer complete.
ftp> bye
221 Goodbye.
$
```

While my email address is shown here as the password, in practice, *ftp* doesn't show you what you're typing in response to the password prompt, so you need to guess that you're entering the information properly. Once connected, the *dir* command lists files on the remote system. You can also type *help* at the ftp> prompt to get a summary of all the commands available. When you're ready to quit, type *bye*.

Command-line ftp

To start the standard Unix *ftp* program, provide the remote computer's hostname:

```
ftp hostname
```

ftp prompts for your username and password on the remote computer. This is something like a remote login (see "Remote Logins," earlier in this chapter), but *ftp* doesn't start your usual shell. Instead, *ftp* has its own prompt and uses a special set of commands for transferring files. Table 8-1 lists the most important *ftp* commands.

Table 8-1. Some ftp commands

Command	Description
put *filename*	Copies the file *filename* from your local computer to the remote computer. If you give a second argument, the remote copy will have that name.
mput *filenames*	Copies the named files (you can use wildcards) from the local computer to the remote computer.
get *filename*	Copies the file *filename* from the remote computer to your local computer. If you give a second argument, the local copy will have that name.
mget *filenames*	Copies the named files (you can use wildcards) from the remote computer to the local computer.
prompt	A "toggle" command that turns prompting on or off during transfers with the *mget* and *mput* commands. By default, *mget* and *mput* will prompt you with mget *filename*? or mput *filename*? before transferring each file; you answer y or n each time. Typing *prompt* once, from an ftp> prompt, stops the prompting; all files will be transferred without question until the end of the *ftp* session. Or, if prompting is off, typing *prompt* at an ftp> prompt resumes prompting.
hash	Displays progress marks on file uploads and downloads so you can gauge progress. Particularly helpful with large transfers.
cd *pathname*	Changes the working directory on the remote machine to *pathname* (*ftp* typically starts at your home directory on the remote machine).
lcd *pathname*	Changes *ftp*'s working directory on the local machine to *pathname*. (*ftp*'s first local working directory is the same working directory from which you started the program.) Note that *ftp*'s *lcd* command changes only *ftp*'s working directory. After you quit *ftp*, your shell's working directory will not have changed.
dir	Lists the remote directory (like *ls -l*).
binary	Tells *ftp* to copy the file(s) that follow it without translation. This preserves pictures, sound, or other data.
ascii	Transfers plain-text files, translating data if needed. For instance, during transfers between a Microsoft Windows system (which adds Control-M to the end of each line of text) and a Unix system (which doesn't), an *ascii*-mode transfer removes or adds those characters as needed.
passive	Toggles the setting of passive mode. This may help *ftp* to run correctly if you are behind a firewall. If you put the command export FTPMODE=passive in your *.profile* file, all your FTP sessions will use passive mode.
quit or bye	Ends the *ftp* session and takes you back to a shell prompt.
!*cmd*	Gives the specified command to a shell, displays its output, then returns to the *ftp* program.

Here's an example. Kiana moves into the local directory she wants to use as a starting point (a good idea whether you're uploading or downloading). She then lists the files in her current directory to see what's there, and then uses *ftp* to connect to an FTP server, located at *rhino.zoo.edu*. After using her username and password to log on, Kiana changes directories to the *work* subdirectory, and she then gets the *todo* file and downloads that to her local machine. After receiving the "Transfer complete" message, Kiana uses the *!ls* command to make sure that the file she transferred is on her local machine, and with the knowledge that the file is there, she quits the FTP session.

```
$ cd uploads
$ ls
afile    ch2    somefile
$ ftp rhino.zoo.edu
Connected to rhino.zoo.edu.
Name (rhino:kiana): ktaylor
Password:
ftp> cd work
ftp> dir
total 3
-rw-r--r--  1 csmith   mgmt     47 Feb  5  2001 for.ed
-rw-r--r--  1 csmith   mgmt    264 Oct 11 12:18 message
-rw-r--r--  1 csmith   mgmt    724 Nov 20 14:53 todo
ftp> get todo
local: todo remote: todo
227 Entering Passive Mode (17,254,16,11,224,18).
150 Opening BINARY mode data connection for todo (724 bytes)
226 Transfer complete.
724 bytes received in 00:00 (94.06 KB/s)
ftp> !ls
afile    ch2    somefile    todo
ftp> quit
$ ls
afile    ch2    somefile    todo
```

We've explored the most basic *ftp* commands here. Entering **help** at an ftp> prompt gives a list of all commands; entering **help** followed by an *ftp* command name gives a one-line summary of that command.

SFTP: FTP to secure sites

If you can only use *ssh* to connect to a remote site, chances are it won't support regular FTP transactions either due to higher security. Fortunately, Mac OS X also includes a version of *ftp* that's part of the *ssh* package and works similarly to regular FTP. To run the program, type *sftp* at the command line. Here's an example:

```
$ cd downloads
$ sftp taylor@intuitive.com
Connecting to intuitive.com...
The authenticity of host 'intuitive.com (128.121.96.233)' can't be
established.
RSA key fingerprint is d0:db:8b:cb:73:c8:37:e4:9a:71:fc:7a:e2:d6:40:81.
Are you sure you want to continue connecting (yes/no)? yes
Warning: Permanently added 'intuitive.com,128.121.96.233' (RSA) to the list
of known hosts.
taylor@intuitive.com's password:
```

```
sftp> cd mybin
sftp> dir -l
drwxr-xr-x    0 24810    100      1024 Jun 26 20:18 .
drwxr-xr-x    0 24810    100      1536 Sep 16 18:59 ..
-rw-r--r--    0 24810    100       140 Jan 17  2003 .library.account.info
-rwxr-xr-x    0 24810    100      3312 Jan 27  2003 addvirtual
-rw-r--r--    0 24810    100       406 Jan 24  2003 trimmailbox.sh
-rwxr-xr-x    0 24810    100      1841 Jan 24  2003 unpacker
-rwxr-xr-x    0 24810    100       946 Jan 22  2003 webspell
sftp> get webspell
webspell                            100%  946      4.7KB/s   00:00
sftp> quit
$ ls -l webspell
-rwxr-xr-x  1 taylor  taylor  946 25 Sep 11:28 webspell
```

The *sftp* program also has a very useful option, which you can specify when you're copying files: *-P* causes the program to preserve date and time information:

```
sftp> get -P webspell
```

Additional helpful commands include *lcd*, *lls*, and *lmkdir* to change your location in the local filesystem, list the files in the current local working directory, and make a new local directory. You can also use the *!* escape to access any Unix command from within *sftp*. Like the *ftp* program, *sftp* also has built-in help, which you can access by typing **help** at the prompt.

FTP with a web browser

If you need a file from a remote site, and you don't need all the control that you get with the *ftp* program, you can use a web browser to download files using anonymous FTP. To do that, enter a URL (location) with this syntax:

```
ftp://hostname/pathname
```

For instance, *ftp://somecorp.za/pub/reports/2001.pdf* downloads the file *2001.pdf* from the directory */pub/reports* on the host *somecorp.za*. In most cases, you can start with just the first part of the URL—such as *ftp:// somecorp.za*—and browse your way through the FTP directory tree to find what you want. If your web browser doesn't prompt you to save a file, use its Save menu command.

If you are using the Safari browser, it will open *ftp:* directories by mounting them in the Finder identically to if you specified the ftp URL in the Finder itself, as explained later in this chapter.

FTP with curl

A faster way to download a file is with the *curl* (copy from URL) command. For example, to save a copy of the report in the current directory, enter:

```
$ curl -O ftp://somecorp.za/pub/reports/2001.pdf
```

Without the -O option (that's a capital letter O, not a zero), *curl* dumps the file to standard output (your screen). If you want to read a text file from an Internet server, you can combine *curl* and *less*:

```
$ curl ftp://ftp.oreilly.com/pub/README.ftp | less
```

You can also use *curl* with web pages, but this brings the page up in HTML source view:

```
$ curl http://www.oreilly.com | less
```

One strategy you could use, though it isn't necessarily optimal, is to save HTML pages locally, then open them in Safari:

```
$ curl http://www.oreilly.com > oreilly.home.page.html
$ open oreilly.home.page.html
```

It turns out that there are better ways to work with HTML pages on the command line, as you'll see in Chapter 10.

FTP from the Finder

You can also mount remote FTP directories using the Finder, and then access them with standard Unix commands in the Terminal. In the Finder choose Go → Connect to Server... then type in *ftp://* followed by the name of the server that you want to access (such as *ftp.oreilly.com*). Figure 8-5 shows how this appears in Tiger's Finder.

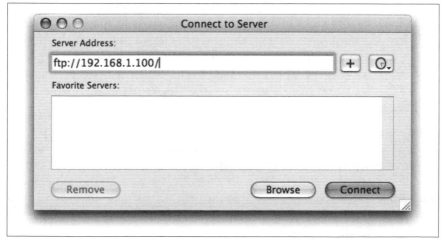

Figure 8-5. Connecting to an FTP server in the Finder

If a password is required, another window pops up, asking you to authenticate with a valid username and password. Enter those correctly and the new FTP disk appears on your Desktop, and is accessible in the /Volumes directory, as shown here:

```
$ ls -l /Volumes/
total 9
dr-xr-xr-x    1 taylor  unknown    512 Jan 13 20:10 192.168.1.100
drwxrwxr-t   39 root    admin     1326 Jan 11 20:40 Hello
drwxr-xr-x    2 taylor  admin       68 Jan 13 19:18 idisk
lrwxr-xr-x    1 root    admin        1 Jan 13 16:23 shuttle -> /
```

When you're done with the FTP server, you can use the *umount* command to disconnect:

```
$ umount /Volumes/192.168.1.100
```

It's considerably easier than using the *ftp* program!

Other FTP solutions

One of the pleasures of working with Unix within the Mac OS X environment is that there are a wealth of great Aqua applications. In the world of FTP-based file transfer, the choices are all uniformly excellent, starting with Fetch, NetFinder, Transmit, Cyberduck, Rbrowser, and Anarchie, and encompassing many other possibilities. Either open the Apple menu and select Mac OS X Software, or try VersionTracker (*www.versiontracker.com*), Mac OS X Apps (*www.macosxapps.com*), MacUpdate (*www.macupdate.com*), or the shareware archive site, Download.com (*www.download.com*).

Transferring Files with Your iDisk

If you have an account with Apple's popular .Mac system, you'll be interested to learn that you can use Terminal commands to mount your iDisk and then standard Unix commands to copy files to and from the remote device. You can't use *ftp* or *sftp*, because neither of those file transfer protocols are available. Instead, iDisk is based on a different networked filesystem called WebDAV (which stands for the clunky name Web Distributed Authoring and Versioning).

The first step is to connect your iDisk to your Macintosh, which you can do by using the *mount_webdav* command, specifying both your account on the remote system and the desired mount point. Unlike the iDisk utility, you'll need to create a destination directory before you run the command: I use *~/iDisk* on my system. My account on .Mac is *dave.taylor*, so here's how my invocation looks:

```
$ mkdir ~/iDisk
$ mount_webdav idisk.mac.com/dave.taylor/ ~/iDisk
```

Rather surprisingly, the command-line program immediately pops up an account and password prompt window, as shown in Figure 8-6.

WebDAV File System Authentication

Enter your user name and password to access the
server at the URL "http://idisk.mac.com/
dave.taylor1/" in the realm "dave.taylor1@mac.com."

Your name and password will be sent securely.

Name

Password

☐ Remember this password in my keychain

Cancel   OK

Figure 8-6. Using WebDAV commands, you can mount your .Mac disk from the command line, but you will be prompted for the correct credentials beforehand

Enter your .Mac account information, and the disk is mounted:

```
$ ls -l ~/iDisk
total 57
-rwxrwxrwx  1 unknown  unknown  10532  9 Jun  2004 About your iDisk
drwxrwxrwx  1 unknown  unknown   2048 14 Sep 10:34 Backup/
drwxrwxrwx  1 unknown  unknown   2048 10 Jul  2000 Documents/
drwxrwxrwx  1 unknown  unknown   2048 14 May  2003 Library/
drwxrwxrwx  1 unknown  unknown   2048  4 Jan  2000 Movies/
drwxrwxrwx  1 unknown  unknown   2048  8 Jan  2001 Music/
drwxrwxrwx  1 unknown  unknown   2048  4 Jan  2000 Pictures/
drwxrwxrwx  1 unknown  unknown   2048  4 Jan  2000 Public/
drwxrwxrwx  1 unknown  unknown   2048 23 Oct  2003 Sites/
drwxrwxrwx  1 unknown  unknown   2048 20 Nov  2003 Software/
```

To copy files to or from the network-based iDisk, simply use *cp*. I can easily upload a backup copy of a PDF document I've been writing:

```
$ cp Business-Blogging.pdf iDisk/Documents
$ ls -l iDisk/Documents
total 1353
-rwxrwxrwx  1 unknown  unknown  692661 13 Jan 19:26 Business-Blogging.pdf*
```

When you're done working with your iDisk, simply *umount* it:

```
$ umount ~/iDisk
```

Working with a remote disk couldn't be easier!

Easy Shortcuts with Connect to Server

The Terminal application has a very helpful feature that can make connecting to remote systems via *telnet*, *ssh*, *ftp*, or *sftp* a breeze, once it's set up. Connect to Server is available in the File menu and is shown in Figure 8-7.

Figure 8-7. Connect to Server offers simple shortcuts

To add a service, click on the + icon on the left side of the window. More commonly, you'll add servers, which you can do by clicking on the + icon on the right side of the window. It produces a window that asks for the hostname or host IP address, which is easily entered, as shown in Figure 8-8.

Once added in one area, the new server is available for all services, so to connect to Apple's anonymous FTP archive site, choose *ftp*, then the new server name, and then enter *ftp* into the User box, as shown in Figure 8-9.

Finally, the connection to Apple's server is a breeze: specify the server, specify the user, and click Connect. The results are shown in Figure 8-10.

Figure 8-8. Adding a new server to Connect to Server

Figure 8-9. apple.com

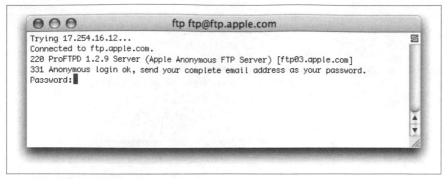

Figure 8-10. Instant connection to Apple's ftp server

Practice

You can practice your *ftp* skills by connecting to the public FTP archive *ftp. apple.com*. Log in as *ftp* with your email address as the password, then look around. Try downloading a research paper or document. If you have an account on a remote system, try using *rcp* and *scp* to copy files back and forth.

## CHAPTER 9

Of Windows and X11

Mac OS X comes with great applications, and a trip to the Apple Store can bag you quite a few more, but there's a flood of applications available to you solely because of Mac OS X's Unix core. Many of these are applications that have been around for a long time, and many are flowing in from other members of the Unix family, including Linux and FreeBSD.

What's different about these applications is that they're not commercial apps like Microsoft Office or Adobe Photoshop, they're not shareware like Graphic Converter and Fetch, and they're not free, public domain applications either. Most of the programs now available to the Mac community from Unix are part of the open source movement. These applications are free to download—including source code, if you want it—but there are constraints on what you can do with the programs, and if you're a programmer and make any modifications to the source, you have an obligation to share those changes with the rest of the open source community. It's a very different distribution model for software, but don't let the lack of a price tag fool you: open source applications are often just as good (and sometimes better) than their commercial equivalents, and having distributed teams of programmers building the apps means that if you do find a bug and report it, the fix often shows up sometime the same day—something that Apple and Microsoft certainly can't match.

Much of this open source software comes from university research, too, and this entire chapter talks about one of these wonderful open source applications, the X Window System, Version 11. X11, as it's called, is a terrific example: it's a graphical interface for Unix that's been around a long, long, time. Although Mac OS X's shiny interface is fantastic, there are many powerful Unix programs that require X11. Fortunately, Apple created an X11 package that runs on Mac OS X Tiger, and once installed, it allows you to run any X11-based Unix application on your Mac.

One warning before we start, however. For typical Mac applications—freeware, shareware, or commercial—they're a breeze to install, thanks to Mac OS X's Installer. However, Unix applications don't have the same easy interface, which means that different programs have different installation methods (sometimes requiring you to type in a sequence of commands in the Terminal, for example). To address this problem, a team of dedicated programmers have created a powerful software distribution and installation system called Fink, which we'll examine in Chapter 10. There's another alternative, too, called DarwinPorts. Both are explored in great detail in the book *Mac OS X Tiger for Unix Geeks* (O'Reilly); pick this up if you'd like to learn more.

X11

The X Window System (commonly called X11), is the standard graphical user interface for Unix systems. Built upon a Unix core, Mac OS X is a significant exception to this rule because its default graphical interface is Aqua, and it's not directly X11 compatible. On Mac OS X, a combination of components called the Quartz Compositor (sometimes just referred to as Quartz), OpenGL, and the CoreGraphics library are responsible for drawing what appears on your screen.

In an X11-based system, an application called an *X server* creates what you see on the screen. The programs that run under X11, such as office applications, web browsers, and terminal windows, are known as *X clients*. X servers and clients talk to each other using standard Unix networking protocols: if an X11 word processor needs to pop up a dialog asking whether you want to save a document, it makes a network connection to the X server and asks it to draw that window. Because X11 is networked in this way, you can run an X client on a Unix system in another office or across the planet, and have it display on your computer's X server.

X servers are typically full-screen applications, which means they completely take over your display. Figure 9-1 shows a full-screen X server running on a Linux computer. Three applications are running: an xterm (which is similar to Mac OS X's Terminal); a meter that shows how busy the Linux computer's CPU is; and a similar meter that's running on a Solaris system nearly 100 miles away, measuring the system load on that box. In addition, a menu is visible. This belongs to the *window manager*, an X11 program that takes care of putting frames and window controls (such as close, resize, and zoom) around application windows. The window manager provides the overall look and feel, and also lets you launch applications and log out of

X11. X11 users have many window managers to choose from; the one shown in Figure 9-1 is *icewm*.

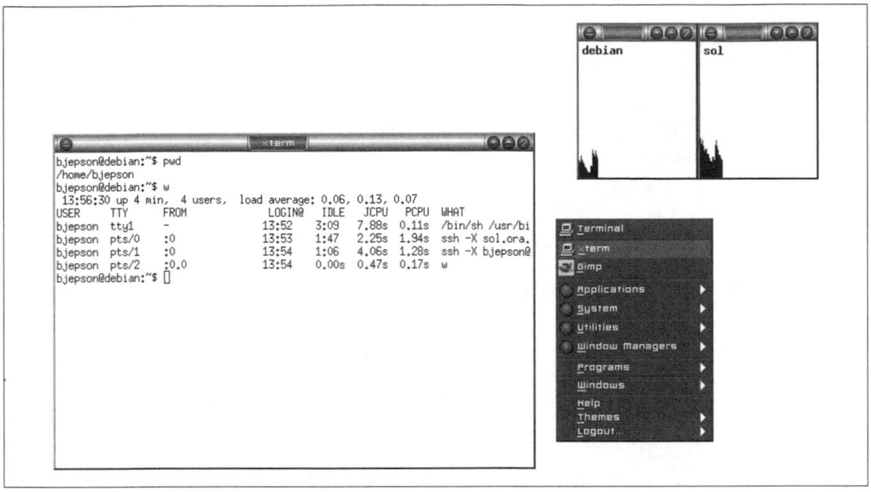

Figure 9-1. An X server running on Linux

Because X11 behaves very differently from Quartz, Apple's solution was to ship a *rootless* X server, which is an X server that won't take over your entire screen. Apple's X11 implementation, which includes the X server, many common X clients, and a software development kit for writing X11 applications, is derived from an implementation of X11, called XFree86 (*www.xfree86.org*). This is the X11 release used on Linux, FreeBSD, NetBSD, OpenBSD, and many other Unix operating systems.

Apple also created an X11 window manager, *quartz-wm*, which draws X11 windows that look and behave much like Quartz windows. As you can see, X11's xterm and Mac OS X's Terminal (shown in Figure 9-2) look remarkably similar.

Installing X11

Apple's X11 is included on Mac OS X Tiger's installation DVD, but it is not installed by default. To locate X11's installer:

1. Insert Mac OS X Tiger's installation DVD into your Mac.

2. Use Spotlight to search for a file named *X11User.pkg*. It is probably in */Volumes/Mac OS X Install DVD/System/Installation/Packages*.

3. Once located, click this package to start the installation process.

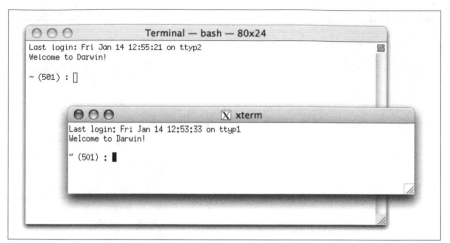

Figure 9-2. Examining an xterm and Mac OS X Terminal side by side

 If you are using an earlier version of Mac OS X, or if you have trouble finding this file, you can go to Apple's X11 page (*www.apple.com/macosx/x11*) for the latest information or to download the X11 package for your system. Please note that X11's download is over 50 MB.

When the installer is finished, you'll have an application called *X11* in your */Applications/Utilities* folder.

Using X11

Once installed, you can launch X11 by double-clicking its icon, located in */Applications/Utilities*. After a few seconds, an xterm window appears. You can start a new xterm by selecting the Terminal item from its Applications menu (or using ⌘-N). Don't confuse this with Mac OS X's Terminal application. Under X11, the program you use to type in Unix commands is also a terminal, except it's an X11-based terminal window, thus the name *xterm*. When you select the Applications menu, you'll see a list of shortcuts to other X11-based applications. By default, there are options for:

- Terminal, which starts a new xterm
- xman, which lets you browse Unix manpages
- xlogo, which pops up a window, displaying the X logo

Figure 9-3 shows X11 running along with these three applications.

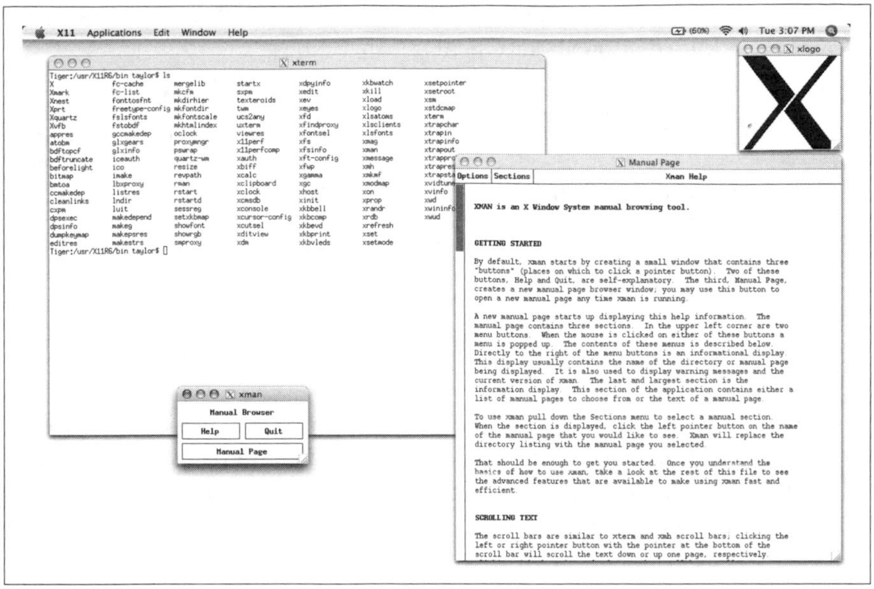

Figure 9-3. Running some X11 clients

X11 includes many other applications. To see a list, examine the X11 application directory with the following command:

```
$ ls /usr/X11R6/bin
```

If you're going to be working with X11 applications often, you'll want to add */usr/X11R6/bin* to your PATH by editing your *.profile* file (if you're using *bash*), or your *.login* file (if you're using *tcsh*). For *bash* users, add this line:

```
PATH=${PATH}:/usr/X11R6/bin ; export PATH
```

tcsh users should add this line:

```
setenv PATH ${PATH}:/usr/X11R6/bin
```

The next time you launch a Terminal or xterm window, you'll be able to type in all the X11 application names at the command line without specifying where they're located.

Here are a few of the most interesting utilities included with Mac OS X:

bitmap
> An X11 bitmap (*.xbm*) editor.

glxgears
> An OpenGL 3D graphics demonstration. OpenGL applications running under Apple's X11 implementation have the benefit of full 3D hardware acceleration.

glxinfo
> Displays information about OpenGL capabilities.

oclock
> An X11-based clock application.

xcalc
> A calculator program that runs under X11.

xeyes
> A pair of eyeballs that follows the mouse cursor around the screen.

xhost
> Gives another computer permission to open windows on your display.

xkill
> Changes your cursor to the "cursor of doom." Any X11 window you click in will be shut down. If you change your mind and don't want to kill an app, press Control-C. This won't kill any Aqua applications; it works only on X11 applications.

xload
> Displays the CPU load.

xwud
> Image display program for X11.

None of these X11 applications included with Mac OS X's X11 package are very interesting, but bear with me, there are a wealth of great X applications available online.

Also, there are some significant differences between X11 and the Mac OS X interface that you need to watch out for. Although Apple's X11 does a great job of minimizing these differences, there are still some quirks that may throw you off:

Mouse focus
> Mac OS X's Aqua interface doesn't care where your mouse is located, as long as you have a given application in the front, that's what sees your keystrokes. X11 doesn't work that way, however, and you'll find that it uses something called *mouse focus* to decide where your typing should be sent. Even having your mouse on the scrollbar or just slightly off the edge of the application window leaves you in limbo. Don't be surprised if this happens, just move your cursor into the middle of the application window and you'll be fine.

Cutting and pasting
> If you press ⌘-C (copy) while you've selected something in an X11 window, you can paste it into another Mac OS X application. But that's where the similarity ends: to paste something into an X11 window, you

can't use ⌘-V. Instead, use Option-click. If you have a three-button mouse, press the middle button to paste into an X11 window.

X11 application menus

The menu at the top of the screen always belongs to X11 itself. Individual X11 applications may have their own menu near the top of their main window. Figure 9-4 shows two different types of X11 application menus: a classic X11 menu from *xmh* (X11 mail reader) and a more modern X11 menu from *gataxx* (a game from the GNOME desktop system).

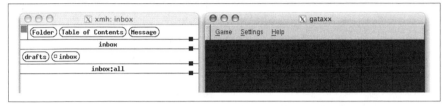

Figure 9-4. Comparing X11 menu styles

Be careful with ⌘-Q

If you press ⌘-Q (quit) while running an X11 application, this shuts down all of X11 and any X applications you're running. Because of this, you'll get a warning if you try to do this when there are X11 clients running. Look for a quit option on the X11 application's own menu, or click the close button on its window.

Scrolling in the xterm

By default, the xterm doesn't have scrollbars. However, like the Terminal, you can use a keystroke to scroll up and down, though, unfortunately, it's not the same keystroke. The Terminal uses Page Up and Page Down (or if you're using a PowerBook or iBook, Shift-Fn–up arrow or Shift-Fn–down arrow), while xterm expects Shift–Page Up and Shift–Page Down.

Launching applications from the xterm

When you type the name of an X11 program in the xterm, it launches, but the xterm window appears to hang because it is waiting for the program to exit. To avoid this problem, you can append the & character after the program name to put it in the background. Another option is to press Control-Z after the program starts, and type **bg** to put the program in the background. (See Chapter 7 for a refresher on how to place Unix processes in the foreground or background.) See Figure 9-5 for an example of launching *xeyes* both ways, specifying different colors for the various elements of the program.

You can also use the *open-x11* command from within an xterm, or from Mac OS X's Terminal to launch an X11 application, as in *open-x11 xterm*.

X11, .bashrc, and .profile

If you've customized your Unix shell by editing *~/.profile*, applications that run under X11, including xterm, won't respect the settings in that file. To correct this problem, put any essential settings in your *~/.bashrc* file, which X11 *does* read. For more information, see the Apple X11 FAQ, which you can find by searching for "X11 FAQ" at *http://developer.apple.com/qa/qa2001/qa1232.html*. There's lots of excellent information about customizing your own X11 installation, particularly having your favorite X11 applications start up automatically when you launch the X11 application.

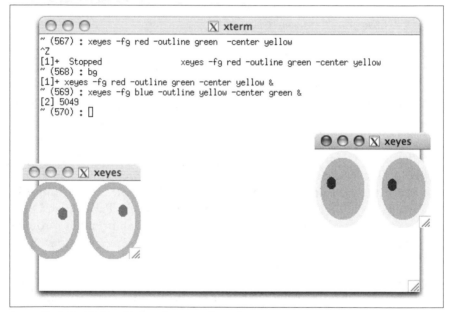

Figure 9-5. Launching X11 applications from the xterm

Customizing X11

One of the big differences between X11 and Mac OS X is that X applications expect that you have a three-button mouse. Meanwhile, Apple still assumes you have a single-button mouse and you don't occasionally mind holding down the Control key to emulate right-mouse-button actions. X11 is built on a three-button mouse, so as an X user, you need to know how to get to all of those buttons. That's one of the key preferences accessible from the X11 → Preferences menu, as shown in Figure 9-6.

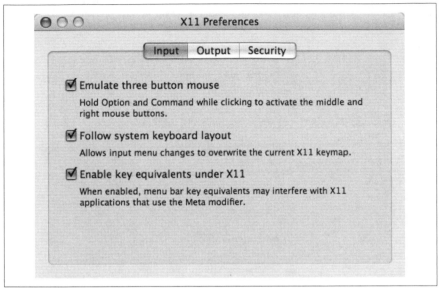

Figure 9-6. Configuring X11 Input preferences

You should leave the other two configuration options set to their default values, unless you're an absolute wizard at working with X and know how to tweak it to match the Apple hardware configuration. Set these wrong and you can throw the proverbial spanner in the works, causing X11 to not work or to display everything unreadably.

The Output tab offers additional preferences, most notably that you can switch out of so-called *rootless* mode, which allows X11 to take over your entire screen. If you do this, make sure that you write down that Option-⌘-A lets you leave full-screen mode, or you might end up having to reboot to figure out how to get back to the familiar world of Aqua and Mac OS X.

Customizing X11's Applications menu

You can customize X11's Applications menu by selecting Applications → Customize Menu. Click the Add button to add an X11 application to the menu. Specify the menu title in the Menu Name column, and use the Command column for the command to execute. You can also add any necessary parameters or switches here. For example, to change the Terminal/xterm menu item so it uses white text on a dark blue background, rather than the boring default of black text on a white background, add the switches *-bg darkblue -fg white*, as shown in Figure 9-7.

> Although the Application menu item for xterm is named Terminal, it's not the same as Mac OS X's Terminal application.

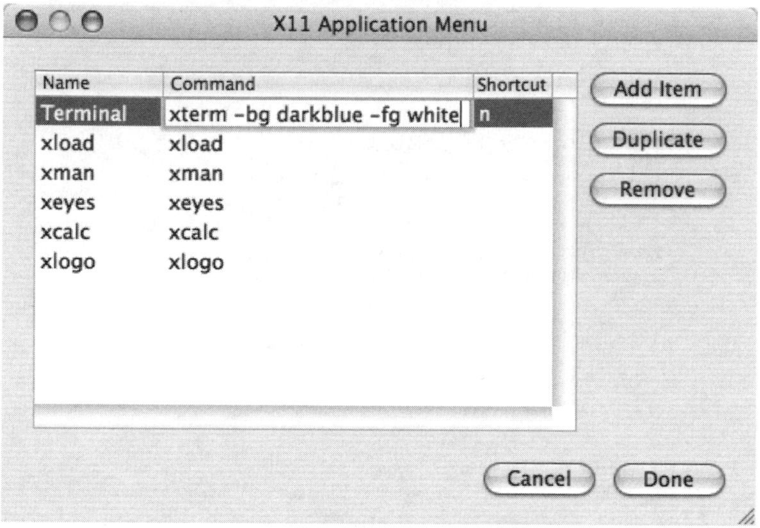
X11 Application Menu
Name
Command
Shortcut
Terminal
xterm -bg darkblue -fg white
n
xload
xload
xman
xman
xeyes
xeyes
xcalc
xcalc
xlogo
xlogo
Add Item
Duplicate
Remove
Cancel
Done

Figure 9-7. Configuring xterm to launch with a different font

You can also specify a shortcut in the shortcut column. The shortcut key must be used with the Command (z) key, so the `n` in the Terminal/xterm entry specifies the ⌘-N keystroke.

X11 and the Internet

Since the X Window System is built on a network model, it should be no surprise that you can launch X applications on your computer and have them actually display on an X11 system somewhere else on the network. What's cool is that you can also do the opposite and have remote computer systems run applications that actually display and work on your own computer.

Remote X11 Access to Your Mac

If you use other Unix systems that run X11 (such as a Red Hat Linux system running XFree86), you can remotely log into your Mac, run X11 applications, and have them display on that Unix system (the applications are still executing on the Mac, but they appear on the Unix system). If you have an always-on broadband connection, you can even do this from afar (perhaps you use a Unix system at school or at work, but want to connect to your Mac at home).

To set up your Mac for remote X11 access:

1. Use the following command to make a backup of the configuration file you'll edit in the next step:

   `$ sudo cp /etc/sshd_config /etc/sshd_config.backup`

2. If anything goes wrong during this process, you can use the following command to restore the original file and restart your Mac:

   `$ sudo cp /etc/sshd_config.backup /etc/sshd_config`

3. Use the following command to edit your remote login configuration file:

   `$ sudo vi /etc/sshd_config`

   Find the line that reads #X11Forwarding no. The leading # tells *sshd* to ignore that line in the file and to use the default value instead. To be absolutely sure that remote X11 access is enabled, regardless of the default, remove the comment character (the #), and change no to yes. So, change this line to read X11Forwarding yes, and save the file.

4. Open System Preferences → Sharing and find the Remote Login setting. If it's disabled, enable it. If it's enabled, stop it and start it again to be sure that the configuration change you made in the previous step takes effect.

Pay attention to the instructions at the bottom of the Sharing preference pane (you need to have Remote Login selected for these to appear). This tells you how to connect to your computer remotely. In Figure 9-8, for example, it specifies the command *ssh taylor@192.168.0.7* for connecting to Brian's computer. This command (with some changes; you'll have a different username and IP address) lets you run X11 applications on your Mac and display them on other Mac OS X systems on the same network as your Mac. It also works with any Unix system on the same network as your Mac that has either the commercial version of SSH from SSH Communications Security (*www.ssh.com*), or OpenSSH (*www.openssh.org*), the open source version included with Mac OS X Tiger.

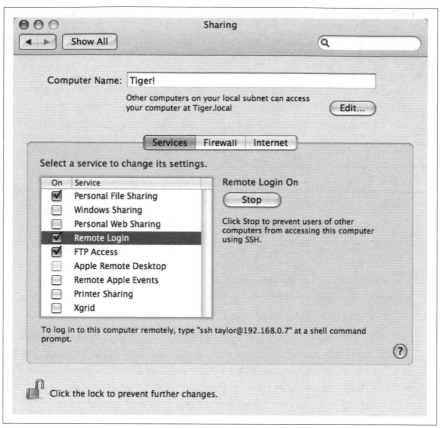

Figure 9-8. Examining the Remote Login settings

To run X11 applications on your Mac and display them on another computer, take the following steps:

1. Log into the remote machine. If it's a Mac, start X11 and bring the xterm window to the front or launch a new xterm from the X11's Applications menu. If it's a Unix or Linux system, start X11 (many systems start it automatically), and open an xterm or other terminal application, such as dtterm.

2. On the remote machine, use *ssh +x hostname* (SSH Communications Security) or *ssh -X hostname* (OpenSSH) to connect to your Macintosh.

3. After you've logged into your Mac over SSH, run the X11 application that you're interested in.

Figure 9-9 shows an example of connecting from a Solaris system and launching the X11 application OpenOffice on the Macintosh (but it appears on the Solaris system instead of the Macintosh).

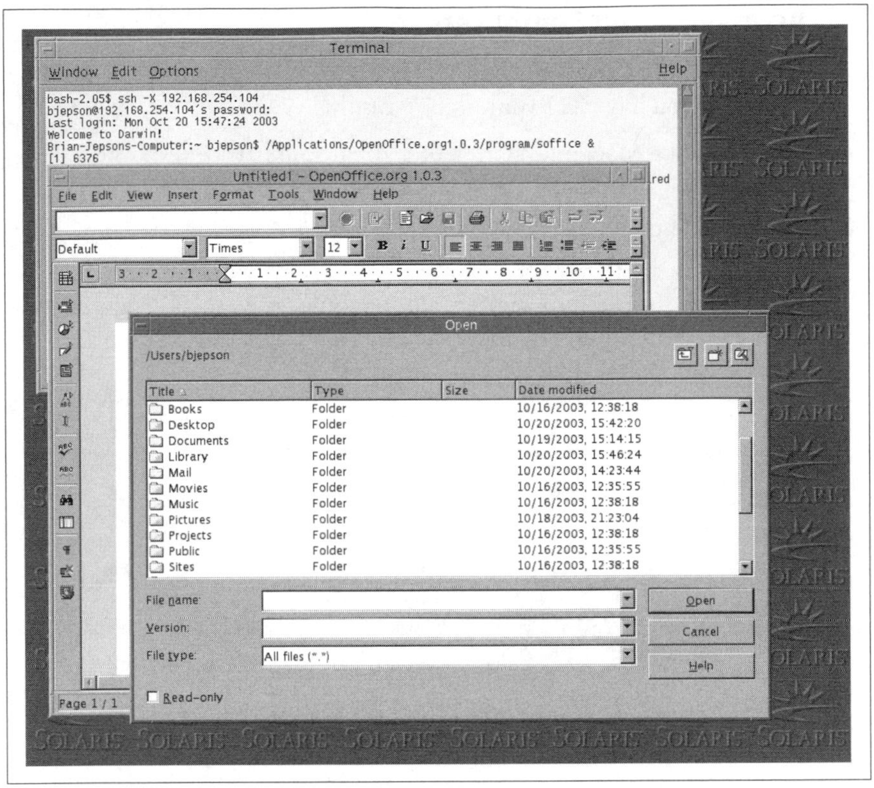

Figure 9-9. OpenOffice.org running on a Mac, but displayed on a Solaris system using remote X11

Opening a Private Network

If your Macintosh is on a private network and you try to connect from the outside, the command shown in the Sharing pane will probably fail, since private network addresses are not reachable from other networks on the Internet. If you use an AirPort Base Station or a non-Apple access point (such as a Linksys router) to connect your home network to a broadband connection, then you are almost certainly on a private network. However, you can use the Port Mapping tab of the AirPort Admin Utility (*/Applications/Utilities*) to open a connection on port 22 (the port that SSH uses) and forward it to your Mac.

If you have a firewall or router, you might well need to map port 22 on that device to your Macintosh, too. Remember that when connecting from the outside world, you need to specify the address of your router, firewall, or, if your AirPort unit is acting as a router, your AirPort Base Station. Even with this configuration, though, remote access may not work, since many Internet Service Providers (ISPs) place restrictions on inbound connections.

X11 Access to Other Computers

You can also run X11 applications on other computers and display them on your Mac once you have X11 running. To do this:

1. Log in to your Mac, and start X11 (*/Applications/Utilities*), and launch an xterm (one should open by default when you launch X11).

2. Issue the command **ssh -X *hostname***, where *hostname* is the name or IP address of the remote computer.

3. After you've logged into the remote machine, run the X11 application that you're interested in. Figure 9-10 shows Netscape running on a Solaris system but displayed on a Macintosh via X11.

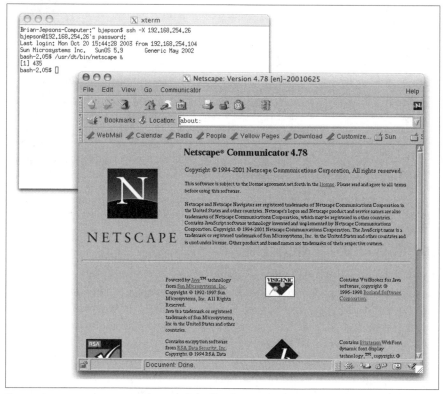

Figure 9-10. Running an application on Solaris, but displaying it on a Mac

What Happened to OpenOffice.org?

Various groups have tried building a suite of applications that would rival the Microsoft Office collection of Word, Excel, and PowerPoint, but few efforts have produced long-term results. The best of the alternatives has been OpenOffice.org (pictured in Figure 9-9), but unfortunately development of a Mac OS X version of this application has ceased. The best alternative today is NeoOffice/J (*http://www.neooffice.org*), a Java-based suite of applications that doesn't rely on X11.

## CHAPTER 10

Open Source Software Via Fink

The Fink Project is a mechanism for obtaining, installing, and keeping up to date a wide variety of open source applications on your Macintosh. The project itself is made up of volunteers who are dedicated to bringing the best open source software to Mac OS X. They fine-tune these open source applications for the Mac OS X environment, and then keep the applications updated so they work with the latest release of Mac OS X.

Many of the programs featured in this chapter are available through Fink, as is a wealth of other applications.

Installing Fink

Since Fink does not come with Mac OS X, you'll first need to download its disk image from *http://fink.sourceforge.net/download*. Once you've downloaded and mounted the disk image by double-clicking it, you're ready to install Fink, with the following steps:

1. Open the mounted disk image in the Finder, and then double-click Fink's Installer package (the *Fink 0.7.7 Installer.pkg* file) inside.

2. Install the application, using all the default configuration options. You will need your administrative password to complete the task.

3. At the end of the installation process, Fink proposes adding a line to your *.profile* file so Fink and its necessary programs are in your shell environment's PATH. You should let it include the line suggested, as shown in Figure 10-1.

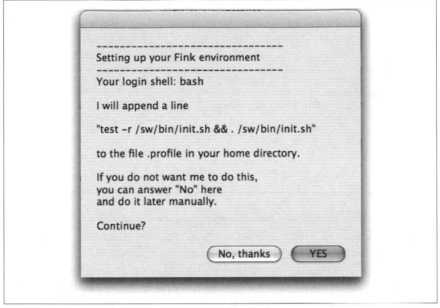

Figure 10-1. When you install Fink, it asks to modify your PATH automatically; just click YES

If you opt not to have Fink add the line to your *.profile* file, you'll need to add it manually. Simply add this command to the end of your *.profile* file (see "Changing Your Prompt" in Chapter 2):

```
. /sw/bin/init.sh
```

You can also find an installer for many open source applications by selecting "Get Mac OS X Software" from the Apple menu. When you select this menu item, your default web browser jumps into action and takes you to Apple's Downloads page for Mac OS X. From there, find and click on the "Unix & Open Source" link, which offers a list of useful Unix applications. The advantage of using Fink is that you can use it to manage thousands of available Unix packages, making sure that you have the latest versions and that different packages cooperate with each other.

Next, close your Terminal window and open a new one. You won't notice anything different, but the addition to your *.profile* file will configure future Terminal sessions for Fink. You can check that everything worked by looking at your PATH. It should look like this:

```
$ echo $PATH
/sw/bin:/sw/sbin:/bin:/sbin:/usr/bin:/usr/sbin:/usr/X11R6/bin
```

After you've installed Fink and started a new Terminal session, you should use the *fink* command to ensure that you have the very latest version of the program. This is done by typing *fink selfupdate*, which immediately prompts you for the administrative password, then asks how you want to update the *fink* package:

```
$ fink selfupdate
/usr/bin/sudo /sw/bin/fink  selfupdate
Password:
fink needs you to choose a SelfUpdateMethod.

(1)  rsync
(2)  cvs
(3)  Stick to point releases

Choose an update method [1]
```

I suggest that you stick with the default *rsync* method, which you can use by just hitting Return. (Then watch as dozens and dozens of lines of output stream past your screen.) Hopefully you won't encounter any errors, but one that might occur, especially if you're an early adopter of Tiger, is that the specified version of the C compiler is out of sync with what *fink* wants. This shows up with the following error message:

```
Setting up fink (0.23.3-1) ...
Checking system... powerpc-apple-darwin8.0.0b2

Since you have gcc 3.3 installed, fink must be bootstrapped or updated using
that compiler.  However, you currently have gcc 4.0.0 selected.  To correct
this problem, run the command:

  sudo gcc_select 3.3

dpkg: error processing fink (--install):
 subprocess post-installation script returned error exit status 255
Errors were encountered while processing:
 fink
### execution of dpkg failed, exit code 1
Failed: can't install package fink-0.23.3-1
```

Scary, but easy to fix:

```
$ sudo gcc_select 3.3
Password:
Default compiler has been set to:
gcc version 3.3 20030304 (Apple Computer, Inc. build 1808)
```

Now just run the *fink selfupdate* command again, and this time you'll see the hundreds of lines of output as it tests, analyzes, and figures out exactly how your system is configured and what packages you have or need to get installed.

Listing Available Packages

To see a list of available packages, use the command *fink list* (this sample shows an abbreviated list):

```
$ fink list | more
Information about 2009 packages read in 2 seconds.
        3dpong          0.4-12      Pong clone
        a52dec          0.7.4-1     ATSC A/52 stream decoder
        a52dec-dev      0.7.4-1     ATSC A/52 stream decoder
        a52dec-shlibs   0.7.4-1     ATSC A/52 stream decoder
        aalib           1.4rc5-22   Ascii art library
        aalib-bin       1.4rc5-22   Ascii art library
        aalib-shlibs    1.4rc5-22   Ascii art library
    i   abiword         1.0.3-12    Open-source word processor
        abook           0.5.2-2     Text-based address-book for use with
mutt
        abs             0.908-12    Opensource spreadsheet
        acct            6.3.5-3     GNU Accounting Utilities package
        acme            2.4.1-5     GNOME multimedia keyboard support
        advancemame     0.79.0-10   SDL-based unofficial MAME emulator
        advancemenu     2.3.0-10    SDL-based frontend for AdvanceMAME
        aesutil         1.0.7-1     CLI tool to encrypt/decrypt with AES
        afni            2.51e-12    Tools for analyzing FMRI data
        agrep           2.04-18     Flexible egrep/fregrep replacement
    [... output deleted for brevity...]
```

An i in the leftmost column indicates that the package is already installed (for example, this shows that *abiword* is installed on my system). The second column is the package name. The third column shows the current version number, and the last column provides a brief description of the package.

Installing Packages

You can use the *apt-get install* command to install a package if you're a long-time Fink user, but the recommended approach is to use the *fink* command itself. Here's a simple demonstration, installing the text-only web browser Lynx:

```
$ fink install lynx
Information about 2009 packages read in 3 seconds.
The following package will be installed or updated:
 lynx
curl -f -L -O http://distfiles.master.finkmirrors.net/lynx2.8.4.tar.bz2
  % Total    % Received % Xferd  Average Speed   Time    Time     Time
Current
                                 Dload  Upload   Total   Spent    Left
Speed
100 1895k  100 1895k    0     0  21992      0  0:01:28  0:01:28 --:--:--
27317
```

```
bzip2 -dc /sw/src/lynx2.8.4.tar.bz2 | /sw/bin/tar -xf -  --no-same-owner --
no-same-permissions
...
hundreds of lines of testing and compilation omitted
...
Writing control file...
Finding prebound objects...
Writing dependencies...
Writing package script postinst...
Writing conffiles list...
dpkg-deb -b root-lynx-2.8.4-24 /sw/fink/dists/stable/main/binary-darwin-
powerpc/web
dpkg-deb: building package `lynx' in `/sw/fink/dists/stable/main/binary-
darwin-powerpc/web/lynx_2.8.4-24_darwin-powerpc.deb'.
dpkg -i /sw/fink/dists/stable/main/binary-darwin-powerpc/web/lynx_2.8.4-24_
darwin-powerpc.deb
(Reading database ... 18227 files and directories currently installed.)
Preparing to replace lynx 2.8.4-22 (using .../lynx_2.8.4-24_darwin-powerpc.
deb) ...
Unpacking replacement lynx ...
Setting up lynx (2.8.4-24) ...
```

When you use *apt-get* to install a package, Fink searches its archive for a prebuilt package for that application. (A prebuilt package is an application that has been bundled up in a manner similar to the installers used by other Mac OS X applications.) Although the *fink list* command lists many packages, not all of them have binary packages. However, if you've installed the Xcode Tools (see Chapter 4), you can use *fink install* to automatically download, compile, and install an application.

The *fink install* command performs a lot of actions on your behalf: downloading source code, locating patches (modifications to the source code that provide Mac OS X compatibility), compiling the source, and installing the compiled programs. This process can take a long time, depending on which packages you have selected. If you select a package that depends on another package, *fink* automatically installs the package you've selected as well as its dependency. If there are many dependencies between packages, you could be in for a long wait, so be prepared.

For this reason, it's best to use *apt-get* to install packages whenever possible. Since *apt-get* uses precompiled packages, you don't have to download all the source and wait for it to compile. Also, *apt-get* warns you if there are any dependencies, and gives you a chance to cancel the installation prior to adding software you're not sure about; for example:

```
$ sudo apt-get install ethereal
Password: ********
Reading Package Lists... Done
Building Dependency Tree... Done
```

```
The following extra packages will be installed:
  libpcap-shlibs pcre-shlibs
The following NEW packages will be installed:
  ethereal libpcap-shlibs pcre-shlibs
0 packages upgraded, 3 newly installed, 0 to remove and 3  not upgraded.
Need to get 8160kB of archives. After unpacking 29.5MB will be used.
Do you want to continue? [Y/n] N
```

If you enter a Y (for yes) or just hit Return, *apt-get* continues with the install;
but if you enter N (for no), *apt-get* quits the installation process.

 At the time of this writing, I had various problems using
both *apt-get* and *fink install* to download and install packages, though they should be fixed by the time you read this
chapter. If one of these commands doesn't work, try the
other one.

Using FinkCommander

While the Fink Project has created a fabulous tool for managing open source
packages within the Mac OS X world, the interface is a bit more complex
than most people prefer. Fortunately, Steve Burr and a group of developers
created a very nice Aqua frontend to Fink, called FinkCommander.

To install FinkCommander, start by going to *http://finkcommander.
sourgeforge.net* and choose the "disk image" link in the Download area of
the page. Choose a download mirror that's close to you, and the program
starts flowing onto your Tiger system.

Once the download is done, a new disk image appears on your Desktop (or
wherever you choose to have downloads saved), and the Finder shows you
its contents (FinkCommander, a license document, a README file, and a
German README file called *LesenSeiMich.html*). Read the license and
README to ensure that there's nothing that might conflict with your com-
pany software policies, and then drag and drop the FinkCommander application into your Applications folder.

Now, finally, open your Applications folder and double-click on the Fink-
Commander application, and you'll see a screen like the one in Figure 10-2.

Notice in the titlebar that there are 2,008 packages available through Fink,
of which only 25 are installed on this system. It's like having free reign in a
computer software store!

The icon bar on the top has nine small icons that allow you easy access to
install a binary package (the default action you'll take), install the source
code so you can read the program and even change it if you'd like, delete

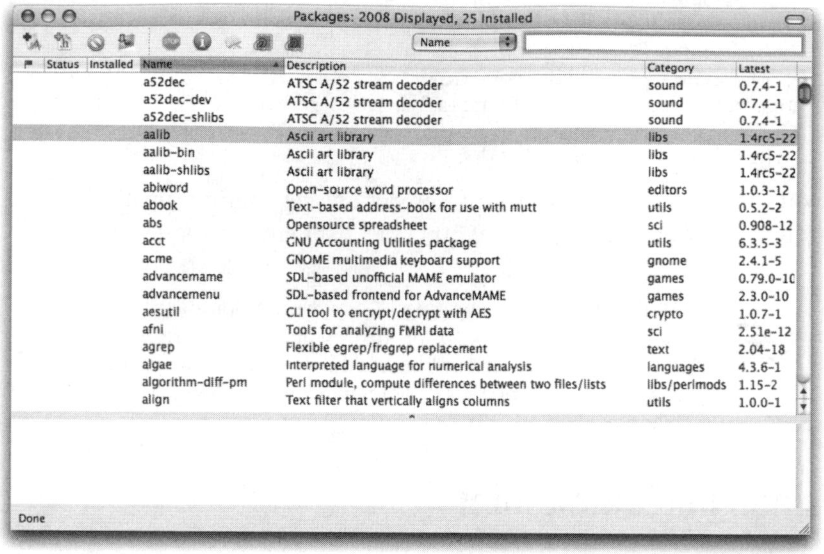

Figure 10-2. FinkCommander makes working with Fink a breeze

specific files in a package (somewhat akin to the uninstall capability on Windows systems), update package descriptions (it generates a *fink updateall* command), terminate the command currently running, plus there's a package inspector, package file browser, and two buttons that let you report that a program is or isn't working on your system.

There are lots of different applications accessible via the Fink system and FinkCommander, including Lynx (a fast text-only web browser), GIMP (a powerful graphics editor and competitor to Adobe Photoshop), and Pine (a simple but powerful text-based email application). Rather than talk exclusively about these applications right now, it's worth highlighting that you can also find lots of games through Fink. At the pop-up menu in the top toolbar of the FinkCommander window, change "Name" to "Category" and type in "games". You'll see a list of 84 different games, including an X11 version of Go, a graphical role playing game called Crossfire, the amazingly sophisticated strategy game FreeCiv (based on the board game, *Civilization*), GNU Backgammon, the SimCity clone LinCity, popular adventure game NetHack, Scrabble, Space Invaders, and much more.

Just for fun, I'll install GNU Backgammon (*gnubg*) using FinkCommander. Clicking on the small blue "i" button (for "Info") in FinkCommander's toolbar pops up information about GNU Backgammon in a small info window, as shown in Figure 10-3.

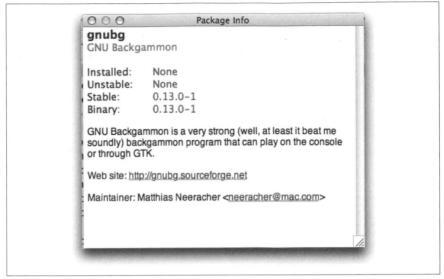

Figure 10-3. FinkCommander displays information about the package you've selected to install if you click the Info button

To install GNU Backgammon, click on the leftmost icon in the toolbar to launch a binary install process. This prompts for the administrative password, then actually runs the *apt-get* utility, showing you each line of output in the lower portion of the FinkCommander window. Sometimes the installation prompts for specific data, in which case FinkCommander stops and asks for your answer, as shown in Figure 10-4.

After an extended period of downloading and building, you'll have a nice new backgammon game on your Macintosh, courtesy of the open software community. Two clicks later, and you can also install *xscrabble* (a version of the Scrabble game) on your system, as shown in Figure 10-5.

Some Picks

This section describes just a few of the applications you can install using Fink. First up is Lynx, a text-based web browser that's great for viewing or downloading web pages quickly. After that, we talk about Pine, an email client and Usenet newsreader. Finally, we discuss the GIMP, a general-purpose graphics manipulation package that can do all sorts of great things with images.

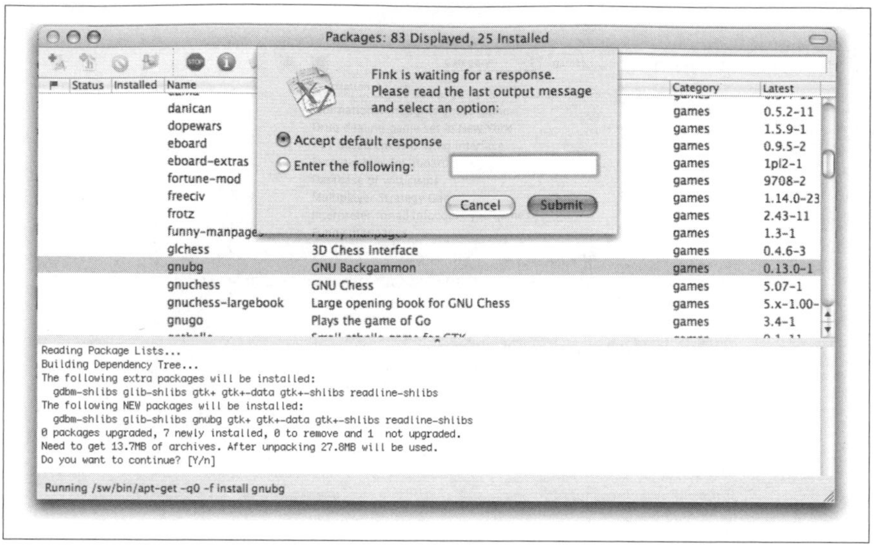

Figure 10-4. Sometimes, it's pretty obvious that FinkCommander is just a graphical layer atop the Fink command

Figure 10-5. XScrabble, a free download via FinkCommander

Browsing the Web with Lynx

There are a number of excellent web browsers available for Mac OS X, including Safari, Firefox, Camino, and OmniWeb. However, attractive, graphically based web browsers can be slow—especially when trying to load flashy, graphics-laden web pages over a slow network.

 To install Lynx, use the command *fink install lynx* (see "Installing Packages," earlier in this chapter).

The Lynx web browser (originally from the University of Kansas and available on many Unix systems) is different because it's a text-based web browser that works within the Terminal application. Because it's text only, Lynx comes with some trade-offs you should know about:

- Lynx indicates where graphics occur in a page layout, but you won't see the graphics, but the bits of text that Lynx uses in their place can clutter the screen.
- Because it doesn't have to download or display those graphics, Lynx is *fast*, which is especially helpful over a dial-up modem or busy network connection.
- Sites with complex multicolumn layouts can be hard to follow with Lynx; a good rule is to page through the screens, looking for the link you want and ignore the rest.
- Finally, remember that in a text-only application, you navigate with the keys on your keyboard, not the mouse. Use Tab or the left and right arrow keys to step from link to link on a page, and use Return/Enter to select a link and jump to another page.

The Lynx command-line syntax is:

```
lynx "location"
```

For example, to visit my Ask Dave Taylor web site, enter:

```
$ lynx "http://www.askdavetaylor.com"
```

Or, you can simply use:

```
$ lynx "www.askdavetaylor.com"
```

Figure 10-6 shows part of the home page.

To move around the Web, use your keyboard's arrow keys, spacebar, and a set of single-letter commands. The third line from the bottom of a Lynx screen gives you a hint of what you might want to do at the moment. In

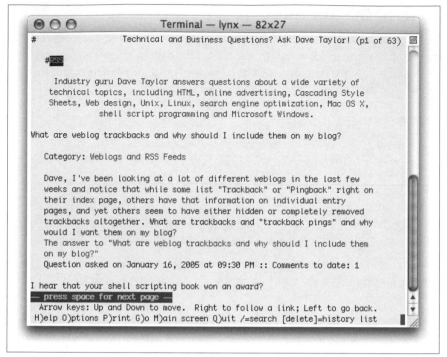

Figure 10-6. Viewing AskDaveTaylor.com in Lynx

Figure 10-6, for instance, "Arrow keys: Up and Down to move. Right to follow a link; Left to go back" means you can follow the link by pressing right arrow. You can hop from link to link by using the Tab key.

The bottom two lines of the screen remind you of common commands, and the help system (which you get by typing h) lists the rest (use the Spacebar to scroll forward one screen, and press b to move back a screen).

When you first view a screen, the link nearest the top is selected and highlighted. To select a later link (farther down the page), press the Down-Arrow key. The Up-Arrow key selects the previous link (farther up the page). Once you've selected a link you want to visit, press the Right-Arrow key to follow that link; the new page appears. Go back to the previous page by pressing the Left-Arrow key (from any selected link; it doesn't matter which one).

Downloading a web page with Lynx

You can use Lynx to download the contents of a web page in plain text, which you can then paste into an email message. Lynx preserves URLs in documents by formatting them as footnotes. To download a web page as text, use:

```
lynx -dump URL
```

For example:

```
$ lynx -dump www.intuitive.com/kana.shtml
Calligraphy
   "Chokkan"

   The calligraphy on the Intuitive Systems Web site was produced by
   Master Japanese Calligrapher [1]Eri Takase, and it means "insight" or
   "intuition":

      The first character means "direct". It is interesting in that it
      originally meant "ten eyes" or clear, transparent, no concealment.

      The second character is constructed of characters meaning "bite the
      heart" and now means "feel" or "sense".

                   Intuition means to "directly sense"

   [2]close this window

References

   1. http://www.takase.com/
   2. javascript:window.close();
```

More interestingly, you can grab the HTML source of a page and then use simple Unix commands to extract certain types of information with the same type of command pipes highlighted in previous chapters.

Want to check the title tag of O'Reilly Media's home page? Try this:

```
$ lynx -source www.oreilly.com | grep -i '<title'
<title>oreilly.com -- Welcome to O'Reilly Media, Inc. -- computer books,
software conferences, online publishing</title>
$
```

To tell you the truth, I use Lynx quite a bit when I'm writing shell scripts and otherwise accessing and using web-based information on the command line. Check out *lynx*'s manpage, because there's quite a bit it can do.

Electronic Mail with Pine

When you install Mac OS X or boot it for the first time, the installer may ask whether you want to sign up for .Mac, Apple's suite of Internet services that includes *electronic mail* (email). If you signed up for .Mac (*www.mac.com*), you probably use Apple's Mail application to send and receive email. If you didn't sign up for .Mac, you may be using an email account provided by your ISP or employer, along with Apple's Mail or some other application such as Mailsmith (*www.barebones.com*) or Thunderbird (*www.mozilla.org/products/thunderbird*).

There are many great graphical mail applications for Mac OS X. However, Terminal-based email programs have some benefits:

- They are not affected by conventional email viruses, although security holes do appear from time to time in nearly every program that interacts with the Internet.

- You can read your email while logged into your Mac from another machine (see "Remote Logins" in Chapter 8).

Pine, from the University of Washington, is a popular program for reading and sending email from a Unix terminal. It works completely from your keyboard, and best of all, you don't need to use a mouse.

Mac OS X does not include Pine by default. To install Pine, use the following command:

```
$ sudo apt-get pine
```

Once installed, you can start Pine by entering its name at a shell prompt. It also accepts options and arguments on its command line; to find out more, enter *pine -h* (help). Figure 10-7 shows the starting display, i.e., the *main menu*.

Configuring Pine

Pine's main menu has a Setup entry for configuring Pine. After you enter S (the "Setup" command), you can choose what kind of setup you want. From the setup screen, you can get to the option configuration area with C (the "Config" command).

The configuration screen has page after page of options. You can look through them with the spacebar (to move forward one page), the – key (back one page), the N key (to move forward to the next entry), and the P key (back to the previous entry). If you know the name of an option you want to change, you can search for it with W (the "Whereis" command).

When you highlight an option, the menu of commands at the bottom of the screen shows you what can do with that particular option. A good choice, while you're exploring, is the ? (help) command, to find out about the option you've highlighted. There are several kinds of options:

- Options with variable values: names of files, hostnames of computers, and so on. For example, the personal-name option sets the name used in

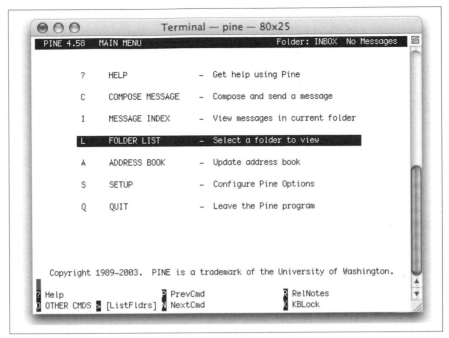

```
    ● ● ●             Terminal — pine — 80x25
    PINE 4.58   MAIN MENU                        Folder: INBOX  No Messages

            ?    HELP               -  Get help using Pine

            C    COMPOSE MESSAGE    -  Compose and send a message

            I    MESSAGE INDEX      -  View messages in current folder

            L    FOLDER LIST        -  Select a folder to view

            A    ADDRESS BOOK       -  Update address book

            S    SETUP              -  Configure Pine Options

            Q    QUIT               -  Leave the Pine program



        Copyright 1989-2003.  PINE is a trademark of the University of Washington.

    ? Help                  PrevCmd                    RelNotes
    O OTHER CMDS  [ListFldrs] NextCmd                  KBLock
```

Figure 10-7. Pine's main menu

the "From: " header field of mail messages you send. The setup entry
looks like this:

```
    personal-name        = <No Value Set: using "Robert L. Stevenson">
```

No Value Set can mean that Pine is using the default from the system-
wide settings, as it is here. If this user wants his email to come from
"Bob Stevenson," he could use the C (Change Val) command to set that
name.

- Options that set preferences for various parts of Pine. For instance, the
  enable-sigdashes option in the Composer Preferences section puts two
  dashes and a space on the line before your default signature. The option
  line looks like this:

```
    [X] enable-sigdashes
```

The X means that this preference is set, or "on." If you want to turn this
option off, use the X (Set/Unset) command to toggle the setting.

- Options for which you can choose one of many possible settings. The
  option appears as a series of lines. For instance, the first few lines of the
  saved-msg-name-rule option look like this:

```
    saved-msg-name-rule     =
            Set    Rule Values
            ---    ----------------------
            (*)    by-from
```

```
( )   by-nick-of-from
( )   by-nick-of-from-then-from
( )   by-fcc-of-from
( )   by-fcc-of-from-then-from
```

The * means that the saved-msg-name-rule option is currently set to by-from. (Messages are saved to a folder named for the person who sent the message.) If you wanted to choose a different setting—for instance, by-fcc-of-from—you'd move the highlight to that line and use the * (Select) command to choose that setting.

These settings are trickier than the others, but the built-in help command (?) explains each choice in detail. Start by highlighting the option name (here, saved-msg-name-rule) and reading its help info. Then look through the settings' names, highlight one you might want, and read its help info to see if it's right for you.

When you exit the Setup screen (with the E command, for Exit), Pine asks you to confirm whether you want to save any changes you made. Answer N if you were just experimenting or aren't sure, and Y to save your changes.

Configuring Pine to send and receive email

Before you can send or receive email with Pine, you must configure it to talk to your email servers. For this, you'll need the following information (if you are not using .Mac, you will need to get this information from your ISP or system administrator):

Your email address
This is supplied by your ISP. If you are using .Mac, your email address is *username@mac.com*.

 Your Mac OS X username must be the same as the username in your email address, since Pine uses your Mac OS X username and your *user-domain* to generate your email address.

Incoming mail server
This is the server where your email messages sit until you're ready to read them. Your ISP may refer to this as a POP or IMAP server. If you are using .Mac, this is *mail.mac.com*.

Incoming mail protocol
Pine supports two protocols for downloading remote email: POP (Post Office Protocol) and IMAP (Internet Message Access Protocol). If you are using .Mac, this will be IMAP.

Outgoing mail server

This is a server that accepts your outgoing email and delivers it to the recipients. Your ISP may refer to this as an SMTP server (SMTP is Simple Mail Transfer Protocol, the network protocol for sending and receiving email). If you are using .Mac, this is *smtp.mac.com.*

 You can configure email clients to gather .Mac's email via POP, but that's beyond the scope of this book. For more information about .Mac's email service and how to configure your Mail client to grab .Mac's email via POP, see *Inside .Mac,* by Chuck Toporek (O'Reilly).

Enter the setup screen by pressing S at Pine's main menu. Then press C to enter the Config screen. To configure your email account, do the following:

1. Look at your email address. Set Pine's *user-domain* to everything after the @ symbol (for example, mac.com).

2. Set the smtp-server to your outgoing mail server (for example, smtp. mac.com).

3. Set your *inbox-path*:

    a. If you are using IMAP, set the inbox-path to {*incoming mail server/* user=*username*}inbox, as in {mail.mac.com/user=dtaylor}inbox.

    b. If you are using POP, set the inbox-path to {*incoming mail server/* pop3/user=*username*}*inbox*, as in {pop3.nowhere.oreilly.com/pop3/ user=dtaylor}inbox.

The exact settings may vary. If you need more help, visit the Usenet newsgroup *comp.mail.pine* and look for the latest posting of the FAQ.

After you've made these changes, press E to exit setup, press Y to commit changes, and then quit and restart Pine.

Reading email with Pine

When you first start Pine, the main menu appears, as shown earlier in Figure 10-7. You may also be prompted for your password, since Pine needs this to connect to your POP or IMAP server.

The highlighted line, which is the default command, gives a list of your email folders.* You can choose the highlighted command by pressing Return, pressing the greater-than sign (>), or typing the letter next to the

---

* Pine also lets you read Usenet newsgroups. The L command takes you to another display where you choose the source of the folders, *then* you see the list of folders from that source.

command. (Here, this is l—a lowercase L. You don't need to type the commands in uppercase.) But because you probably haven't used Pine before, the only interesting folder is the inbox, which is the folder where your new messages wait for you to read them.

Let's go directly to the inbox by pressing I (or by highlighting that line in the menu and pressing Return) to read the new mail. Figure 10-8 has the *message index* for our inbox.

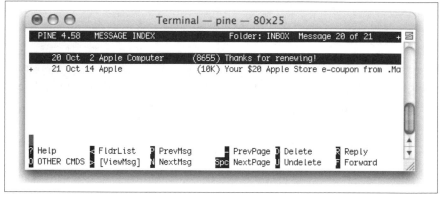

Figure 10-8. Pine's message index

The main part of the window is a list of the messages in the folder, one message per line. If a line starts with N, it's a new message that hasn't been read. (The first message has been sitting in the inbox for some time now.) Next on each line is the *message number*; messages in a folder are numbered 1, 2, and so on. That's followed by the date the message was sent, who sent it, the number of characters in the message (size), and, finally, the message subject.

Let's skip the first message and read number 2. The down-arrow key or the N key moves the highlight bar over that message. As usual, you can get the default action—the one shown in brackets at the bottom of the display (here, [ViewMsg])—by pressing Return or >. The message from Apple appears.

Just as > takes you forward in Pine, the < key generally takes you back to where you came from—in this case, the message index. You can type R to reply to this message, F to forward it (send it on to someone else), D to mark it for deletion, and the Tab key to go to the next message without deleting this one.

When you mark a message for deletion, it stays in the folder message index, marked with a D at the left side of its line, until you quit Pine. Type Q to quit. Pine asks if you really want to quit. If you've marked messages for deletion,

Pine asks if you want to *expunge* ("really delete") them. Answering Y here deletes the message.

Sending email with Pine

If you've already started Pine, you can compose a message from many of its displays by typing C. (Though, as always, not every Pine command is available at every display.) You can also start from the main menu. Or, at a shell prompt, you can go straight into message composition by typing pine *addr1 addr2*, where each *addr* is an email address such as *taylor@intuitive.com*. In that case, after you've sent the mail message, Pine quits and leaves you at another shell prompt.

When you compose a message, Pine puts you in a window called the *composer*. (You'll also go into the composer if you use the Reply or Forward commands while you're reading another mail message.) The composer is a lot like another Unix text editor (Pico), but the first few lines are special because they're the message *header*—the "To:," "Cc:" (carbon copy), "Attchmnt:" (attached file), and "Subject:" lines. Figure 10-9 shows an example, already filled in.

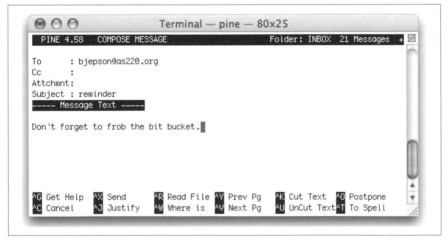

Figure 10-9. Pine's message composer

As you fill in the header, the composer works differently than when you're in the message text (body of the message). The list of commands at the bottom of the window is a bit different in those cases, too. For instance, while you edit the header, you can attach a file to the end of the message with the "Attach" command, which is Control-J. (Pine uses the ^ symbol to indicate a control character.) However, when you edit the body, you can read a file into the place you're currently editing (as opposed to attaching it) with the Control-R "Read File" command. But the main difference between editing the body and the header is the way you enter addresses. If you have more than one address on the same line, separate them with commas (,). Pine rearranges the addresses so there's just one on each line.

Move up and down between the header lines with Control-N and Control-P, or with the up-arrow and down-arrow keys. When you move into the message body (under the "Message Text" line), type any text you want. Paragraphs are usually separated with single blank lines.

> If you put a file in your home directory named *.signature* (the name starts with a dot (.), the composer automatically adds its contents to the end of every message you compose. (Some other Unix email programs work the same way.) It's good Internet etiquette to keep this file short—no more than four or five lines, if possible.

You can use editing commands such as Control-J to justify a paragraph and Control-T to check your spelling. When you're done, Control-X (exit) leaves the composer, asking first if you want to send the message you just wrote. Control-C cancels the message, though you'll be asked if you're sure. If you need to quit but don't want to send or cancel, the Control-O command postpones your message; then, the next time you try to start the composer, Pine asks whether you want to continue the postponed composition.

Editing Graphics with the GIMP

The GIMP (GNU Image Manipulation Program, available at *www.gimp.org*) is a powerful free graphics manipulation program. You can use the the GIMP to manipulate photos and other bitmap images in ways previously possible only with expensive graphics software.

> To install GIMP, use the command *sudo apt-get install gimp* (see "Installing Packages," earlier in this chapter). If you run into problems using *apt-get*, try using *fink install gimp* as a workaround.

To run the GIMP, you'll need to launch X11 and run the command *gimp &* in an xterm window. You can also add the GIMP to the X11 Applications menu (see "Customizing X11" in Chapter 9). The first time you run the GIMP, it walks you through its user installation process (see Figure 10-10).

Figure 10-10. When you install the GIMP, you'll see this message, alerting you to its terms of use

After you've finished setting the GIMP up, several windows appear, as shown in Figure 10-11.

Clockwise from the top, the options are:

Main Window and Toolbar
Use the menus in this window to open a file (File → Open), create a new file (File → New), or quit the GIMP (File → Quit). You can also select the active tool. Click this window to bring it to the front, and hover the mouse over the toolbar to see its name. Click a tool to select it.

Tool Options
Use this window to set configurable options for the current tool.

Brush Selection
> Many tools, such as the paintbrush and eraser, use a certain brush shape. Use this window to select the brush properties.

Layers, Channels, and Paths
> This window lets you work with multilayered documents.

GIMP Tip of the Day
> This window displays some helpful tips to help you use the GIMP.

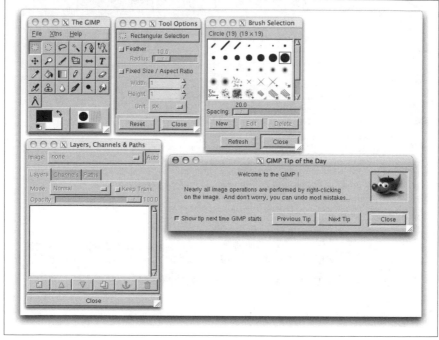

Figure 10-11. The GIMP's default windows

To open an existing file, select File → Open, and choose a file. Command-Click or click the wedge in the upper-left corner of the window to bring up a menu. The options are too numerous to describe completely, but the following list describes some you may find useful. Figure 10-12 shows a JPG photographic image open in the GIMP.

File → Save
> Save the file.

File → Revert
> Abandon all your changes and revert to the saved version.

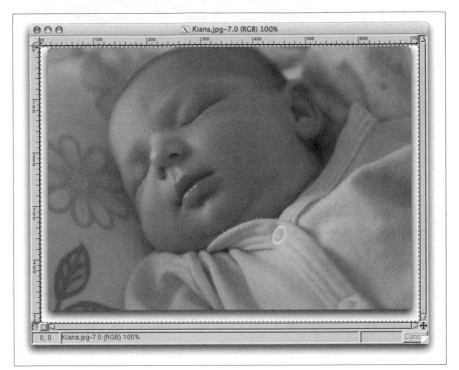

Figure 10-12. Editing a photograph in the GIMP

Edit

Contains the usual suspects: Undo, Redo, Cut, Copy, and Paste. It also includes Paste as New, which creates a new image out of whatever's in the GIMP's clipboard.

Image → Scale Image

Change the size of the image.

Image → Filters

Runs a filter over the image; you'll find filters that sharpen, despeckle, blur, and many more.

Script-Fu

Performs more complicated transformations to the image. You'll want to play around here, but be sure you are working on a backup copy. Figure 10-13 shows the result of the Filters → Artistic → GIMPressionist transformation.

Also notice in Figure 10-13 that the actions menu is shown in the top left of the image, with its many different function options. Among the many, many features included with the GIMP are a set of extensions for generating various types of graphics, including buttons and logos. Switch to the GIMP main window and select Script-Fu from the Xtns menu (see Figure 10-14).

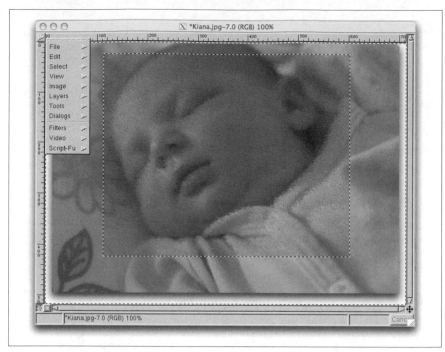

Figure 10-13. A more artistic photograph created with the Filters → Artistic → GIMPressionist filter

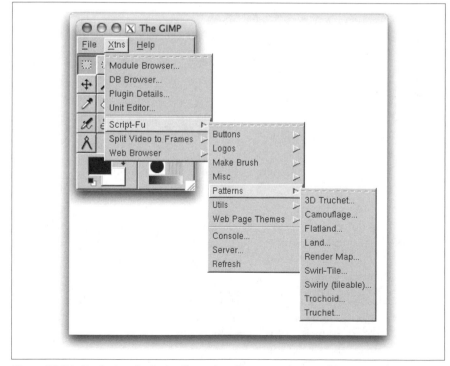

Figure 10-14. Exploring the Script-Fu options for generating graphics

The GIMP is a deep and broad application, and this section of the chapter has barely scratched the surface. You can use the GIMP to resize images, clear up red-eye (in your photos, that is; you're on your own for your own eyes), and perform sophisticated image enhancements. For more information on the GIMP, see the *GIMP Pocket Reference*, by Sven Neumann (O'Reilly).

CHAPTER 11

Where to Go from Here

Now that you're almost to the end of this guide, let's look at some ways to continue learning about the Unix side of Mac OS X. Documentation is an obvious choice, but it isn't always in obvious places. You can also learn how to save time by taking advantage of other shell features—aliases, functions, and scripts—that let you shorten a repetitive job and "let the computer do the dirty work."

We'll close by seeing how you can use Unix commands on non-Unix systems.

Documentation

You might want to know the options to the programs I've introduced and get more information about them and the many other Unix programs. You're now ready to consult your system's documentation and other resources.

The Terminal's Help Menu

An excellent first place to seek further information is the Apple Help system included with the Terminal application. Lots of Mac users automatically ignore the Help menu, mainly because Apple's version of "help" in the early days didn't amount to much. But with Mac OS X Tiger, that's a mistake, because therein lies plenty of useful information. Many of the Terminal's Help topics are specifically about the Terminal application itself, but you'll also find plenty of other interesting topics to read about, including:

- Copying a file
- Finding out which directory you're in
- Learning about Unix commands

- Listing the contents of a directory
- Paths in Unix
- Printing a Terminal session
- Root or administrator privileges
- Setting Unix permissions

Figure 11-1 shows a sample Help topic, this one explaining how you can split a Terminal window to both see what's already been displayed in the Terminal window and what you're working on currently.

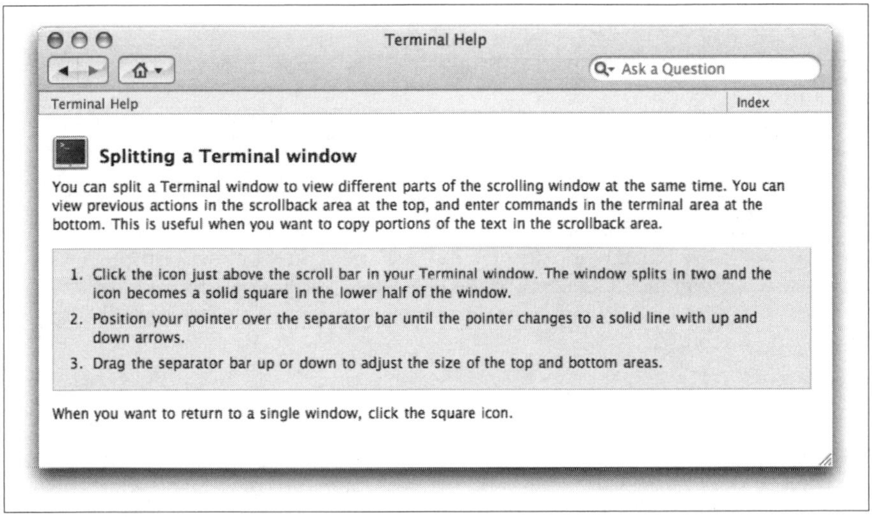

Figure 11-1. Terminal Help topics can be quite informative

If you've diligently read through all the material in this book, almost all of the material in Terminal Help will be redundant, but knowing that you can get a quick reminder of key Unix information without having to leave this book on your desk is still a boon.

The man Command

Different versions of Unix have adapted Unix documentation in different ways. Almost all Unix systems have documentation derived from a manual, originally called the *Unix Programmer's Manual*. The manual has numbered sections; each section is a collection of manual pages, often called *manpages*; each program has its own manpage. Section 1 has manpages for general Unix programs such as *who* and *ls*.

Mac OS X has individual manpages stored on the computer, and you can also read them online (*www.manpage.org*). If you want to know the correct syntax for entering a command or the particular features of a program, enter the command *man*, followed by the name of the command about which you need information.

For example, if you want to find information about the program *vi*, which allows you to edit text files, enter:

```
$ man vi
.
.
.
$
```

The output of *man* is filtered through the *less* pager in Mac OS X, as mentioned in Chapter 4.

> Manpages are displayed using a program that doesn't write the displayed text to Terminal's scroll buffer. This can be quite annoying, because if you need to scroll back, you can't. Fortunately it's an easy fix: just specify `TERM="ansi"` on the command line, or add the line export `TERM="ansi"` to your *~/.bashrc* file, and the manpages remain in the Terminal's scroll buffer.

After you enter the command, the screen fills with text. Press the spacebar or Return to read more, and press q to quit.

Mac OS X also includes a command called *apropos*, or *man -k*, to help you locate a command if you have an idea of what it does but aren't quite sure of its correct name. Enter *apropos* followed by a descriptive word, and you'll get a list of commands that might help. To get this working, however, you need to first build the apropos database. This is done when Mac OS X runs its weekly maintenance job, which you can also run manually with the following command:

```
$ sudo periodic weekly
Password:
$
```

Don't be surprised if it takes 10 minutes or more for the *periodic* command to complete; it's doing quite a lot of work.

> If you don't want to wait for periodic to finish up, don't forget that you can append an & and have the job run in the background (as discussed in Chapter 7).

Once you've rebuilt your apropos database, you can use *apropos* (or its easier to remember cousin, *man -k*) to find all commands related to AppleTalk, for example, with:

```
$ man -k appletalk
appleping(1)  - exercises the AppleTalk network by sending packets to a
named host
appletalk(8)  - enables you to configure and display AppleTalk network
interfaces
at_cho_prn(8) - allows you to choose a default printer on the AppleTalk
internet
atlookup(1)   - looks up network-visible entities (NVEs) registered on the
AppleTalk network system
atprint(1)    - transfer data to a printer using AppleTalk protocols
atstatus(1)   - displays status information from an AppleTalk device
```

If you use *man -k* and get tons of output, don't forget that you can use a standard Unix pipe to trim the results. Only interested in regular user commands, for example? Add **grep "(1"** and it'll eliminate all the uninteresting matches by constraining the results to just those that are from section one of the manpage database (similarly, "(2" would limit it to section two, and so on):

```
$ man -k postscript | grep "(1"
enscript(1)   - convert text files to PostScript
grops(1)      - PostScript driver for groff
pfbtops(1)    - translate a PostScript font in .pfb format to ASCII
dpsexec(1)    - Display PostScript Executive
dpsinfo(1)    - Display PostScript Information
makepsres(1)  - Build PostScript resource database file
pswrap(1)     - creates C procedures from segments of PostScript language
code
```

Documentation on the Internet

The Internet changes so quickly that any list of online Unix documentation I'd give you would soon be out of date. Still, the Internet is a great place to find out about Unix systems. Remember that there are many different versions of Unix, so some documentation you find may not be completely right for you. Also, some information you'll find may be far too technical for your needs (many computer professionals use and discuss Unix). But don't be discouraged! Once you've found a site with the general kind of information you want, you can probably come back later for more.

The premier place to start your exploration of online documentation for Mac OS X Unix is the Apple web site. But don't start on their home page. Start either on their Mac OS X page (*www.apple.com/macosx*) or their Darwin project home page (*http://developer.apple.com/darwin*). Another excellent place to get information about software downloads and add-ons to your Unix world is the Fink project (see Chapter 10).

Many Unix command names are plain English words, which can make searching hard. If you're looking for collections of Unix information, try searching for the Unix program named *grep*. One especially Unix-friendly search engine is Google (*www.google.com*). Google offers a specialized Macintosh search engine at *www.google.com/mac*, and a BSD search engine at *www.google.com/bsd* (which is useful because Mac OS X's Unix personality derives from its BSD heritage).

Here are some other places to try:

Magazines
> Some print and online magazines have Unix tutorials and links to more information. Macintosh magazines include MacTech (*www.mactech. com*), MacWorld (*www.macworld.com*), and MacAddict (*www. macaddict.com*).

Publishers
> Publishers such as O'Reilly Media, Inc. (*www.oreilly.com*) have areas of their web sites that feature Unix and have articles written by their books' authors. They may also have books online (such as the O'Reilly Safari service) available for a small monthly fee—which is a good way to learn a lot quickly without needing to buy a paper copy of a huge book, most of which you might not need.

Universities

Many schools use Unix-like systems and will have online documentation. You'll probably have better luck at the Computer Services division (which services the whole campus) than at the Computer Science department (which may be more technical).

Mac OS X–related web sites

Many Mac OS X web sites are worthy of note, though they're run by third parties and may change by the time you read this. Mac OS X Apps (*www.macosxapps.com*) offers a wide variety of Aqua applications. Information on Darwin can be found at Open Darwin (*www. opendarwin.org*), and Mac OS X Hints (*www.macosxhints.com*) offers valuable information and hints. I also have a popular Q&A site that addresses many Unix and Mac OS X questions, and I invite you to visit with your questions: Ask Dave Taylor (*www.AskDaveTaylor.com*). One more site well worth a bookmark is O'Reilly's MacDevCenter (*www. macdevcenter.com*).

Books

Bookstores, both traditional and online, are full of computer books. The books are written for a wide variety of needs and backgrounds. Unfortunately, many books are rushed to press, written by authors with minimal Unix experience, and are full of errors. Before you buy a book, read through parts of it. Does the style (brief or lots of detail, chatty and friendly, or organized as a reference) fit your needs? Search the Internet for reviews; online bookstores may have readers' comments on file.

Customizing your Unix Experience

One of the great values of Unix is that it's flexible, and what's the point of all this flexibility if you can't bend it to meet your own needs? Let's finish up this book with a brief tour of the different ways you can reshape your Mac OS X Unix world.

Shell Aliases and Functions

If you type command names that are hard for you to remember, or command lines that seem too long, you'll want to learn about *shell aliases* and *shell functions*. These shell features let you abbreviate commands, command lines, and long series of commands. In most cases, you can replace them with a single word or a word and a few arguments. For example, one of the long pipelines (see Chapter 6) could be replaced by an alias or function (for instance, *aug*). When you type **aug** at a shell prompt, the shell would list files modified in August, sorted by size. This might look like:

```
alias aug="ls -l | grep Aug"
```

Making an alias or function is almost as simple as typing in the command line or lines that you want to run. References earlier in this chapter have more information. Shell aliases and functions are actually a simple case of shell programming. For more information on aliases, see Chapter 2.

Programming

There are a number of different ways that you can delve into the world of programming, ranging from the lightweight interpreted shell script to full C++ or Java development. They're all supported within the Mac OS X environment.

Shell scripts

I mention earlier that the shell is the system's command interpreter. It reads each command line you enter at your terminal and performs the operation that you call for. Your shell is chosen when your account is set up.

The shell is just an ordinary program that can be called by a Unix command. However, it contains some features (such as variables, control structures, and so on) that make it similar to a programming language. You can save a series of shell commands in a file, called a *shell script*, to accomplish specialized functions.

Programming the shell should be attempted only when you are reasonably confident in your ability to use Unix commands. Unix is quite a powerful tool, and its capabilities become more apparent when you try your hand at shell programming.

Take time to learn the basics. Then, when you're faced with a new task, take time to browse through references to find programs or options that will help you get the job done more easily. Once you've done that, learn how to build shell scripts so that you never have to type a complicated command sequence more than once.

Let's have a closer look at a shell script to give you some flavor of what can be done. First, to list all known user accounts on the system, you need to extract the information from the NetInfo database, which can be done by using *nireport*.

You can try this script, *listusers*, by entering the following few lines into *vi*, Pico, or another Unix text editor of your choice. See Chapter 4 for additional information on editing files.

```
#!/bin/sh


echo "UID      NAME    FULLNAME      HOME
SHELL"


nireport . /users uid name realname home shell | \
   awk '$1 >= 500 { print $0 }'
```

After typing in this script, save the file and name it something like *listusers*—since that's what the program does. (Giving the script a similar name helps you quickly identify the script later when you need to use it.) The first line indicates what program should run the script, and, like most scripts, this is written for the Bourne shell, */bin/sh*. The *nireport* program extracts user information from the NetInfo database, and by using the *awk* utility to test for user IDs greater than or equal to 500, this script screens out any account information for system accounts (which, by convention, have an ID value of less than 500).

To make a shell script act as if it's a new program rather than just a text file, you use *chmod +x* to make it executable, then you can run it by typing in its name if it's in your current PATH (see Chapter 2 for more information on setting and customizing your PATH), or with the ./ prefix to indicate that it's in the current directory, as shown here:

```
$ chmod +x listusers
$ ./listusers
UID     NAME    FULLNAME      HOME            SHELL
501     taylor  Dave Taylor   /Users/taylor   /bin/bash
502     tintin  Mr. Tintin    /Users/tintin   /bin/bash
```

This is really the tip of the iceberg with shell scripts. For more information, look at *Unix in a Nutshell*, by Arnold Robbins, and *Unix Power Tools*, by Shelley Powers, et al. (both published by O'Reilly), or *Wicked Cool Shell Scripts*, by Dave Taylor (No Starch Press).

Turning shell scripts into AppleScript droplets

A very cool trick with Mac OS X is to turn a shell script into a droplet, an application that can have files dropped onto it from the Finder. To accomplish this feat, you'll need to have download and launch a copy of Fred Sanchez's DropScript utility (*http://www.mit.edu/people/wsanchez/software/darwin/DropScript-0.5.dmg*).

You can also find DropScript on VersionTracker (*www. versiontracker.com*) by searching for "dropscript." Version-Tracker is well worth exploring to help you keep up to date on system and application updates.

At its simplest, a droplet script accepts one or more files, which are given as command-line arguments, which are then processed in some manner. As a simple example, here's a droplet script that prints whatever files you give it:

```
#!/bin/sh
pr "$@" | lpr
```

This can be turned into a droplet by dragging the shell script icon over the DropScript application in the Finder. It creates a new version called *dropfilename* that's fully drag-and-drop-enabled. For example, if this script were called *print-text*, the droplet would be called *dropprint-text*.

Perl, Python, and Ruby

If shell script programming seems too limiting, you might want to try learning Perl, Ruby, or Python. Like the shell, these languages are interpreted from source files full of commands. These programming languages have a steeper learning curve than the shell. Also, because you've already learned a fair amount about the shell and Unix commands by reading this book, you're almost ready to start writing shell scripts now; on the other hand, a programming language takes longer to learn. But if you have sophisticated needs, learning one of these languages is another way to use even more of the power of your Mac OS X system.

C and C++

In addition to Perl, Python, and Ruby, Mac OS X also includes compiled programming languages, where there's an intermediate step between writing a program and having it ready to run on your system. These are how Mac applications themselves are written, including both Unix commands and the graphical Aqua utilities that make the Mac such a great environment. They're also quite complex and can take years to fully master. Three of these that you might have heard of are Objective-C (another variant of the C programming language that's popular with Mac developers), Cocoa (a Mac OS X–only development environment), and Carbon (an API set that allows Mac OS 9 applications to also run on Mac OS X; Carbon apps are often referred to as "Carbonized"). But if you want to begin learning, you'll be glad to know that a full development environment is included with your Mac OS X system.

Index

We'd like to hear your suggestions for improving our indexes. Send email to *index@oreilly.com*.

shell script wrappers, 179
Shell settings of Terminal, 20
.signature file, 234
Silverman, Richard, 188
-size (find primary), 129–131
sizes of files, matching by, 129–131
slash (/)
    in absolute pathnames, 52
    indicating root directory, 7, 51
    starting pattern in vi, 98, 101
sleep command, 174–175
SMTP (Simple Mail Transfer Protocol)
    server, supported by Pine, 230
sockets, 58
sort command, 153–155
    uniq command and, 155
[:space:] option (regexes), 123
spaces in filenames, 16
    copying/pasting, 29
    refrain from using, 84
Spafford, Gene, 72
special characters, in filenames and
    directory names, 84
Spotlight application, xiv, 137–142
ssh program, 181–188
    syntax for, 187
SSH: The Secure Shell, 188
standard input, 143–148
standard output, 143–148
    filtering, 149
status of background processes,
    checking, 165–172
storage space used by directories, 63
Strang, John, xviii
string encoding, nonstandard, 25
subdirectories, 51
subshells, logging out of, 40
sudo apt-get install gimp
    command, 234
sudo command, 43, 72, 79–81
superuser, 35
    sudo command and, 79–81
suspend character, 47, 165
swapping pages in memory, 171
symbolic links, 58
    creating, 114
system administration, x
system log, viewing, 173
system resources, monitoring
    consumption of, 169

T

-t option (pr command), 159
Tabbed C shell (tcsh), 34
tail command, 152
    viewing system log with, 173
tar (tape archiver) program, 116
tcsh (Tabbed C shell), 34
telnet program, 186
.term files, 31
Terminal application, x, xii
    changing preferences, 19–28
    customizing sessions, 30–32
    default shell used by, 15
    frozen sessions, 47
    in X11, 204
    launching, 10, 14–30
    starting, 33
    using the ps command, 2
Terminal Inspector
    Buffer settings, 23–24
    Color settings, 25
    Display settings, 24
    Emulation settings, 22
    Keyboard settings, 27
    Processes settings, 21
    setting defaults using, 20
    Shell settings, 20
    Window settings, 27
Terminal Pal utility, 32
Terminal session, 33
text editors
    BBEdit, 93
    choosing, 93
text, redirecting to files, 145–148
TextEdit graphical text editor, 93
time tests, searching for files by, 133
titles of windows, fine-tuning, 27, 30
Todino, Grace, xviii
top command, 13, 169–172
tr command (translator utility), 94, 150
    input redirection, 144
transferring files between
    computers, 188–198
troubleshooting
    cat command, entering without a
        filename, 145
    cd to filenames not allowed, 56
    chmod problems, 77
    cp command errors, 108
    exit command errors, 40

About the Author

Dave Taylor is a popular writer, teacher, and speaker focused on business communications and technology issues. The author of almost 20 books, including *Growing Your Business with Google, Wicked Cool Shell Scripts,* and *Teach Yourself Unix in 24 Hours*, he is also a visionary in the business blogging and communications space. His primary weblogs are The Intuitive View (*www.intuitive.com/*) and Ask Dave Taylor (*www.askdavetaylor.com*). Dave has an MS Education and MBA and has been involved with the Internet since 1980 and the Macintosh since his first dirty beige 512K Mac in 1985. He has contributed software to the 4.4 release of Berkeley Unix (BSD) and his programs are found in all versions of Linux and other popular Unix variants.

Colophon

Our look is the result of reader comments, our own experimentation, and feedback from distribution channels. Distinctive covers complement our distinctive approach to technical topics, breathing personality and life into potentially dry subjects.

The animal on the cover of *Learning Unix for Mac OS X Tiger* is a Siberian tiger cub. Tiger cubs are born blind and weigh only about as much as a small domestic housecat. Litters average two to four cubs. They feed on their mother's milk for six to eight weeks (and remain blind for the first two), until their she begins to bring them solid food at the age of three months. After roughly a year, the mother tiger will begin teaching her young how to hunt. Cubs develop the lethal teeth of an adult and begin killing their own food when they are approximately 18 months old, but will remain with their mother until they are two to three years old. Once they are old enough and can ably take down large kills of deer, buffalo, and other prey, the tiger cubs must strike out to find their own hunting territory. The Siberian tiger can live up to 15 years in the wild.

Philip Dangler was the production editor for and proofreader for *Learning Unix for Mac OS X Tiger*. Sanders Kleinfeld and Colleen Gorman provided quality control. Lydia Onofrei provided production assistance. Julie Hoer wrote the index.

Ellie Volckhausen designed the cover of this book, based on a series design by Edie Freedman. The cover image is an original illustration created by Susan Hart. Karen Montgomery produced the cover layout with Adobe InDesign CS using Adobe's ITC Garamond font.

David Futato designed the interior layout. This book was converted by Keith Fahlgren to FrameMaker 5.5.6 with a format conversion tool created by Erik Ray, Jason McIntosh, Neil Walls, and Mike Sierra that uses Perl and XML technologies. The text font is Linotype Birka; the heading font is Adobe Myriad Condensed; and the code font is LucasFont's TheSans Mono Condensed. The illustrations that appear in the book were produced by Robert Romano, Jessamyn Read, and Lesley Borash using Macromedia Free-Hand MX and Adobe Photoshop CS. The tip and warning icons were drawn by Christopher Bing. This colophon was written by Philip Dangler.

Related Titles Available from O'Reilly

Macintosh

AppleScript: The Definitive Guide

Appleworks 6: The Missing Manual

The Best of the Joy of Tech

FileMaker Pro 7: The Missing Manual

GarageBand: The Missing Manual

iLife '04: The Missing Manual

iMovie 4 and iDVD: The Missing Manual

iPhoto 4: The Missing Manual

iPod & iTunes: The Missing Manual, *2nd Edition*

Mac OS X Panther in a Nutshell

Mac OS X Panther Pocket Guide

Mac OS X Panther Power User

Mac OS X: The Missing Manual, *Panther Edition*

Mac OS X Unwired

Macintosh Troubleshooting Pocket Guide

Modding Mac OS X

Office X for the Macintosh: The Missing Manual

Revolutionaries in The Valley: Their Incredible Stories of How the Mac was Made

Running Mac OS X Panther

Mac Developers

Building Cocoa Applications: A Step-By-Step Guide

Cocoa in a Nutshell

Learning Carbon

Learning Cocoa with Objective-C, *2nd Edition*

Learning Unix for Mac OS X Panther

Mac OS X for Java Geeks

Mac OS X Hacks

Mac OS X Panther Hacks

Mac OS X Panther for Unix Geeks

Managing & Using Mac OS X Server

Objective-C Pocket Reference

RealBasic: The Definitive Guide, *2nd Edition*

Keep in touch with O'Reilly

1. Download examples from our books

To find example files for a book, go to:

www.oreilly.com/catalog

select the book, and follow the "Examples" link.

2. Register your O'Reilly books

Register your book at *register.oreilly.com*

Why register your books? Once you've registered your O'Reilly books you can:

- Win O'Reilly books, T-shirts or discount coupons in our monthly drawing.
- Get special offers available only to registered O'Reilly customers.
- Get catalogs announcing new books (US and UK only).
- Get email notification of new editions of the O'Reilly books you own.

3. Join our email lists

Sign up to get topic-specific email announcements of new books and conferences, special offers, and O'Reilly Network technology newsletters at:

elists.oreilly.com

It's easy to customize your free elists subscription so you'll get exactly the O'Reilly news you want.

4. Get the latest news, tips, and tools

http://www.oreilly.com

- "Top 100 Sites on the Web"—PC Magazine
- CIO Magazine's Web Business 50 Awards

Our web site contains a library of comprehensive product information (including book excerpts and tables of contents), downloadable software, background articles, interviews with technology leaders, links to relevant sites, book cover art, and more.

5. Work for O'Reilly

Check out our web site for current employment opportunities:

jobs.oreilly.com

6. Contact us

O'Reilly & Associates
1005 Gravenstein Hwy North
Sebastopol, CA 95472 USA

TEL: 707-827-7000 or 800-998-9938
         (6am to 5pm PST)

FAX: 707-829-0104

order@oreilly.com
For answers to problems regarding your order or our products.
To place a book order online, visit:

www.oreilly.com/order_new

catalog@oreilly.com
To request a copy of our latest catalog.

booktech@oreilly.com
For book content technical questions or corrections.

corporate@oreilly.com
For educational, library, government, and corporate sales.

proposals@oreilly.com
To submit new book proposals to our editors and product managers.

international@oreilly.com
For information about our international distributors or translation queries. For a list of our distributors outside of North America check out:

international.oreilly.com/distributors.html

adoption@oreilly.com
For information about academic use of O'Reilly books, visit:

academic.oreilly.com